ZARATHUSTRA'S SISTERS:
WOMEN'S AUTOBIOGRAPHY AND
THE SHAPING OF CULTURAL HISTORY

SUSAN INGRAM

Zarathustra's Sisters: Women's Autobiography and the Shaping of Cultural History

UNIVERSITY OF TORONTO PRESS
Toronto Buffalo London

© University of Toronto Press Incorporated 2003
Toronto Buffalo London
Printed in Canada

ISBN 0-8020-3690-2

Printed on acid-free paper

National Library of Canada Cataloguing in Publication Data

Ingram, Susan
  Zarathustra's sisters : women's autobiography and the shaping of
cultural history / Susan Ingram.

  Includes bibliographical references and index.
  ISBN 0-8020-3690-2

  1. Autobiography – Women authors.   2. Women authors –
Biography – History and criticism.   3. Prose literature – Women
authors – History and criticism.   4. Man-woman relationships.
5. Nietzsche, Friedrich Wilhelm, 1844–1900.   I. Title.

PN471.I54 2002   809'.93592072'0904   C2002-901794-7

'Kremlin's Mountaineer' is reproduced from Nadezhda Mandel'shtam,
Hope against Hope: A Memoir, translated by Max Hayward (New York:
Modern Library, 1999).

University of Toronto Press acknowledges the financial assistance to
its publishing program of the Canada Council for the Arts and the
Ontario Arts Council.

This book has been published with the help of a grant from the Humanities
and Social Sciences Federation of Canada, using funds provided by the
Social Sciences and Humanities Research Council of Canada.

University of Toronto Press acknowledges the financial support for
its publishing activities of the Government of Canada through the
Book Publishing Industry Development Program (BPIDP).

Contents

Acknowledgments

This book's underlying theme, the relationality of subjectivity, is reflective of my own good fortune in this regard. During the course of my research and writing, I incurred many debts in many places – from St Petersburg and Riga to Sosnowiec and Saarbrücken, Vienna, Prague and Ljubljana, New York, Montreal, and Toronto – but starting in and always returning to Edmonton. Those are the signposts of this project – the special faces and memories that found their way into, and indeed made possible, the following pages. Now that the project is drawing to its far from inevitable conclusion, it is a real pleasure to acknowledge the support that has made the past several years so enjoyably productive.

First, I am most grateful to the Social Sciences and Humanities Research Council of Canada and the University of Alberta for the funding without which this project would not have been possible. In addition, a Research Associateship courtesy of the Russian and Eastern European Summer Laboratory at the University of Illinois allowed me access to both its fine library and a group of wonderfully engaging interlocutors. Working in the Jerome Robbins Dance Division at the New York Public Library for the Performing Arts, as well as in the Theater Museum and the Andrejs Upits Museum in Riga, was facilitated greatly by their knowledgeable, personable staffs. Maria Kalnina, in particular, has been a tremendous source of material and inspiration. It was great luck to have Catherine Frost at University of Toronto Press as my copy-editor and to be so well chaperoned through the publishing process by Barb Porter.

At the University of Alberta, I had the privilege of working with Elena Siemens, a generous, rigorous reader, whose critical suggestions infused the following pages with whatever life they have and whose never-wavering encouragement, optimism, and support continue to keep me dreaming of possibilities. To Bob Burch, Ray Morrow, Leo Mos, and Edward Mozejko I am grateful for our always motivating meetings, both fortuitous and planned. I also very much appreciate the time taken by Birgit Wagner and the anonymous readers in the ASPP process to so attentively read and so helpfully comment on my work. Special thanks go to Markus Reisenleitner, whose tenure at the Canadian Centre for Austrian and Central European Studies was instrumental in this book's completion and who makes the future a far more inviting, exciting, promising place.

Heartfelt thanks are also due my family. My cher frère proved, as always, a veritable pillar of encouragement, advice, solace, sources, summer lodgings, and *Korrekturlesen*. My parents were there for me when the worst came to the worst, as it repeatedly did. And my generous aunt and uncle also made sure at a critical venture that I had the best writing environment possible.

That leaves to be acknowledged my trusty Powerbook 100, whose whirrings and clickings so often provided a much-needed pick-me-up, as did very dear friends, who, scattered between new worlds and old, help me to make sense of, and find my way in, all of them. Finally, I dedicate this work to the biggest and grandest of grandmas.

Lou Andreas-Salomé. Photograph courtesy of the Freud Museum, London.

Simone de Beauvoir. Photograph courtesy of Magnum Photos.

Asja Lacis. Private collection.

Nadezhda Mandel'shtam. Photograph courtesy of Magnum Photos.

Romola Nijinsky. Photograph courtesy of the Jerome Robbins Dance Division of the New York Public Library for the Perfoming Arts.

ZARATHUSTRA'S SISTERS:
WOMEN'S AUTOBIOGRAPHY AND
THE SHAPING OF CULTURAL HISTORY

Zarathustra's Sisters

[O]ne morning [Zarathustra] rose with the dawn, stepped before the sun, and spoke to it thus: 'You great star, what would your happiness be had you not those for whom you shine?

For ten years you have climbed up to my cave: you would have gotten fed up with your light and with the journey had it not been for me and my eagle and my serpent.'

'Prologue,' 1, *Zarathustra*[1]

Companions the creator seeks, not corpses, not herds, not believers. Kindred creators, the creator seeks, those who write new values on new tablets.

Companions the creator seeks, those to harvest with: for everything is ripe for harvesting around them. But the creator lacks a hundred sickles: so the ears of corn are husked in great annoyance.

Companions the creator seeks, and such as know how to whet their sickles. Destroyers they will be called, and despisers of good and evil. But they are the ones who harvest, and who celebrate.

'Prologue,' 9, *Zarathustra*[2]

It is necessary to learn to *look away* from oneself in order to see *much* – every climber of mountains needs this hardness.

'The Wanderer,' *Zarathustra*[3]

The six women who serve as subject for this study share the experience of being in and writing about a relationship with a man who is significant to the tradition of western letters. One would be justified in expecting a critical survey of the extent to which their reception has been shaped by their relationships. Simone de Beauvoir is also known as *'la grande Sartreuse.'*[4] Lou Andreas-Salomé's name is often found with the further hyphenation 'Nietzsche-Rilke-Freud.'[5] Mandel'shtam and Nijinsky are generally taken to be the names of the renowned Russians poet Osip and dancer Vaslav, not of their wives, Nadezhda and Romola. What little academic attention Asja Lacis and Maitreyi Devi receive is due to the Benjamin-Brecht-Piscator-Meyerhold and Eliade-Tagore connections, respectively.

It is not, however, on account of their relationships per se that I was drawn to work on these particular six women. They have much more in common than simply the fact of their involvement with 'names' and their subsequent autobiographical output. In the same suggestive way all encourage a focus on the cultural implications of self-representation, specifically on the question of how the autobiographical or documentary genre has been mobilized to intervene with discernibly didactic intent in hostile, condescending, or indifferent cultural force fields.[6] I first became interested in the topic when I worked on Nadezhda Mandel'shtam's memoirs. Her verve, gumption, and unrelenting sense of purpose captured my imagination. While reading a wide sampling of autobiographical texts, I began to distinguish a 'Mandel'shtam response' among women who came into their own and wrote autobiographically in the post-Nietzschian 'Old World.' These women led long, active, productive, transitive lives, during which they experienced the Kafkaesque periods of upheaval that so tragically mark the first half of the twentieth century.[7] They had received better educations than women of their time were generally encouraged to attain.[8] They were very quick to shed whatever shackles of bourgeois restraint they encountered, and their precocity brought them into what would in today's North America be considered rather highbrow circles, circles that remained closed to their less feisty, less favourably situated contemporaries and, whether literary, theatrical, or philosophical, that have come to be recognized as among the crème de la crème of their respective fields. These women wrote with the same sense of urgency and engagement. They valued the documentary nature of the autobiographical genre rather than its interpretative character. They painted their relationships with their fathers in unusually positive colours and those with their mothers in less flattering, though often touchingly compassionate, shades.[9] Their precocity far from having dissipated with age, they saturated their autobiographical writings with an earnest determination, cultivated and represented with great pride and leaving little room for dissension or disbelief. They knew how it was, they had been there, and it was important that the reader recognize the value of and benefit from that experience. The values and benefits of their experience deserve a less partial reading than they have thus far 'enjoyed' in Anglo-America and its scholarship; this belief certainly was a factor in my selection of these particular six women.

There was, however, a further consideration. The main impetus for this study is the very suggestive constellation these women form, one that I see as precursory of a particular part of the academic postmodern and thus contributing to our understanding of the postmodern continuum as it has been and continues to be played out within the academy.[10] As David Simpson discusses in his 1995 *The Academic Postmodern and the Rule of Literature*, the spectrum of academic postmoderns is broad. Whereas Simpson chooses to focus on 'the conservative, "establishment" incarnations, those that have achieved a certain prestige and reproductive power in the academy: the writings of Geertz and Rorty, the new historicism, and so on' (18), I find that the more personal forms of academic criticism, which have come to be known as 'intimate,' 'confessional,' and 'personal,' offer a more productive entry point into postmodern academic production.

When they are considered together, which is the purpose of this study, the six autobiographical projects in question encourage a reconsideration of the current preoccupation with 'getting a life'[11] from the critical, 'anti-aesthetic' perspective, which Hal Foster, in the preface to his 1983 essay collection, *The Anti-Aesthetic*, links with postmodernism: 'the sign not of a modern nihilism – which so often transgressed the law only to confirm it – but rather of a critique which destructures the order of representations in order to reinscribe them' (xv).[12] The readings in this study work towards demonstrating the extent to which questions of reinscription are at work in the texts, not simply transgression for its own sake, as is so often the case with the more aesthetically inclined.[13]

It is here that the invocation of 'Zarathustra's sisters' proves useful. The reinscriptive, 'anti-aesthetic' stance of the women in this study will be attributed to consonances in situation, character, and hearing, to delicate ears resonating to the same rumblings heard by Zarathustra. Utilizing Nietzsche's productively provocative and ambiguous positioning vis-à-vis the postmodern, I aim to transfer scholarship and context from the seat of this debate to works that have received less of such attention.[14] As the previous reference to Foster's 'anti-aesthetic' is intended to indicate, however, my reading of Nietzsche is completely in agreement with neither critical theorists nor poststructuralists, for whom Nietzsche represents an aesthetic, affirmative model of human freedom.[15] Rather, in situating myself at the intersection of scholarship on Nietzsche, autobiography, and modernity, I draw on each of these areas to cross-pollinate the others. In the rest of this chapter I will specify how. First I will set up the two axes against which the six texts in this study can be located: the first generic and the second socio-historical. In a concluding section I will address the ethical issues shown to arise from Nietzsche's interstitial positioning.

Reading Up, Going Down: Autobiographical Writing and the Modern

They have discovered themselves who say, 'This is *my* good and evil'; with that they have reduced to silence the mole and dwarf who say, 'Good for all, evil for all' ... 'This is *my* way; where is yours?' – thus I answered those who asked me 'the way.' For *the* way – does not exist.

'Of the Spirit of Gravity,' 2, *Zarathustra*

'A' Is for Autobiography

The generic terms currently available for the denotation of the texts to be considered in this study present certain problems.[17] The formal, more traditional definitions of autobiography, memoir, autobiographical novel, and biography are too narrow to adequately encompass the body of work in question, while the more recent term, 'life-writing,' also is not entirely unproblematic. The purpose of introducing life-writing as a conceptual category was, in part, to overcome this earlier rigidity.[18] It quickly assumed a more political, reformatory function, however, one of creating cultural and academic space within which to create and discuss types of writing traditionally subject to little academic attention, such as those of women, other 'minorities,' and the newer, hybrid, less formal writing modalities such as internet interaction. In that sense, both the present project and the texts I will be examining could conceivably be considered life-writing, which makes a terminological distinction desirable.

Autobiographical writing, as introduced here, is intended not to supplant life-writing but rather to supplement it. It would be reserved for texts that involve intervening with one's own lived experience in one's surrounding written culture and would be marked by being based on one's own lived experience and its realization into writing. More fundamentally, autobiographical writing, as opposed to life-writing, would be restricted to works that deliberately invoke Lejeune's autobiographical pact, which 'supposes that there is identity of name between the author (such as he figures, by his name, on the cover), the narrator of the story, and the character who is being talked about' (1989, 12). Maitreyi Devi's supposed roman-à-clef, *It Does Not Die: A Romance*, for example, is not at all operating under the same kind of pact with the reader as either Beauvoir's *The Mandarins* or Andreas-Salomé's *Fenitschka*. While *The Mandarins* and *Fenitschka* are obviously written out of the autobiographical experiences of their authors, in *It Does Not Die* Devi invites, indeed challenges, the reader to accept it as her version of her actual real-life encounter with Eliade. The same type of claim is made in Beauvoir's *Memoirs of a Dutiful Daughter* and Andreas-Salomé's *Looking Back* and deliberately is not being made in their more fictional writing. It is precisely in the willingness of the reader, inherent in the autobiographical pact, to accept the story as more than mere fiction and the willingness or determination of the author to have the story read as the true story of at least part of her life that the ethical potential of the genre resides (a point to which I will return in the concluding section of this chapter on the relevance of Nietzsche to the project).

The choice of the term 'autobiographical writing,' as opposed to both autobiography and life-writing, is dictated by subject matter. While the present project would like to plant itself in the fertile post-structural soil, where the inclusive notion of life-writing has taken firm root, it cannot do so unconditionally. Without wishing to negate in any way the theoretical gains of the conceptual shift that has allowed theorists to target and clarify the power matrices that give shape to our lives,[19] I do want to stress here the ways in which the texts that will be examined here do not allow for an unquestioned acceptance of these new terminological developments. While demanding consideration of the implications of the new generic category of life-writing, they simultaneously reinforce its challenge to philological categories of periodic classification. The following overview is intended to briefly illustrate the way in which autobiographical texts have traditionally been approached as purely aesthetic objects and the way academic periodization reflects this priority.

The traditional view of autobiography is as a truthful representation of its author's life history, an approach founded on the ontology of an observable and comprehensible self. Problems began to arise, however, among those who have come to be known as the literary modernists, when authors not only recognized that the self was neither coherent nor knowable but began to explore what it meant to live within the 'incomplete' paradigm of modernity.[20] However, at a time when, pace Yeats, 'Things fall apart; the centre cannot hold/ Mere anarchy is loosed upon the world,' even this consciously stylized, despairing vision of increasing fragmentation and human powerlessness in the face of blind technology could not be expected to last. As the very possibility of representation, immutable disciplines and genres, Truth, History, Science, and the Author fell under attack by what Gadamer has called 'the French challenge,' the effects of, in particular, its rather acidic American fallout could not but be felt in the area of autobiography.[21] Even the most radically poststructural French flank of the postmodern condition, however, has been shown to suffer from a certain orthodoxy, which has left it open to attack from forces Theo D'haen has termed 'counter-postmodern.' The counter-postmodern, according to D'haen, 'counters orthodox postmodernism in putting its finger on the latter's complicity with what it purports to subvert or problematize ... [and] writes the subjectivity, history, and language of those hitherto suppressed by the discourse of modernity as emanating from Western bourgeois society' (1996, 194). That is, destabilized poststructural subjectivities have been found to be as notably Eurocentric, patriarchal, straight, and so on as their essentialist Enlightenment counterparts. It is this counter-postmodern that has lately been causing a great splash in the already murkied waters of autobiography. To briefly summarize, as conceptions of the self · changed from truthful, enlightened representation to anguished anathema, destabilized multiplicity, and downtrodden but embodied victim, so too did the form of the stories of those selves, as the following examples illustrate. Whereas Rousseau's *Confessions* and Goethe's *Dichtung und Wahrheit* can be seen as classical instances of the traditional introspection of great men, Gertrude Stein's *The Autobiography of Alice B. Toklas* and Michel Leiris's *L'âge d'homme* are prototypically modernist in their purely formal type of experimentation. Barthes's *Roland Barthes* and bp nichol's *Selected Organs* are their postmodern equivalents in playfully experimenting with fragments, while the heart-wrenching episodes in Maxine Hong Kingston's *The Woman*

Warrior and Maya Angelou's *I Know Why the Caged Bird Sings* are exemplars of the rapidly expanding canon of the counter-postmodern. As will become apparent during the course of this study, the above chronology leaves no room for discussion of the texts under consideration here. Neither classical nor modernist, postmodernist nor counter-postmodernist, the autobiographical texts of these six women chafe uncomfortably under categories of periodization and genre designed with others in mind.[22] In thus eluding generic and periodic capture, they serve to draw attention to the bases on which these categories are constructed. Just as life-writing has its own agendas, so the varieties of 'modernisms' outlined above have theirs. They are explicitly literary labels that affix to texts read as, and only as, literature. As we will see, not one of the women in question here considered or constructed herself, or has been considered or constructed by scholarship, as a primarily literary artist; not one understood her autobiographical project as a solely aesthetic undertaking.[23] Thus, in contradistinction to Elliott and Wallace's commitment in *Women Artists and Writers: Modernist (Im)positionings* 'to rethinking modernism as a discursive and historical *field*' (1994, 1; italics in original), in the present study I proceed rather in the spirit of the Adornian force field.

(B)uilding up a 'Matrioyshka' Modern

Modernity, as Octavio Paz reminds us, is a tradition divided against itself. Thus, it seems fitting, if not inevitable, that my response to it in this study is also divided. In order to encompass the various levels of criticism on this tradition and distance myself from the Anglo-American tendency in scholarship to conflate modernism with the avant-garde, I approach the concept as a 'matrioyshka' modern.[24] Like the smoothly shaped, colourfully painted wooden dolls that have so gleefully been appropriated of late for political and pop-cultural purposes,[25] my 'matrioyshka' modern unpacks into progressively smaller, more specific figures, ranging from the grand narrative of philosophical modernity through the period of literary history known as modernism to the brief moment in high modernism of the avant-garde.

The innermost figure of this matrioyshka modern, then, belongs to Peter Bürger and his socio-historical distinction between the avant-garde and modernism in *Theory of the Avant-Garde*. His analysis of the institutionalization of modern art is particularly useful for the present study, since it encourages one to think in terms of the institutional implications of the work of these women. For Bürger, 'the development of the avant-garde has nothing to do with a critical consciousness about language; it is not a continuation of tendencies already present in Aestheticism. Rather, for him the turning point from Aestheticism to the avant-garde is determined by the extent to which art comprehended the mode in which it functioned in bourgeois society, *its comprehension of its own social status*. The historical avant-garde of the twenties was the first movement in art history that turned against the institution "art" and the mode in which autonomy functions. In this it differed from all previous art movements, whose mode of existence was determined precisely by an acceptance of autonomy' (1994, xiv; italics added). Bürger's approach focuses on the way in which avant-garde artists worked to overcome their societal isolation 'to alter the institutionalized commerce with art' (xv). While I am not arguing that the women who comprise this study are by any means avant-garde artists, I do think they lived and wrote avant-garde lives in very non–avant-garde ways, as Bürger understands that term, a point that will prove crucial to my concluding argument. Keeping Bürger's methodological framework in the background will help to focus on and contextualize the mechanisms by which these women strove towards an ambiguously autonomous status, matters that hitherto have served as an academic bone of contention.

Involvement with culturally significant figures has neither aided nor abetted scholars in dealing with these six women. As one might expect, early studies and those of a more traditionally philological bent have tended to treat them as glorified appendages, helpmates who happen to be a useful source of valuable biographical material but in themselves of no intrinsic interest. The title of Althaus-Schönbucher's (1981) 'Nadezhda Mandel'shtam: *Vospominanija* und *Vtoraja kniga*. Memoiren als Ergänzung der Literaturforschung' (Nadezdha Mandel'shtam: *Hope against Hope* and *Hope Abandoned*. Memoirs as a Supplement to Literary Studies) and the comment in Grigulis's introduction to Lacis's *Red Carnation* that it is a 'rich source of information' (1984, 5) are cases in point. Theoretically informed feminist scholarship has since intervened to 'right/write' these 'wrongs' by concentrating on the conditions under which these women wrote and were written. While studies such as Toril Moi's work on Beauvoir and that of Biddy Martin on Andreas-Salomé do provide an important, sociologically informed background for their subjects, as feminists these authors choose to highlight their subjects' struggles for, not with, autonomy. Moi, for example, concludes: 'On the threshold of the twenty-first century, [Beauvoir] still makes it easier for us to live our lives as we wish, without regard to patriarchal conventions ... When I realize how hard it was for her to gain a sense of autonomy and independence, I find her achievements all the more admirable' (1994, 256–7). Instead of assuming that the women in the present study strove for autonomy and independence, I proceed from Bürger's work on the avant-garde to suggest that their aim was ambiguity and interdependence.

Bürger targets a social dynamic within the larger artistic movement of modernism, which is the second figure in the matrioyshka modern. Continental and Russian criticism on the modernist movements in literature is useful for its attention to the questions of the creation of cultural myths and *zhiznetvorchestvo*, which has been variously translated as 'life-art' and 'life-creation.' Gasparov explains the development of modernism from romanticism:

Modernism breathed new life into the romantic cult of the creative personality and of the artist's messianic calling. Here too, however, Modernism reinterpreted a traditional motif in accordance with the Modernist concept of total eschatological synthesis. Romantic individualism and eccentricity, the Romantic's flight from the 'vulgarity' of everyday life, and his dedication to the creation of lofty spiritual values were replaced by the idea of 'life-creation' (*zhiznetvorchestvo*) which demanded that the antinomy between 'life' and 'art' be obliterated and the entire life of the artist-messiah be transformed into a continuously unfolding and totalizing artistic text. Where the Romantic artist 'fled' from the quotidian to serve his creative calling, the Modernist artist refused to live in historical time at all. Every moment of the Modernist artist's life was seen as a synthetic creative act that occurred in a paradigmatic time where all his potential symbolic reflections were mythologically co-present. (1992, 3–4)

While I am not suggesting that the modernist relation between life and art, which tended to degenerate into dandyism and caricature, is evidenced in the texts under consideration, the modernist cultural landscape the women in this study inhabited was dominated by the social fact of cultural mythologies, and, as we will see, it is important to consider how these mythologies were recreated through their writing.

What is the significance of these mythologizing tendencies?[26] As will be addressed in greater detail in the first chapter on Lou Andreas-Salomé, mythological figures function to allow for the expression of an epoch's obsessions, its inner tensions and fears, under the guise of historical distance and objectivity. By creating or inventing themselves and their relationships as mythologies, these women were actively intervening in and providing for a subtle shift in the societal basis of consensus. One could speak here more of an 'anti-tradition' than an 'anti-aesthetic.' That is, this cultural mechanism operates in a similar yet counter fashion to that identified in Hobsbawm and Ranger's essay collection, *The Invention of Tradition*, in which traditions, such as those surrounding the British monarchy in its public ceremonial manifestations, are unmasked as late nineteenth- and early twentieth-century products: 'practices, normally governed by overtly or tacitly accepted rules and of a ritual or symbolic nature, which seek to inculcate certain values and norms of behaviour by repetition, which automatically implies continuity with the past.' It was not always the case that the tradition of Scottish national identity was represented by kilts, tartans, and bagpipes; rather, it is a relatively new, modern, 'retrospective invention.' Inventing traditions proved crucial, for example, in the success of colonizing Africa in the late nineteenth century: 'the invented traditions imported from Europe not only provided whites with models of command but also offered many Africans models of "modern" behaviour. The invented traditions of African societies – whether invented by the Europeans or by Africans themselves in response – distorted the past but became in themselves realities through which a good deal of colonial encounter was expressed' (1983, 1, 15, 212). So, too, were the mythologies these women created of themselves and their relationships projected into the cultural fray as alternative models of 'modern behaviour,' as 'anti-traditions,' as subversively inimitable examples.

Further, *zhiznetvorchestvo* is tantalizingly related to Beauvoir's notion of *l'entreprise de vivre*, or art of living, which is the undercurrent informing Karen Vintges's *Philosophy as Passion: The Thinking of Simone de Beauvoir*. Vintges looks at how Beauvoir 'continues to emphasize her life as active subject ... I think we can conclude this is what Beauvoir had in mind with her art of living ... [T]hrough her own life, she wanted to prove a woman could live as subject. Her own life was to form a refutation of Freud's theory; it would give other women a successful example of life as an active woman and thus mean something for them' (1996, 107). Like Lynn Tirrell, in 'Sexual Dualism and Women's Self-Creation: On the Advantages and Disadvantages of Reading Nietzsche for Feminists,' though in much greater depth, Vintges is interested in Beauvoir's project of self-articulation. While Tirrell finds it 'significant that both Nietzsche and Beauvoir were concerned with their own need to tell their stories of their lives, working on the borderland between philosophy and literature, and that both tried to recreate the self that was telling in the process of the articulation' (1994, 159), Vintges sharply distinguishes Beauvoir from Nietzsche and 'neo-Nietzschean postmodernism' along ethical lines. Her central thesis – now that 'postmodernism has swept away all foundations for a positive ethics ... Beauvoir's idea of ethics as art of living can fill the hiatus that is left' – has the disadvantage of rather nonchalantly dismissing the context of 'neo-Nietzschean postmodernism' for both Beauvoir's and her own work (1996, 160–1, 189–90, 162). It is this 'neo-Nietzschean postmodernism' and the larger debate it has spawned about and within the philosophical project of modernity that provide the backdrop against which the accomplishments of Beauvoir and the other five subjects in this study can be best appreciated. As such, it forms the outermost shell of my matrioyshka modern.

The groundwork for such a discussion of the postmodern has already been staked out in Mary Evans's 1996 study of Simone de Beauvoir. Evans begins by situating Sartre and Beauvoir as moderns: 'Both these people, frequently regarded as pariahs by their own society, were nevertheless entirely integrated into its central, modernist, belief: that there are universal, general laws and the world, through properly developed and understood "laws," can be rendered coherent. To understand de Beauvoir, and indeed Sartre, it is essential to situate her not just in France (and urban, cosmopolitan France at that) but in the intellectual climate of European modernity.' She then makes the following contrast: 'As de Beauvoir confronted Sartre in London in the mid-1930s, she puts forward an argument which was to reappear later in feminism and postmodernism, namely, that the world's diversity cannot, or indeed need not, be understood in terms of single epistemologies. Sartre's search for a universal theory of knowledge ... looks, in the 1990s, like a pointless and redundant exercise, whereas de Beauvoir's resistance has about it more than a suggestion of the way in which postmodernism was to fracture the great universalistic expectations and assumptions of the Enlightenment' (1996, 22, 32). Evans's efforts to salvage something of Beauvoir for postmodern scholarship sidestep the underlying difficulties that Beauvoir's well-reasoned and often masculinist writings present. Nonetheless, it should be stressed that the jump Evans is making is not to the literary movement of modernism but to the philosophical and social paradigm of modernity, just as Biddy Martin does in her study of Lou Andreas-Salomé. What are the methodological implications of making a such jump? As the editors of the series 'Reading Women Writing,' to which it belongs, point out, 'Martin's *Woman and Modernity* is not simply a reading of Lou Andreas-Salomé's writing ... this book attempts to read Salomé the "writer, thinker, and lay analyst" institutionally, that is to read her life and work *in* as well as *against* its historical, political, and intellectual context' (1991, ix; italics in original). A further step along this critical path is to ask what kind of readings ensue from assuming a self-reflexive stance towards the lives and works in question, that is, not simply situating them in and against their social contexts but reading them as active interventions in that context, that is, as examples of the autobiographical writing outlined above.

This matrioyshka modern thus allows for consideration of all relevant, interrelated layers of criticism. It also helps to clarify my choice of the texts of these six women rather than those of others. The reason for not including, for example, a section on the diaries of Anais Nin and Frida Kahlo, or one in which the liaison of Lily Brik and Vladimir Mayakovsky is compared with that of Baroness Elsa von Freytag-Loringhoven and Frederick Philip Grove, or one in which the texts of Anglo-American authors such as Lilian Hellman and Mary McCarthy are examined is that these texts do not evince the same 'modern' (in the sense of Nietzschean avant-garde) spirit as that of my six subjects.[27] The six women in this study have other, more didactic, less aesthetic priorities; they read and write themselves, and set themselves up to be read, in different ways from these other authors. It is these differences that I am attempting to highlight in dubbing them 'Zarathustra's sisters.'

Life and Writing as a Bridge to the *Übermensch*[28]

For *that* is who I am through and through: reeling, reeling in, raising up, raising, a raiser, cultivator and disciplinarian, who once counseled himself, not for nothing: Become who you are!

'The Honey Sacrifice,' *Zarathustra*[29]

Nietzsche's writings, especially *Also Sprach Zarathustra* and its infamous whip comment, were traditionally regarded as too incendiary to be of any use for approaching women's writing.[30] As writers in the 1989 special issue of *History of European Ideas* on 'Turning Points in History' make apparent, however, the Berlin Wall did not fall on its own: its collapse was concurrent with those of other barriers, such as that between Nietzsche's and women's writings. In the past decade, 'Nietzsche' has marked a site of critical intervention in Anglo-American academia. Since 1991 when the translation of Irigaray's 1980 *Amante marine* into *Marine Lover of Friedrich Nietzsche* appeared, it is not uncommon to find comments such as: 'Nietzsche's misogyny is tempered by a surprising understanding of the situation of the (white, European, upper-class) women of his day ... [he] enjoins women, in contemporary feminist terms, to stop being male-defined and to actively engage in creating their own identities' (Tirrell 1994, 176) and 'Nietzsche's objections to feminism contain the "post-feminist" message that women's attempts to define woman as such commit the same essentialist fallacies as the masculinist tradition of Western philosophy' (Ansell-Pearson 1992, 327). As pointed out in the previous section, none of the subjects in this study was completely onside as far as the succeeding waves of feminisms were concerned, and this has created difficulties for their rehabilitation in the hands of feminist scholars. Even, or perhaps especially, Beauvoir, the 'mother' of feminism, has had a most problematic relation with the feminist movement both in her own country and abroad.[31] In drawing on Nietzsche, I hope to overcome these difficulties. I recognize that each particular scene of writing is not a neutral space but rather one that in turn resists and is to be resisted, thus heeding Shoshana Felman's warning in *What Does a Woman Want?* that 'resisting reading for the sake of holding on to our ideologies and preconceptions (be they chauvinist or feminist) is what we tend to do in any case.' Like Felman, I am not keen to attempt 'a dogmatic summary of feminist theory and scholarship as yet another legislating process of codification of the real and another institutional legitimation and authorization' and would rather 'experiment pragmatically with strategies for reading sexual difference insofar as it specifically eludes codification and resists any legitimizing institutionalization' (1993, 6). Like Seyla Benhabib in *The Reluctant Modernism of Hannah Arendt*, I aim at steering a course between disinterested historicism, 'which kills the interest of contemporary readers in past texts by blocking the asking of any questions that transcend the immediate historical context in which these texts were written,' and the self-righteous dogmatism of latecomers: 'This [Adrienne Rich's] kind of reading of past texts is particularly prevalent among activists of social movements who, very often, simply juxtapose the misunderstandings of the past to the truths of the present. For the collective self-understanding of social movements, this kind of simplistic heuristic may be part of an inevitable process of political identity formation that requires a breaking away from the past and an assertion of one's identity as distinct from the legacy of the past. For the art of reading and appropriating the past, however, such an attitude is inadequate. If we approach tradition and thinkers of the past only to "debunk" them, then there really is no point in seeking to understand them at all' (1996, 4–5).

Likewise, I share the impatience Joanna Hodge sees in Habermas's 1981 lecture, 'Modernity: An Incomplete Project,' with the production of the terms 'postmodernity' and 'postmodernism' as responses to the demands of a product-hungry market for cultural goods, rather than as the result of identifying genuinely new phenomena for analysis (1989, 90). However, the phenomenon targeted by these theorists, which I have tentatively followed along in calling a 'postmodern' academy and will return to in more detail in the conclusion of this study, does seem, if not genuinely new, then a rather disturbing mutation. Certainly, the star-studded, groupie-dominated, Anglo-American academy against which Barry Olshen rails in 'Subject, Persona, and Self in the Theory of Autobiography' (1995) is a much different beast from its staid counterpart of a few decades earlier, dominated as it was by great-yet-humble men of letters who wrote confidently on topics such as 'Truth and Design in Autobiography,' as though both were not only possible but self-evident. I found in Nietzsche's philosophy of the self an adroit context in which to situate not only the autobiographical writing in question but also this not unrelated academic mutation.

When viewed through an autobiographical lens, three of what are arguably Nietzsche's most critical, and contentious, concepts – the eternal return, the will to power, and the *Übermensch* – fit together like so many pieces of a jigsaw puzzle. In *Nietzsche: Life as Literature*, Alexander Nehamas finds in Proust's *Recherches du temps perdu* 'the best possible model' for explicating Nietzsche's idea of a perfect life:

The life of Proust's narrator need not have been, and never was, Nietzsche's own specific ideal. But the framework supplied by this perfect novel which relates what, despite and even through its very imperfections, becomes and is seen to be a perfect life, and which keeps turning endlessly back upon itself, is the best possible model for the eternal recurrence ...[32] Nietzsche seems to think that to lead a perfect life is to come to know what the self is that is already there and to live according to that knowledge. But to live according to that knowledge will inevitably include new actions that must be integrated with what has already occurred and the reinterpretation of which will result in the creation or discovery of a self that could not have been there already. This paradoxical interplay between creation and discovery, knowledge and action, literature and life is at the center of Nietzsche's conception of the self. (1985, 168)

Such interplay is also at the centre of autobiographical writing. What more appropriate way is there to 'become what one is' than by living autobiographically? In autobiographical writing, a character, a cultural persona replete with personal narrative is created,[33] one that comes to function metonymically for its author; and that character is recreated by reviewing, by overviewing, one's life in Nietzschean style, asking questions such as: Can one accept one's life exactly as it has been? How does one handle the return of one's memories? Has one lived in such a way that they can be fashioned into a narrative that one is willing to acknowledge as one's own story, to affirm as one's inevitable fate, à la *amor fati*? While the question of fashioning a self-narrative is answered more often by the burning of bridges than in building ones to Nietzsche's *Übermensch*, the act itself inherently can provide for a Nietzschean expression of the will, for a demonstration of the power it takes to create in life and then recreate in writing a coherent self-narrative.

Another way of approaching 'coherent self-narrative' is, of course, as identity. In *Situating the Self*, Seyla Benhabib defines identity as follows: 'Identity does not refer to my potential for choice alone, but to the actuality of my choices, namely, to how I, as a finite, concrete, embodied individual, shape and fashion the circumstances of my birth and family, linguistic, cultural and gender identity into a coherent narrative that stands as my life's story ... The self is not a thing, a substrate, but the protagonist of a life's tale.' The question arises, however, as to how to read the stories of these selves. In her critique of Habermas's, Rawls's, and Kohlberg's universalist moral theories based on a 'generalized' (i.e., bourgeois, white, male property owner) other, Benhabib concludes that what is necessary is to recuperate a sense of a 'concrete' other and thereby 'to reconsider, revise, and perhaps reject the dichotomies between justice and the good life, interests versus needs, norms versus values,' that is, the dichotomies between *Sittlichkeit* and *Moralität*, ethics and morality (1992, 161–2, 170).

Although Nietzsche might perhaps strike the reader as an odd bridge for such a context, seen within the history of philosophical thought he is not. For Nietzsche wrote to fill a platonically induced lack in nineteenth-century European society to which his classical training was attuned. In the introduction to *Love's Knowledge*, Martha Nussbaum paints for us this prelapsarian intellectual idyll: 'for the Greeks of the fifth and early fourth centuries B.C., there were not two separate sets of questions in the area of human choice and action, aesthetic questions and moral-philosophical questions, to be studied and written about by mutually detached colleagues in different departments. Instead, dramatic poetry and what we now call philosophical inquiry in ethics were both typically framed by, seen as ways of pursuing, a single and general question: namely, how human beings *should* live.' It is thanks to Plato's inaugurating such a difference that we find ourselves trapped in particular disciplinary boundaries: 'Before Plato came on the scene the poets (especially the tragic poets) were understood by most Athenians to be the central ethical teachers and thinkers of Greece, the people to whom, above all, the city turned, and rightly turned, with its questions about how to live' (1990, 15; italics added). In answering for himself the question of how one should live – as a continual revaluing of all values, a process of creative self-revaluation that would eventually drive him mad[34] – Nietzsche proved himself a tragic poet, both stylistically and fatally. In briefly turning to *Ecce Homo*, we find the form that Nietzsche put to his tragic fate and the key in which to listen to our examples of autobiographical writing.

In *Ecce Homo* Nietzsche begins: 'In the predictability of shortly having to appear before humanity with the most difficult of demands' and ends in a tirade against Christian morality, in which he likens this tirade (and himself) to a *'force majeure*, a destiny – he sunders the history of humanity in two.' By placing his story within these bookends of 'humanity' and beginning with this imperative, Nietzsche demonstrates the seriousness and the scale with which he perceives his life-project. He sees it as his duty to tell his story: 'Under these circumstances, there is a duty against which strictly speaking my habit, even more the pride of my instincts revolts, namely, to say: listen to me! For I am so-and-so.' Nietzsche thus opens the story he tells of himself by placing it not under the rubric of ambition or of scandal but of obligation. He does not want to say who he is – his entire being revolts against this task – but he feels that he must. Such an opening immediately imparts to his writing a sense of urgency. I really don't want to have to tell you this, so runs the subtext of Nietzsche's opening lines: it goes against my nature; but I must; therefore, it must be important. He then explicitly declares the feelings of responsibility that propel his project: 'Life has become easy for me, easiest when it makes the hardest demands of me. Whoever saw me during those seventy days this fall, where I without interruption did a whole pile of first rate things, for which there is no equal and no teacher (*die kein Mensch mir nachmacht – oder vormacht*) with a responsibility for all millennia after me, will have noticed no trace of tension in me, and all the more overflowing freshness and levity.' By the end of the work, Nietzsche has justified his feeling of urgency and responsibility in summarizing his oeuvre as one long, lonely cry against false morality: 'And this all was believed, as morality! – *Ecrasez l'infâme!*' (1988, 257, 373, 297, 374).[35] He constructs himself as an inimitable example and urges his readers to do the same, to pay attention to the basic concerns of life itself, and to shape and value their existence for themselves.

The same sense of revaluing drives *Zarathustra*. In the opening of Zarathustra's speeches in Part I, three metamorphoses are outlined, according to which a spirit might learn its own will and in(ter)dependence: those of the camel, the lion, and the child. The first 'weight-bearing' spirit must traverse its own desert, laden with the heaviest of burdens; the second 'preying' spirit must track, pounce on, and dismember existing 'thou shalts' that the camel would otherwise bear; and the third 'innocent and forgetful' spirit must begin afresh in its own newly created world. Analysts taking these spirits as their guide would approach a work with questions such as: Are burdens borne or portrayed as being borne, and, if so, how? Does any kind of moral disembowelment take place, and, if so, how graphically? Does a new, individual, unique world-view emerge, and, if so, what are its parameters? Immediately preceding these speeches is a prologue that sets the stage for this revaluing. The prophet goes down to the people and comes across a market scene with a tightrope walker who falls. During his self-imposed vigil over the body of the tightrope walker, Zarathustra equates the *Übermensch* with giving life meaning: 'Human existence is uncanny and still without meaning: a jester can be fateful to it. I want to teach humans the meaning of their existence: which is the *Übermensch*, a bolt out of the dark cloud of humankind' (1994, 18).[36] The context of these words is important. Confronted with an other who has literally fallen from the sky and landed at his feet, Zarathustra, and only he, not only feels but acts on his feelings of responsibility in the face (or body) of this other: 'The crowd rushed pell-mell apart, and especially where the body was about to fall. Zarathustra, however, remained where he was' (1994, 17). While the sudden presence of this body confronts all with the same ethical obligation, Nietzsche demonstrates that not all have the courage necessary to shoulder it. His earlier exhortations to readers to shape and value their existence for themselves must be amended to 'for themselves and for others.'[37]

In following from Nietzsche in this style, I propose here to enact a kind of ethics of reading that is neither general ethics nor moral philosophy.[38] If it is akin to anything, it would be to an 'ethics of personality' which, as Agnes Heller contends in her reading of Nietzsche in the third volume of her series, Theory of Morals, is the culmination of all modern ethics: 'All modern ethics culminates in an ethics of personality. An ethics of personality tells us that we are morally responsible for ourselves and our fellow creatures and that we should leap – yet it provides no crutches. This is why modern men and women still need a general ethics and a philosophy of morals.' Nietzsche's ethics of personality, however, does not represent any kind of culmination or lead Heller out of any ethical quandries: 'a merely formal concept of the ethics of personality is too broad (for example, even Hitler would qualify for it). The substantive determinations offered by Nietzsche either narrow down ethics to the most preferred type (to Nietzsche himself, to his overman, his Dionysus) or remain unfit for intersubjective generalization.' Heller argues that Wagner's Parsifal is much better fitted for an ethics of personality because one 'substantively determined by Mitleid alone already contains morality.' Nietzsche's growing obsession with Wagner can be accounted for when understood in this context: 'Nietzsche revolts [against Parsifal]: man is free; he must be fully autonomous.' That is, he must not kneel before a Grail, as Parsifal does, he must not look upward, he must not humiliate himself before something (or someone) that stands higher than himself. But Parsifal chooses to do so: 'No one tells Parsifal "you should empathize"; he simply does.' While my reading of Nietzsche credits him with a more ethical stance than Heller does, I take as my sounding board her query of Nietzsche's revolt against all morality: '[b]ut is there such a thing as full autonomy? And if there were, could it be still called "human"?' (1996, 6, 89, 90, 91). In approaching the autobiographical writing in this study as the stories of selves and their 'concrete others,' I will be reading them empathetically in search of empathy. I will argue that each in her own way (as befitting an ethics of personality, which is always in the indefinite singular) struggled with Nietzsche's injunction, and that each in her own way found her own answer to the riddle of human autonomy, precisely in making a 'Parsifalian' choice, one which in the conclusion of this study I will link to modern art and the challenges of postmodern production.

The study is structured comparatively. It consists of three parts, in each of which two projects are compared with respect to their choices and to the cultural implications of mythologizing the gender-specific self / other representations that assured the cultural relevancy of their writings. Before proceeding to the sisters themselves, however, I will set the stage, in Zarathustrian fashion, with a prologue. I began the introduction by raising the question of reception. Because all the women in this study were very much public personae, and because the nature of that publicity was in each case bound to a well-known male figure, the challenge with which their autobiographical writing confronts the reader – how to negotiate between life, text, and culture without becoming unduly mired in any of the many varieties of ideological quicksand – is magnified. As Toril Moi emphasizes in her work on Simone de Beauvoir, it is due to both Beauvoir's unorthodox lifestyle and her success as a writer that she became 'the stuff that myths are made of' and that is why 'traditional biography actually has come closer than literary criticism to capturing something of the importance of Beauvoir for our century' (1994, 5). In the prologue, I tackle the nebulous status of the biographical in scholarship in addressing the biographical relevance of *Zarathustra*. In Part 1 I read the autobiographical writings of Lou Andreas-Salomé and Simone de Beauvoir against each other as the responses of canny, culturally established writers to uncontrollable cultural and personal forces, predictable in their perversity, that dictated the terms against which they lived and wrote. What emerges in Part 2, in which the works of Maitreyi Devi and Asja Lacis are examined, are eerily similar images of the ghosts of attachments past on the parts of both the women in question and the men with whom they were fleetingly involved, Walter Benjamin and Mircea Eliade, respectively. The focus of Part 3 is the means by which Nadezhda Mandel'shtam and Romola Nijinsky establish and represent their cultural authority in telling the stories of their husbands' heroic artistic accomplishments. Thus, all three parts are designed to establish the modern, mythological parameters operating in the production of the autobiographical writing in question and to determine how they work as ethics of personality. In the conclusion I tackle the question of art and/in postmodernity and argue that, like Nietzsche, these women were important precursors of a movement in the academy that has been considered postmodern. Whereas Habermas saw in Nietzsche a 'turning point' to contemporary 'postmodern' French philosophy, I argue that in their ambiguous autonomy, these women paved the way and offer us important reading strategies for the autobiographical criticism increasingly prevalent within the Anglo-American academy.

This study, then, is founded on the following convictions: that there is a difference between simply assuming the story of one's own life narratively and actually writing it down, that is, becoming not simply text but a tangible part of one's cultural history; that it makes a difference whether one understands one's life in terms of obligation, and to whom or what that obligation is directed; and, finally, that autobiographical writing, as it is understood here in its ethical dimension, plays the role of keystone in these matters.

Getting a life is a Heraclean, if not Sisiphean, task. In setting the voices of my women in counterpoint to the voice of Nietzsche's controversial prophet, I hope to harness some of their spirit and thereby bring out harmonies in the melody of modernity that may modulate the abrasive muzak to which our postmodern condition has grown so alarmingly accustomed.

Prototypically Zarathustrian: A Prologue

It's strange. Zarathustra knows little of women, and yet he's right about them! Is this because nothing's impossible with women? And now take a little truth as thanks! I'm certainly old enough for it! ... Are you going to the ladies? Don't forget the whip!

'Of Old and Young Women,' *Zarathustra*[1]

In *Ecce Homo* Nietzsche claims that the first part of *Zarathustra* 'overtook' him in ten tumultuous days in January 1883. While the actual length of Nietzsche's creative outburst has been questioned, that it occurred in the traumatic aftermath of his encounter with Lou Salomé has not. Not only does their story make manifest the socio-historical stakes inherent in the designation 'Zarathustra's sisters,' but it allows us to redress the nebulous status of the biographical in scholarship. Before proceeding to the sisters themselves, let me first set the stage by turning to the romantic circumstances surrounding *Zarathustra*'s conception and the consideration they have been granted in the reception of the two main protagonists.[2]

Nietzsche first met Lou Salomé in late April 1882 in the full bloom of a Rome spring. Lou Andreas-Salomé[3] recounts in her memoirs that this meeting took place in St Peter's Basilica, where their mutual friend, Paul Rée, was in the habit of working. 'From which stars have we fallen to each other here?' is how Lou Andreas-Salomé recalls being greeted by Nietzsche (LRB 80/47).[4] It was not the first attempt at such a meeting. At the end of March Lou had made a detour through Genoa in the hope of meeting Nietzsche, but he had already embarked on a Columbus-like sea voyage to Messina. 'Through this step you've shocked and worried the young Russian girl the most,' a reproachful Rée wrote Nietzsche when he learned of the news. 'You absolutely must meet her,' the letter continued (Dok 106).[5] When they did meet, however, it exposed the crossed purposes of the self-proclaimed 'holy trinity.' Both men raced to propose marriage to the 'energetic, unbelievably clever creature with the most girlish, even childlike of features' (Dok 106), while that creature had her own dream, which she found 'particularly convincing,' perhaps because it 'flew directly in the face of all social conventions. In it I saw a pleasant study filled with books and flowers, flanked by two bedrooms, and walking back and forth between us, a cheerful, earnest circle of collegial comrades in work' (LRB 76/45). Lou was not a stranger to marriage proposals. Back in her native St Petersburg, not only had the Dutch Protestant pastor whom she had approached as a seventeen-year-old for spiritual and intellectual guidance agreed to provide her with instruction in Goethe and Schiller, Spinoza and Kant (and could she possibly learn Dutch and help him with the translation of Otto Pfeiderer's *Philosophy of Religion on a Historical Foundation*? Of course she could), but he eventually could not resist offering to leave his marriage and two children of her age in order to be better able to instruct her in more worldly topics as well. Her response? 'When the decisive moment unexpectedly required me to descend from the heavenly to the earthly I could not [*ich versagte*]. At one blow, that which I had worshipped fled from my heart and mind into foreign lands' (LRB 29/13), and she departed for Switzerland and university studies forthwith.

The 'Lou affair,' as it is commonly referred to in the scholarship on Nietzsche, lasted approximately six months.[6] Shortly after their first encounter in Rome, on 5 May 1882, Lou, her mother, Nietzsche, and Rée again met in a small mountain town north of Milan, where Lou and Nietzsche took much longer climbing Monte Sacro than their companions thought necessary. Nietzsche would later thank her for 'the most exquisite dream of my life' (Dok 183), while Lou Andreas-Salomé would later claim not to remember whether or not she had kissed Nietzsche during the hike (LRB 236/167). A week later, after Nietzsche had paid a visit to friends in Basel, they all met again for a few days in Lucerne where the infamous 'whip' photograph was taken. It has come to be seen as epitomizing the dynamics of their platonic threesome and as inspiring the eminently quotable 'Going to the ladies? Don't forget the whip' barb in *Zarathustra*. Against a painted Alpine background, the two men are standing, as Nietzsche insisted, harnessed to a cart in which Lou is crouched holding a stick with a rope and a sprig of lilac dangling from it. After a few short days together, they once again set off on their separate ways. After mother and daughter Salomé had made stops in Zurich, Hamburg, and Berlin, Lou was able, with the written assurances of her respectable, trustworthy male protectors, to convince her mother to leave her for the rest of the summer in their care.

Lou stayed at the Rée homestead in Stibbe in western Prussia (now northern Poland) until the Bayreuth première of *Parsifal*, the last festival of Wagner's lifetime. There she was introduced to the Wagners and to Nietzsche's sister, Elisabeth, with whom she then travelled (and quarrelled on the way) to Elisabeth's summer residence in Tautenburg where Nietzsche was waiting. The prudish, spinsterly, jingoistic, thirty-six-year-old Elisabeth – who would later marry the anti-semitic founder of an Aryan colony in Paraguay and whose coffin would be crowned with a laurel wreath by the same Nazi *Führer* who had paid the eighty-nine-year-old a surprise visit at her Nietzsche Archives ten days before her death in 1935 – was not likely to take kindly to an irreverent, uninhibited, twenty-one-year-old, foreign beauty who mesmerized both Bayreuth society and her beloved brother, especially when she was then shut out of the following three weeks of lively philosophical conversation. In her memoirs, Lou records a letter she sent to Rée on 18 August: 'We will live to see him as the prophet of a new religion, one which recruits heroes as disciples. How similarly we think and feel about all this, practically taking the words from each other's mouths. We've talked ourselves practically to death these past three weeks, and strangely enough he's suddenly now able to talk almost ten hours a day' (LRB 84/50). Elisabeth did not realize how little she had to worry about. It was a point of pride with Lou not to assume any subservient duties; she was not about to become either a good little disciple or a good little wife. Judging from her correspondence and from the diary she was keeping for Rée of the intense visit, Lou seemed relieved when it drew to a close and she could leave for Stibbe. When Lou, Rée, and Nietzsche met again in Leipzig a month later, plans for a winter of living and studying together in Paris were marred by Nietzsche's jealous undermining of Rée. On 5 November Rée and Lou left for Berlin to visit Rée's mother. They parted amicably from Nietzsche, who did not suspect that they would not meet again in Paris as planned, that, in fact, he was never to see either of them again. As the following weeks confirmed the treachery of his two friends,

Nietzsche fell into despair and wrote letters threatening suicide and otherwise giving vent to his suffering, just as his sister was mounting a poison-pen campaign of her own designed to get Lou sent back to Russia. Neither epistolary effort had the intended effect, yet the correspondence briefly united them. Nietzsche allowed himself to believe Elisabeth's vindictive stories of the past summer and a year later was even motivated to dispatch a libellous missive to Rée's brother in which he called Rée, among other things, a slimy liar and likened Lou to a 'scrawny, dirty, smelly, little ape with false breasts' (Dok 325). By the following spring (1884), however, he realized the extent of his sister's meddling and wrote to ask her why he must continually regret their reconciliation. The letter continued: 'I have never hated anyone, except you ... Of all acquaintances I have made, the most valuable and full of consequence is that with Fräulein Salomé. Only since knowing her was I ripe for my Zarathustra' (Dok 353).

The extent to which this chronology should be understood to imply causality has been subject to scholarly debate. As Walter Kaufmann would have it in his influential 1950 monograph, *Nietzsche: Philosopher, Psychologist, Antichrist*: 'The relationships between Nietzsche, Lou, and Rée have been a matter of controversy ever since Nietzsche broke with Lou and Rée' (1968, 49). The spin that Kaufmann thus tries to put on Nietzsche's agency in the situation – as though the break was Nietzsche's idea! – does not negate, or sublate, the question of how to read Lou's relation to Nietzsche's subsequent work. In a letter in which she unburdened herself to a sympathetic friend in Basel, Clara Gelzer, in late September 1882, Elisabeth Nietzsche delivered the first dart at a Zarathustrian Lou by seeing in the cunning little vixen her brother's philosophy 'personificiert' (Dok 252). Her brother provides further fuel for such speculation. In another letter to Basel, sent a few weeks before his sister's missive, Nietzsche updated his close friend, Franz Overbeck, on the developments of the late summer: 'Unfortunately, my sister has developed into a deadly enemy of Lou's, she was full of moralistic indignation from beginning to end, and now claims to know just what my philosophy is about. She wrote to my mother, she "experienced in Tautenb. my philosophy in person and was shocked: *I* love evil, *she* however loves good ..." My sister (who didn't want to come to Naumburg as long as I was there, and is still in Tautenburg) ironically quotes in this context "Thus began Zarathustra's going under/downfall [*Untergang*]." – In fact, it is the *beginning* of the *beginning*' (Dok 229; italics in original).

A passage in a reworked version of the Columbus poem, which Nietzsche gave Lou in Leipzig before their parting, further hints at a connection between Lou and Zarathustra. While the final version counsels her against trusting 'Genoans,' there exists a version entitled 'Towards New Seas' ('Nach neuen Meeren'), which ends with the suggestive lines, 'There, suddenly, girl-friend, one was two – / And Zarathustra passed me by' ('Da, plötzlich, Freundin! wurde eins zu zwei – / Und Zarathustra ging an mir vorbei' (Dok 462–3), while a letter he wrote to Lou at the beginning of September 1882, just after her departure, ends with the entreaty: 'Finally, my lovely Lou, the old, deep, heartfelt request: *become that which you are!* First one has need of emancipating oneself from one's *chains*, and then one must *emancipate* oneself from this emancipation!' and is signed 'In fond devotion of your destiny – for in you I also love *my hopes*. F.N.' (Dok 224; italics in original). Although Nietzsche's friends expressed no doubt concerning this co-mingling in Nietzsche's mind – Peter Gast writing that 'He saw in her someone rather extraordinary. Lou's intellect and her femininity sent him into ecstasies. Out of his illusion about Lou the spirit of Zarathustra was born' (cited in Etkind 1993, 21; Peters 1977, 142) – Nietzsche scholars have remained singularly unconvinced, seeing in the circumstances nothing but the possibility of Nietzsche's influence on Lou. Kaufmann's fellow Nietzsche English translator, R.J. Hollingdale, admonishes in his *Nietzsche: The Man and His Philosophy*: 'At the time, Nietzsche thought it [the "affair" with Lou Salomé] very important and his disappointment at its failure threw him off balance for a while: but there is no ground for thinking it changed him in any way or that his work from 1883 onwards would have been any different in its essentials if he had never met Lou Salomé' (1965, 179). There is, of course, ample ground for such thinking. The facts will remain that Nietzsche did meet Lou, that he did fall in love with her, that they did spend an intense summer together, and that her rejection of him instigated the writing of *Zarathustra*. There is no point in engaging in idle speculation as to what might have occurred had circumstances been different. They were not. What is important, however, is to remember that such commentary was made in the name of scholarship a comparatively short time ago, and that it still holds academic currency. The title of Mike Gane's 1993 book, *Harmless Lovers? Gender, Theory and Personal Relationships*, would seem to declare an intention to go beyond the philosophical and sociological pale and interrogate the effect of personal relationships on the works of noted social theoreticians. However, it is a sober, skeletal rendering of the encounter that Gane offers in his chapter on Nietzsche and Lou. While careful to avoid making any outrageous statements about the 'Lou affair,' Gane is equally careful not to see in the involvement of others, especially a notorious femme fatale, anything more than background lighting for the development of philosophical thought.

Scholarship on Lou Andreas-Salomé, on the other hand, is marked by a welcome heterogeneity. While some work to establish Lou as the model for Zarathustra, others reflexively question such an approach. Biographers H.F. Peters, Angela Livingstone, and Aleksandr Etkind devote sections of their works to the ways in which 'in creating the Superman, Nietzsche was merely translating Lou into the masculine' (Livingstone 1984, 57), while feminist scholars, such as Biddy Martin and Brigid Haines, make frequent mention of the Nietzschean elements of her Weltanschauung: her lack of 'ressentiment,' her serene optimism, and her *amor fati* (Haines 1993, 78–9) without attention being drawn to their 'Nietzscheness.' Lou Andreas-Salomé's biography is a decidedly 'mixed blessing' for feminists, as Haines elaborates: 'While it is advantageous that, unlike many female authors before and since, she is well-known, it is nevertheless to be regretted that her fame should result almost entirely from a fascination on the part of succeeding generations of critics with her biography, in particular her connections with the many famous men that she knew (Nietzsche, Rilke and Freud, to name but a few), and that so much of the writing on her should be underwritten by often prurient speculation as to the nature of her relationships with them.' In order to compensate for 'this overemphasis on the biographical,' which has meant that Lou Andreas-Salomé's literary, essayistic, and psychoanalytical works 'have not been looked at for their own intrinsic interest,' this latest surge of scholarship has caught the 'Death of the Author' wave and ridden its liberating poststructural discourse in order to establish 'gender as a product of the conflict between competing forms of subjectivity' (Haines 1991, 416, 417). The biographical had its day; it was misused and its plug was deservedly pulled, draining away the tepid fascination of critics as well as the baby so often subject to prurient speculation.[7]

While it is admittedly not enough to faciley attribute or deny causality to real-life encounters such as the 'Lou affair,' I believe that one must nonetheless heed and respect the historical resonances of texts. They are not, as the above *récit* amply demonstrates, written in vacuums. Zarathustra need not be directly equated with Lou, yet her part in it should be neither whitewashed, aggrandized, nor ignored.[8] In order to capture the complexity of the situation, I suggest reading *Zarathustra* as addressed in the first instance to Lou, as speaking with and thereby trying to continue at least intellectual contact with her, his friend, and with others like her:

> My gift is poor, my voice is not loud,
> And yet I live – and on this earth
> My being has meaning *for someone*:
> My distant heir shall find it
> In my verses; how do I know? my soul
> And his shall find a common bond,
> As I have found *my friend* in my generation,
> I will find a reader in posterity.
>
> (E.A. Baratynsky; cited in O. Mandel'shtam 1979, 68; italics added)

In a similar spirit, the following readings of 'Zarathustra's sisters' will be attuned to the frequencies on which Zarathustrian echoes register and will be focused on them as, in Toril Moi's words, 'the stuff that myths are made of' (1994, 5). Attention will be drawn to the ways in which Lou Andreas-Salomé and Simone de Beauvoir mobilized their autobiographical writing to counter societal mythologies and entrench their positions as sovereignly established figures of literary and cultural import. The autobiographical writings of Maitreyi Devi and Asja Lacis will be presented as anti-mythologies, setting the record straight about their fatefully fleeting relationships with young scholars whose work was destined for substantial academic capital. Finally, the texts of Nadezhda Mandel'shtam and Romola Nijinsky will be analysed to reveal the mythologizing means by which these literary widows offered up both their husbands and themselves as heroic figures. Let us now turn to Lou Andreas-Salomé's memoir and listen to the echoes against which it is heard, to names insidiously twisted in slanderous whisper.

Part 1 Writing Over

ISHTAR: important Babylonian-Assyrian goddess, also with male attributes, a goddess of war and of love, also of fertility. She often appears as the sister of the weather god. The main goddess of Ninive, the capital of the Assyrian empire which was destroyed by the Babylonians and the Meders.

Reclams Bibel Lexikon

CHAPTER ONE

Lou Andreas-Salomé

Still is my sea's floor: who would guess that it harbours jocular monsters!
Imperturbable is my depth: but it glistens with swimming riddles and
laughter.

'Of Those Who Are Sublime,' *Zarathustra*[1]

When her memoirs were first published in 1951, fourteen years after
her death, under the editorship of her literary executor, Ernst Pfeiffer,
Lou Andreas-Salomé was a forgotten remnant of a lost age. Born Luise
von Salomé in St Petersburg on 12 February 1861, just as Russia was
emancipating its serfs and almost exactly five years after it had lost the
Crimean War, this not particularly dutiful daughter of a Germanic Balt,
highly placed in the service of the tsars Nicholas I and Alexander II,
was to let nothing and no one tie her down. The youngest of six children, and the only girl, little Ljolja found herself afloat in a world of
fluid boundaries, both at home and not at home in her family, her religion, and her country. She had a Russian nurse, a French governess,
the family spoke German, and at age eight she was sent to an English
private school. The family's sumptuous living quarters across from the
tsar's Winter Palace and their summer house in Peterhof seemed the
stuff of fairytales, as did the beggars outside in the street. While her
older brothers played at being adult, her soon-to-be-pensioned father
played like a child with her, his long-desired daughter. She soon lost
faith in the strict, pietistic religion that a family of Huguenot descent
was bound to practise but, not wanting to hurt her father, long kept up
the pretence of prayer. The lines separating fantasy, play, and reality
were smudged for little Ljolja. She belonged nowhere and everywhere

and felt tied to no one and everyone, a dynamic that would characterize her later life and writing.

It was the spectre of confirmation that drove her to secretly seek out Hendrik Gillot at age seventeen, and the Dutch pastor responded not only with an education which would later stand her in good stead, in Zurich, with Nietzsche, and beyond,[2] but also, since he found the Russian diminutive of her name unpronounceable, by rechristening her. When her father died in February 1879 at age seventy-four, 'Lou' felt free to tell her mother about her secret education; Gillot felt free to propose marriage and, when she refused him, obliged to organize the necessary religious certification for her in Holland so that she could obtain the Russian passport she needed to study abroad. With her mother as travel companion, she arrived in Zurich, where the phenomenon of the foreign female revolutionary student was prominent, just in time to hear the news of Tsar Alexander's assassination. Despite being impressed by the drive of her female compatriots to study medicine and return to minister to their countrymen and women, she did not feel that pull and made no attempt to join their ranks or their all-night political discussions. Her studies were soon marred by the poor health that was to plague her incessantly and that forced her to seek sunnier climates.[3] Leaving a strong impression on professors and fellow students alike, she was soon the new favourite of Malwida von Meysenbug's salon. A witness at the nuptials of her close friends, Richard and Cosima, this 'patroness of the revolutionaries ... celebrated as *the* idealist of her day' (Sorell 1975, 141; italics in original) had just returned from a recuperative winter in Sorrento spent with Nietzsche, Rée, and another student. Appreciative as Lou may have been of her new friend's emancipatory fervour, she found certain of its elements problematic: 'But I realized a long time ago that we two are constantly talking about different things, even when we agree. She keeps saying "we" mustn't do this or that, "we" have to do this – and I really don't have any idea who this "we" is – some ideal or philosophical entity no doubt – but the only thing I know about is "I." I can't live according to some model, and I could never be a model for anyone else; but I intend to shape my life for myself, no matter how it turns out' (LBR 78/46). Lou was less than appreciative of Meysenbug's bourgeois propriety and her attempts to encourage special friendships, that is, those that would result in societally sanctioned marriage, with first Rée, then Nietzsche, and then again with Rée. As discussed above, Lou was not so inclined: 'it was precisely *this* which prevented me from allowing myself to become his [Nietzsche's] apostle, his successor. I would always have been leery of going in *that* direction, one which I had to escape in order to find clarity' (LRB 84–5/50; italics in original).[4]

She preferred or (as she insisted and as will be discussed presently) felt compelled to have Gillot marry her to the Orientalist Friedrich Andreas, who had been born in Batavia (now Jakarta). So it happened, on 20 June 1887, that she once again participated in a religious ceremony of dubious meaning to her in the small Dutch church in Santpoort. Unlike Nietzsche, Andreas was prepared to accept her on her own terms. When, ten years later, his thirty-four-year-old wife took up, albeit most discreetly, with a twenty-one-year-old poet of modest repute by the name of René Maria Rilke (which she immediately suggested he change to Rainer), Andreas did not complain. When, in the summer of 1897, she, Rilke, and their mutual friend Frieda von Bülow rented a small Bavarian farmhouse, which they named 'Loufried' after Wagner's 'Wahnfried,' he was happy for the five weeks he and their dog could visit. When she and Rilke became engrossed in Russian, he left them to their studies and expressed interest in combining the trip to Russia the two were eagerly planning with the return visit to Persia he had long been intending.[5] He even allowed them to return for a second time to Russia in the summer of the following year (1900), this time unaccompanied. He did not try to stop his wife from attending the 1911 conference of the International Psychoanalytic Association in Weimar, or from becoming the only woman in Freud's Wednesday evening circle, or from accepting psychoanalytic patients in the lean and crazily inflationary post-war years when Freud's generosity was the only thing putting butter on their daily bread. Perhaps most remarkably, Andreas did not insist that Lou consummate the marriage or that she play housekeeper either in his Berlin-Tempelhof bachelor apartment where they spent their first married years or in Göttingen where he received a university appointment in west Asiatic languages in 1903.[6]

Perhaps Andreas felt he had no right to demand anything wifely of Frau Lou, since it was her pen that was supporting them. When they met, his was a hand-to-mouth existence, offering private instruction in Turkish and German to soldiers and diplomats (his tutoring someone living in her apartment building had occasioned their first chance encounter), whereas she was already a respected member of the European literary scene with a well-received publication to her credit. Under the pseudonym Henri Lou (Gillot's first name was Hendrik), she had penned the 1885 *Im Kampf um Gott* (*Struggling with God*), a weighty, quasi-autobiographical novel in the form of memoirs of a parson's son who wreaks unintentional havoc on three women, the first dying giving birth to his illegitimate child, the second poisoning herself after nobly relinquishing him to his freedom, and the third drowning herself after discovering that he cannot become her husband, as she had hoped, because he is her father. After her marriage, Lou Andreas-Salomé turned to scholarly writing as a means of securing the 'family' livelihood. At the centre of the Naturalist movement in Berlin, she began publishing articles in Otto Brahm's newly founded *Die Freie Bühne* and in the *Vossische Zeitung*, the *Neue Deutsche Rundschau*, and *Die Frau*. Her timely 1892 *Henrik Ibsens Frauen-Gestalten* (*Henrik Ibsen's Female Figures*) and 1894 *Friedrich Nietzsche in seinen Werken* (*Friedrich Nietzsche in His Works*) were recognized as ground-breaking additions to scholarship. The majority of her almost twenty books are autobiographically influenced fiction, while her hundred-odd articles range from literary reviews to treatises on religion and sexuality.

It was in Göttingen in the early 1930s that her health began to deteriorate. If she were to leave a testament to her life as a writer and participant in some of the key cultural developments of her day, she had to do it quickly, and thus, as she notes in the margins at the conclusion of the addition, 'What's Missing from the Sketch': 'This all was written too quickly because my eyes no longer dare wait for anything' (LRB 307/145). While it is not surprising that the writings of the psychoanalytically tainted 'Hexe von Hainburg' ('Witch of Hainburg,' her Nazi nickname) did have to wait, their author was lucky enough to make her final exit on 5 February 1937 without any Nazi prompting. *Lebensrückblick: Grundriß einiger Lebenserinnerungen* was published posthumously in 1951, and although Italian, French, Danish, and Spanish translations were to appear in 1975, 1977, 1979, and 1980, respectively, an English translation, *Looking Back: Memoirs*, did not appear until an even forty years after the publication of the German original.

In 1991, the year of Breon Mitchell's English translation, a full-fledged rehabilitation of Lou Andreas-Salomé by feminist scholarship appeared in the form of Biddy Martin's *Woman and Modernity: The (Life)Styles of Lou Andreas-Salomé*. While earlier scholarship had tended to be male and hostile (e.g., Peters 1962; Binion 1968; Andrews 1972) and women biographers in the 1980s were inclined to emphasize Lou Andreas-Salomé's mystical femininity (cf. Livingstone 1984; Koepcke 1986), Martin's feminist focus is on the way 'Salomé's constructions and negotiations of sexual difference open up interesting conceptual possibilities and tell us a great deal about the significance of sexuality and sexual difference in late nineteenth century Germany' (1991, 8). Martin's work has since been substantially supplemented, most recently by a special issue of *Seminar* edited by Raleigh Whitinger. Having served as subject for fiction and poetry, stage and screen,[7] Lou Andreas-Salomé is now firmly established not only within the German (feminist) canon but in European cultural history as well (see, e.g., Hahn 1994).

This change, or evolution, in the focus of Andreas-Salomé scholarship provokes both the question of how to go about reading 'Lou' without getting tangled in the well-laid web of stories surrounding her person and her writing and the question of how to negotiate the many 'Lous' and 'Salomés' that have become part of our tradition. For if the figure of Lou Andreas-Salomé is nothing else, it is prismatic, split into a series of well-defined, well-known, hardly reconcilable characters: the young 'Ljolja' who was enraptured by the religious and, in turn, enraptured her Dutch pastor; the slightly older 'Lou' who beguiled the European literary-salon scene in general and one lonely, sickly, former Herr Professor from Basel in particular; the established, married 'Lou Andreas-Salomé' whose work and person dazzled a young poet from Prague; and the older, stately 'Frau Lou' whose influence in psychoanalytic circles was subtle yet profound. All are highly programmatic figures, isolated into manageable slivers of mythology, all with 'something fairytale-like' about them (Ross 1992, 115). Lou Andreas-Salomé herself has done much to contribute to this tendency by fragmenting *Looking Back* into distinct chapters, each encapsulating a formative 'experience'[8] in her life – with God, with love, with friendship, with Russia, with Rainer, and so on. These sections do not seem intended to be united into a larger narrative; they are autonomous pieces, as though each were from a different jigsaw puzzle. One is not to reassemble them so much as to string them along, forming a necklace of semi-precious stones whose smooth surfaces and mottled colours encourage a kind of peaceful, seaside contemplation. There is a tendency in the scholarship on Lou Andreas-Salomé to simply trip from stone to stone along this biographical path. The following reading will situate *Looking Back* along that path, acknowledging its zigzag nature, as does Martin – Lou Andreas-Salomé insisted that all women run a zigzag path between the feminine and the human – but focusing on what she was dodging.

That the names 'Lou' and 'Salomé' were an integral part of the fin-de-siècle zeitgeist has not gone unnoted in the literature: 'Salomé entered a Europe in which the woman question and the perils and promises of modernity constituted a virtual obsession and in which the name of Salomé, that murderous seductress of old, Herod's daughter, inspired the creative imaginations and the fears of male artists and thinkers ... She has been read not only as the proponent but also as the literal personification of the misogynist turn-of-the-century stereotype, the living reflection of the Lulus and Salomés, the femmes fatales who dominated the imaginations of turn-of-the-century male artists' (Martin 1991, 19, 21). Rose-Maria Gropp offers the following summary: 'As a "phantom woman" in pure culture, Lou Andreas-Salomé is here something of a figure of integration. The fascination of the beautiful man-destroyer as well as the tendency to eliminate the disturbing "woman" factor, which has been aptly described as "revirginaliza-tion," are united in an exemplary way in her: "Salomé: the name prom-ises contradictory images of passion and prudery." This *nomen-est-omen* analogy evokes the monstrousness of the involuntary "femme fatale," while at the same time dulling the fictionalisation: one then would have to show her what she *actually wanted*' (1988, 12; italics in original). The phenomenon of *nomen-est-omen*, while thus glossed, has yet to be mined for its potential influence on Lou Andreas-Salomé's creation of a cultural persona for herself in her memoirs. Lou Andreas-Salomé's memoirs will be considered here to constitute a sophisticated response to the mythologizing pressures of the zeitgeist and its zigzag path to represent a concerted attempt to dodge, or at very least dilute, the harshness of predatory cultural rays.

Lou-Lou Strikes First

The figure of Salomé and, more specifically, the Salomé of the Dance of the Seven Veils was one of the most popular themes in fin-de-siècle European art. The brief biblical episodes – Matthew 14:1–12 and Mark 6:14–29 – were to prove the stuff of scandalous decadence beginning with Heine's 1842 *Atta Troll* and cresting in Huysman's 1874 epoch-making *À Rebours*. They also served as one of the French symbols sine qua non[9] in addition to providing the subject matter for over 100 picto-rial works of European art between 1870 and 1920 (cf. Wäcker 1993), the very period when Lou von Salomé was establishing herself on the European cultural scene. The attraction of the biblical Salomé at this

time is not difficult to account for: 'hardly any other subject corre-
sponded with so many of the epoch's preferences: the orient and the
exotic, dance and seduction, demonization and eroticization, hedo-
nism and death' (ibid., 1). The figure of Salomé functioned, as myths
do, to allow for the expression of the epoch's obsessions, its inner tensions and fears, under the guise of historical distance and objectivity:
'Representation professes to re-present these origins but does so
according to a mythology upheld by the society which invents it. What
representation re-presents, then, is the need for a society to believe in
forgetting, in order to cover up the arbitrariness and mortality of consensus' (Meltzer 1987, 216). By turning the obedient, shy, biblical
daughter into a 'deathly pale, cold, tyrannical virgin' (Schaffner 1965,
5), the inherently misogynistic fin-de-siècle zeitgeist betrayed the
threat it felt women represented, at the same time allowing for its
expression and for it to be forgotten, covered up.

The centrality, indeed scapegoating, of Lou Andreas-Salomé in this
process of cultural representational repression can be seen by turning
to a second very popular female figure at the time – Lulu. The heroine
of two Wedekind dramas, *Der Erdgeist* (1898, *The Earth Spirit*) and *Die
Büchse der Pandora* (1904, *Pandora's Box*), is the quintessential femme
fatale.[10] At the opposite end of the spectrum from the 'hooker with a
heart of gold' theme so prevalent in North American culture, Wedekind's Lulu leaves not broken hearts but a trail of male corpses in her
wake, prompting one critic to dub her 'the most ambitious whore in
the history of the German theater' (Andrews 1972, 203). An indicator
of the resonance that Wedekind's plays found among his contemporaries is the success of G.W. Pabst's 1929 film *Die Büchse der Pandora*, and
Alban Berg's 1937 opera *Lulu*, both based on the Wedekind plays.

The connection between the character Lulu and Lou Andreas-
Salomé has become part of German literary legend.[11] Lou Andreas-
Salomé describes becoming acquainted with Wedekind in Paris in the
spring of 1894, at which point he was riding the success of his 1891
Frühlings Erwachen (*Spring Awakening*), as follows: 'I spent almost the
most time in Paris with Frank Wedekind. But that was later on. For at
first, after we had met at the home of the Hungarian Countess Neme-
thy, and accompanied the others to the onion soup restaurant across
from "Les Halles," where we continued our lively conversation into
the early hours of the morning, a Wedekindian misunderstanding
arose, as he later recounted with touching openness and without any
attempt to exonerate himself (and which I also later made use of as

padding for a novella [*Fenitschka*; written 1896, pub. 1898])' (LRB 100/ 60). Ernst Pfeiffer felt it appropriate, in his capacity as editor, to intercede and attribute to Lou the words she has her female protagonist in *Fenitschka* utter: 'The delicate situation in which Lou A.-S. involved herself by her innocence regarding signs of male interest is recognizable in this story [*Fenitschka*] – as are the words (even if not actually spoken) Lou used in order to extricate herself and Wedekind: "The blame is mine, Mr W., for I have never yet met a dishonourable man"' (187, n60). Lou Andreas-Salomé's biographers, in not neglecting to include mention of the passage, have assured that it has become yet another facet of the Lou legend (Livingstone 1984, 232; Koepcke 1986, 177). This episode reveals Lou Andreas-Salomé's strategy in negotiating cultural space, a strategy that could be summed up as a 'first strike' approach. Astutely anticipating both the likelihood of Wedekind's using her character and her name in a less than charitable way and the resonance that it would find in the zeitgeist, she made sure that her version of events was made available, first in the fictional form of her novella and then in her last text of autobiographical writing.[12]

Looking Back can be read as a compendium of first strikes. In the first episode, in which she concretely presents the figure of herself as a young child, she attributes to herself an anticipatory approach: 'A small memory makes believable to me this method whereby I tried to hold off doubt: in a splendid pop-open package which my father had brought home from some festival at court, I got the idea that there were golden dresses. When I was made aware of the fact that the clothes in it were simply made of satiny paper trimmed in gold – I decided not to open it. Thus what *remained* in the box were still to a certain extent the golden clothes' (LRB 13/3; italics in original). Lou Andreas-Salomé thus introduces herself as a strong-minded little girl who already had begun to attempt to control how reality is thought of. Anticipating the truth of the allegations that the clothes will indeed turn out to be not real gold, she finds a way of minimizing the damage of this revelation and manages to keep the clothes, 'to a certain extent' (*gewissermassen* – not in the English translation), golden.

The rest of the book then falls into a pattern of keeping things to some extent golden in the face of serious challenges to her expectations, particularly in her relations with others, particularly those of the opposite sex. The stuff of the second chapter, 'The Experience of Love,' marks the beginning of her rejection of God-substitutes, of which she writes with evident pride: 'But aside from this negative result, the childish aspect of God's disappearance also had a positive side: it thrust me into real life with equal irrevocability. I am certain that – judged autobiographically to the best of my ability – any substitute concepts of God which might have got caught up with my feelings would only have restricted, deflected, impaired me' (LRB 23/10). Her relationship with Gillot and her not so much rejection of as moving beyond him set the tone for later relationships, both recorded (with Nietzsche, Rée, Rilke, and her husband) and unrecorded (Ledebour and Pineles). While the later chapters offer little of the theorizing of the earlier ones, the pattern thus established with Gillot was to carry on interminably. With the important exception of Freud,[13] Lou Andreas-Salomé invariably found her 'childlike dreams and fantasies pushed aside in the real world' as she writes of her experience with Gillot, and she felt helpless to do anything about it. In the case of Paul Rée, 'in spite of the honest and open discussions we had ... a fundamental misunderstanding persisted.' Neither, in the case of Nietzsche, is there anything she can do: 'I was protected from much of the ugliness of this period ... it even appears that some of Nietzsche's letters never reached me.' In the case of Rilke, 'deep in the heart of anyone who saw it happen a realization remains of how little could be done to alleviate Rainer's final loneliness ... Those who saw it happen could only let it happen. Powerless and reverent.' In the case of her husband, she again wrote of her helplessness, that she had married out of compulsion (*Zwang*): 'what brought about this compulsion was the power of the *irresistible* to which my husband himself succumbed' (LRB 28/12, 92/55, 85/50, 200/125; italics in original German). In each case, she did what she could but felt herself helpless to change the situation – she could neither resist her husband, nor alleviate Rilke's anxiety, nor communicate with Rée or Nietzsche.

Yet her reputed helplessness is infused with a distinct sense of agency; for in the text there is considerable value placed on women's being the helmspersons of their own existence and banishing all others if not down into the hold then from the ship entirely. Certainly the element of independent choice is glorified in her description of her mother's final years: 'Her greatest problem toward the end was that we children saddled her with a companion in her old age, so that we would know she was well cared for – a relative she liked of course, but not quite as much as she liked being alone and free to do exactly as she wished. Despite the circle of sons and grandchildren with which she was surrounded, she enjoyed being on her own, and she kept wonderfully busy to the last. Even her reading was seldom dependent on the recommendation of others; one of the very last books she read, with great enthusiasm, was the *Iliad*.' The explanation Lou Andreas-Salomé gives for rejecting friendship with Malwida von Meysenbug – that Malwida allows herself to be influenced by bourgeois propriety, whereas 'I can't live according to some model' – demonstrates a similar sentiment. The comment 'so we *let* motherhood happen to us' (LRB 53/28, 35/18; italics added)[14] is a further indication of her indicting attitude towards and expectations of women.

What is one to make of Lou Andreas-Salomé's account of this paradoxical choosing of helplessness in her relationships with men, her choosing to portray herself as sovereignly helpless, while insisting that women, in particular, maintain an independence of spirit? One possible explanation lies in the nature of the 'passion of belief' that she attributes to the Russian character: 'I felt then ... that there was really no contradiction between that small group of revolutionary bomb-throwers who were willing to sacrifice their private lives totally for a murderous mission in which they believed, and the equally total passivity of the pious peasant, who accepts his fate as God-given. It is the passion of belief which in the one case calls for worship and in the other calls to action. Over both lives, over everything privately expressed within them, is a guiding principle which does not arise from the personal sphere, from which they are able for the first time to realize themselves, and which allows both types – the peasant martyrdom as well as the terrorist martyrdom – to incorporate the consolation of their patience and the power of their violent acts.' One senses in Lou Andreas-Salomé's autobiographical writing a desire to ascribe to this 'passion of belief,' a certain wistful yearning to enter 'the circle of that which fully links a man and woman.' Her praise of female freedom, however, indicates that she senses a fundamental flaw in such passions – that they necessarily demand martyrdom. In every case she encounters a God-substitute, a mere human towards whom it would be inappropriate, and unworthy of her, to direct such passion. If she were to have a guiding principle (*ein Motto*), it would be somewhere between these calls for worship and to action. Such a possibility of impersonal guiding principles, however, is firmly rejected: 'And it's not that I have any principle to represent, but rather something much more wonderful – something that's inside of one and that's hot with the heat of life and that's itching and wants out' (LRB 65/36–7, 146/90, 78/46). It is something wonderful (*das Wunderbare*) that provides her with orientation, that substitutes for guiding principles and a passion of belief.

For Lou Andreas-Salomé would have us believe that she does not believe in anything else, that for her, the most important challenge lies in maintaining a sense of wonder when confronted with the differences between 'what we expect and what we find.' In her own experience, the catalyst is reported to be her loss in faith resulting from a rather mundane joke played on her by one of the hired help: 'A servant who each winter brought fresh eggs to our city residence from our house in the country announced one day that in front of the miniature house in the middle of the garden which I alone possessed he had found a "couple" requesting entrance, but he had told them to go away. The next time he came, I immediately asked about the couple, no doubt because I was worried that they might have starved or frozen to death in the meantime; where could they have turned?' (LRB 15/4). The snow couple's disappearance is crucial in Lou Andreas-Salomé's self-portrait. Not only does it trigger her loss of faith, it brings her to the realization that it is not only *her* loss: 'the God painted upon the curtain didn't just disappear for *me*, he disappeared *totally* – he was lost to the entire universe as well' (LRB 16/5; italics in original). Her knowledge of this loss awakens in her 'a sort of instinctive sympathy for my parents. I didn't want to cause them trouble since, like me, they had suffered a blow – for God was lost to them as well – *they just didn't know it*' (LRB 17/6; italics in original). No sooner is the burden of religion shed than a multitude of other burdens are assumed in its place. Even the characters in the stories she tells as a child come under the cloak of her responsibility: 'I recall a nightmare ... In it I saw a multitude of characters from my stories whom I had abandoned without food or shelter. No one else could tell them apart, nothing could bring them home from wherever they were in their perplexing journey, to return them to that protective custody in which I imagined them all securely resting' (LRB 18/7). In recognizing that 'something of the sort [like her experience with the Snowmen pair] happens to each of us,' she then sets this break as a pivotal moment: how we deal with it determines our future orientation. For her, this break results in an 'uncanny' relation with the world, in 'serving to increase the difficulty of making myself at home in the real world, the world without God' (LRB 16/5, 17/6). At the very outset of her life-story, Lou Andreas-Salomé presents herself as separated from, not fitting in with, and suspicious of, her surroundings. The reason, in this case her knowledge of the loss of God, is not as pertinent as its result. She is 'like a little stranger called from the outermost edge of an immense solitude into an unbelievably distant land' (LRB 17/6).[15] The world in which she found herself was to remain strange, a place without God in which she recognized a weighty responsibility, a place that, for one's own protection, must be anticipated and parried.

The organization of *Looking Back* is an integral part of these anticipatory, parrying efforts, proving Lou Andreas-Salomé an experienced, canny writer. The chapters come, like God's creatures onto Noah's ark, in twos. The first two chapters – 'The God Experience' and 'The Experience of Love' – are heavily general and theoretical, the former beginning 'Our first experience ... is that of loss' and the latter 'In every life there is an attempt to begin again' (LRB 9/1, 27/12). In the next two chapters – 'Family Life' and 'The Russian Experience' – the tone changes completely, to one more conventional to the memoir genre. Here, she relates the background and characters of her parents and brothers. The two following chapters – 'The Experience of Friendship' and 'With Other People' – have a more gossipy, society-page tone, as she enumerates her encounters with the literary establishments first in Switzerland and then in Berlin, Paris, Vienna, and Munich. The next two chapters are dedicated to Rilke – 'With Rainer' and 'Epilogue 1932' – and the next two to Freud – 'The Freud Experience' and 'Epilogue: Memories of Freud (1936).' After the solitary chapter entitled 'Before the World War and After,' which serves as an appropriate caesura, the final two chapters are dedicated to her husband – 'F.C. Andreas' and 'What's Missing from the Sketch (1933).' By parcelling her life experiences into such symmetrical, vaguely chronological chunks, she can more easily bypass episodes she does not feel it proper to include. Her intention not to write anything tabloid-trashy, 'that kind of "gossip about people" made up of hasty formulations and accidental emphases making up the great majority of our judgments' (LRB 95/57) is stated explicitly elsewhere,[16] as well as being implicit in the subtlety with which she alludes to her 'friends.' Gillot, to whom the second chapter is dedicated in spirit if not directly, is never named, although in giving both his profession (pastor) and nationality (Dutch), she obviously makes no attempt to withhold his identity. Ledebour, the Socialist statesman who begged her to leave her husband for him, receives similar, though more limited, treatment. It is not difficult to guess the identity of this 'friend' – a member of Parliament who has just finished serving time for lese-majesty. The complete absence of her lovers – Pineles, by whom she conceived although did not bear a child, and Tausk, the 'Brudertier' in her *Freud Journal* – is also indicative of the discretion that characterizes *Looking Back* as a whole.

Like the poem with which she closes the chapter on love (the poem that Nietzsche set to music and that had not been to Freud's taste), *Looking Back* is intended as a hymn to life, with an appropriately joyful, peaceful, Sunday afternoon tone. The adoption of such a tone is also a canny choice, since it is harder to lambaste – one feels, or should feel, slightly ridiculous attacking the devotional act of a simple, kindly soul. The epigraph at the beginning of Lou Andreas-Salomé's memoirs reads: 'Human life – indeed all life – is poetry. It's we who live it, unconsciously day by day, like scenes in a play, yet in its inviolable wholeness It lives us, It composes us. This is something far different from the old cliché "Turn your life into a work of art": we are works of art – but we are not the artist.' In living her life as a work of art, a hymn to life, Lou Andreas-Salomé found a way to elude the hostile cultural mythologies of her times. As the above reading of its tone, organization, subject matter, and personal philosophy demonstrates, *Looking Back* is, ironically, a very forward-looking book, guaranteeing that future generations would find an impressively, yet ambiguously, sovereign figure as a counterweight to the demonic shapes she had seen spring up around her bearing her names. While Lou Andreas-Salomé had early recognized and had come to appreciate via her training in psychoanalysis that what was to be found in her own personal box was satiny paper with gold trim, she provided in the form of autobiographical writing a cultural persona that is, to a definite extent, golden.

CHAPTER TWO

Simone de Beauvoir

'Why?' said Zarathustra. 'You ask why! I do not belong to those of whom one may ask of their "why." Is then my experience of yesterday? It was long ago that I experienced the reasons for my opinions. Would I not have to be a barrel of memory, should I want to have my reasons with me? It's already too much for me, keeping my opinions myself, and many a bird flies away.'

'Of the Poets,' *Zarathustra*[1]

Another highly programmatic, highly stylized, and highly fragmented cultural icon, Simone de Beauvoir also left behind an autobiographical legacy, a comparative reading of which mutually illuminates both its own and Lou Andreas-Salomé's anticipatory stance.[2]

As befitted her haut bourgeois background, Simone Lucie Ernestine Marie Bertrand de Beauvoir was given many names at her christening, but unlike little Luise von Salomé, her mother's name wasn't one of them.[3] While both were, theoretically, of similarly minor nobility, the situation into which the young Mlle Bertrand de Beauvoir was born on 8 January 1908 was neither as serene nor as secure as that little Fräulein von Salomé had enjoyed over a half century earlier and over a half continent away. Simone's father was not a gracefully ageing general but a young man of aristocratic education and habits who had found in the legal profession the only socially sanctioned outlet for his theatrical aspirations. Her mother was not the daughter of a prosperous owner of a confectionary plant who had dared to leave the security of Hamburg to seek his fortune in the Russian capital, but the daughter of a provincial banker whose imprudent business dealings would lead to bankruptcy, a thirteen-month stint in jail, default on his daughter's dowry, and general disgrace. As Ljolja's father had not married for a dowry, he would not have felt its loss so deeply; but Simone's father had done so and did feel the loss. As Ljolja's mother had been born in the capital and grown into the rhythms and customs of family life there, she was able to take the running of her husband's household in stride; but Simone's mother had not been so situated and thus did not easily enter into such management. Simone's mother did not have the experience of five previous children to draw on, since Simone was her first baby; Simone's father did not have the benefit of military discipline or contacts; he was easily distracted and shiftless. If, as Deidre Bair maintains in the opening of her biography, Simone de Beauvoir's memories of her childhood were painted black, it is little wonder.

Yet for all the differences, there are marked similarities in their upbringing. First, consider the role of religion. Although Mme de Beauvoir was a staunch Roman Catholic and Frau von Salomé a devout Protestant, both so insistently inflicted upon their daughters such heavy burdens of belief that in both young women a traumatic, lasting loss of God resulted. Second, examine the role of education. Both daughters were sent to properly bourgeois private schools whose specialization was churning out products ready for the 'marriage market.' Neither found her early education in any way instructive, except in the negative, but both were born autodidacts with a penchant for philosophy and theology. From the cocoons of these precocious, spoiled little darlings emerged single-mindedly rebellious, fiercely intellectual young women: girls who would be men; girls who aspired to study and debate rather than engage in society gossip and diapers; girls who felt their rightful place to be in philosophy books, not kitchens, their rightful companions to be intellectuals, not maids; girls who would take delight in standing their social worlds on end, in setting off and then placing themselves out of the hearing range of wicked tongues.

There is one question in Beauvoir scholarship that seems destined to return eternally: Why was a nice girl like Simone wasting her time sucking up to a boring old fart like J.-P.? (Angela Carter; cited in Moi 1994, 253). Why did she not reject him the way Lou had Nietzsche? It is a good question, one that has long perplexed and infuriated feminists. Why was Beauvoir content, nay proud, to accept second place to Sartre, the second place she was accorded when competing with him for the 1929 *agrégation* in philosophy? No matter that the eminent French philosopher and Benjamin translator, Maurice de Gandillac, was later to report that two of the judges 'told [him] later, it had not been easy to decide whether to give the first place to Sartre or to her. If Sartre already showed great intelligence and a solid, if at times inexact, culture, everybody agreed that, of the two, she was the real philosopher' (Cohen-Solal 1987, 74). No matter that it was Sartre's second attempt at the prestigious exam. No matter that Sartre, at twenty-four, was three years older and had enjoyed the high-quality education of the École Normale Supérieure. No matter that he had not been the one to baptise her 'Castor' during their exam preparations; it had been their study mate, René Maheu, who had playfully punned on her last name: '"You're a little Beaver," he told me, "always fussing and working ..." At first I didn't know if I should be insulted or not, but Maheu was never sarcastic with me, only to others."' Maheu was married and therefore safe. He became her trusted companion, her Rée, and the only one of the group who failed the *agrégation*. Sartre was something else. Of the study companions, he was, as Beauvoir was later to recollect for her last biographer, 'the dirtiest, the most poorly dressed, and I think also the ugliest' (Bair 1990, 129, 143). He was also the most brilliant and the most needy, a combination to which, as will be noted later, Beauvoir was particularly susceptible. As he wrote to her during his military service: 'because it's only to you that I can say what I think, what I want to write, and only you can understand my daily state, the smoke and fire of ideas' (Sartre 1993, 43–4). In short, because of Sartre, Beauvoir's being had meaning for someone; she felt she had found in him the friend with whose soul hers was to find a common bond. As will be discussed below, it was a commitment she was making as much to herself as to him, and one that was therefore irrevocable.

As Simone de Beauvoir herself found, it is difficult to recount her life *après études* without referring to Sartre. The rest of her life hinges upon their pact of 'essential' love in which Sartre promised to be faithful for two years if afterwards, as he magnanimously suggested, both agreed to have 'contingent' affairs, which each would then share in brutal honesty with the other. Personal glasnost without perestroika, it would lead to triangular and pentagonal constellations of dizzying moral complication, all nicely subsumed under their umbrella term 'The Family.' At the conclusion of the final volume of her memoirs, Beauvoir wrote: 'It is just because I loathe unhappiness and because I am not given to foreseeing it that when I do come up against it I am deeply shocked or furiously indignant – I have to communicate my feelings' (ASD 426).[4] Having been made deeply unhappy for most of her adult life, she knew of what she wrote.

The academic year 1931–2 was particularly unhappy. It was the year Sartre finished his military service and, because Beauvoir refused on principle to marry, they were posted to different lycées: he to Le Havre, she to Marseille. Both considered themselves writers and neither found teaching particularly rewarding. The next year was marginally better, since she received a requested transfer to Rouen, a mere half-hour train ride from Sartre; the following year, 1933–4, Sartre spent in Berlin studying phenomenology in a blissfully apolitical bubble. When he returned to France, Olga Kosakiewicz, the eighteen-year-old student who had been Beauvoir's solace during Sartre's absence, became her nemesis, exciting Sartre's passions and playing the two off against each other for her affections. The roller-coaster ride of the threesome, on which Beauvoir's first novel, L'Invitée (She Came to Stay), is based, continued when they returned to Paris for the 1936–7 term and soon took on a more florid complexion when their soap-operatic ranks expanded to include Olga's younger sister, Wanda; Sartre's prize pupil from Le Havre, Jacques-Laurent Bost; as well as some of Beauvoir's new students.[5]

The imminence of war changed the tenor of their licentiously self-absorbed lifestyle and thrust them out into the rive gauche café scene. With the 1938 publication of La nausée, Sartre made his literary debut. In 1943 Gallimard published not only Sartre's L'être et le néant (Being and Nothingness) and Les mouches (The Flies), but also Beauvoir's L'Invitée. With the October 1945 launch of Les Temps Modernes, they had an organ for their increasingly political writings, beginning with Sartre's manifesto for a literature of commitment. Officially, they were not merely a writing couple, but were the phenomenally productive, highly visible, existential pulse of a roiling Parisian intellectual scene that included the likes of Camus, Koestler, Bataille, Leiris, Gide, Claudel, Malraux, Cocteau, Genet, and Merleau-Ponty.[6] But what kind of a couple were they? The first issue of Temps Modernes was dedicated 'To Delores,' a vivacious Frenchwoman, whose estranged husband was a wealthy American doctor and whom Sartre had fallen for on a journalistic junket to the United States earlier that year. When Beauvoir undertook her American lecture tour two years later, she followed in Sartre's footsteps in more ways than one, beginning a torrid romance with Nelson Algren, a grittily virile Chicago writer with two modestly successful novels under his belt, whose The Man with the Golden Arm would serve in 1955 as a motion picture vehicle for Frank Sinatra. From their own accounts, these other relationships were wonderfully intense. Both Delores and Nelson came to Paris; both insisted on exclusivity; both became frustrated with their lovers' steadfast commitment to the by now mythical 'pact'; and both were unceremoniously set adrift when they wouldn't accept and conform to their contingent fates.[7]

In many ways Beauvoir's 'America affair' was to the inception of *The Second Sex* what the 'Lou affair' was to *Zarathustra*.[8] The infamous revelation in her controversial 1949 tome, that woman is not born but made, sharply raised her cultural profile, especially when both it and *The Mandarins* were placed on the Vatican Index of Banned Books in 1955. Her other writings, philosophical, autobiographical, and fictional, further served to establish her reputation as an unflinching, uncompromising intellectual. In the 1950s and 1960s, as intellectual interest in existentialism waned in France, she and Sartre found themselves in the eye of one highly political international hurricane after another. They threw their support behind Algerian independence and became the targets of extremist bombs. Sartre refused the Nobel Prize in Literature for 1964[9] and became the target of international scorn and abuse. They both sat on the Russell Tribunal, the international commission organized to protest U.S. involvement in Vietnam. They were on the barricades during May 1968, and their controversial Maoist publications provided a barometer on state repression. Throughout, they lived hard, drank hard, and travelled extensively.

Travel had always been one of Beauvoir's 'most burning desires' (PL 81),[10] and, since she and Sartre first took a train to Spain in the summer before they began teaching, it was part of their routine.[11] While they tended to holiday in the south of France, Switzerland, or Italy, invitations from abroad also kept them moving. She and Sartre were feted as official guests of Communist governments in China (September/October 1955), Yugoslavia (summer 1956), Cuba (February/March 1960), and the Soviet Union (June 1962 and again each summer until 1966, when Brezhnev assumed power and put an official end to the Thaw by sending two popular dissident writers, Sinyavsky and Daniel, to labour camps for 're-education'). In Brazil and Japan, Finland and Estonia, Poland and Czechoslovakia, Egypt and Israel, Sweden and Denmark, 'at home and abroad Sartre and de Beauvoir remained an indivisible institution' (Francis and Gontier 1987, 329).

Only in 1970 was Beauvoir first approached to support a political organization on her own, without Sartre. The request was made by the MLF (*Mouvement de Libération des Femmes*), and Beauvoir promptly threw the weight of her public persona behind it and spoke out for abortion. Her presence in the feminist movement served to show up its fault lines. Many could not accept the way she had always idolized Sartre, had made admissions such as, 'philosophically I only had the role of a disciple' (Bair 1990, 144), and had considered his work more important than hers. It was particularly difficult for American feminists to understand her attraction to Sartre, since they had come to know him during his final years, which were not his most elegant. Despite dramatically deteriorating health, he continued to drink, smoke, pop pills, and cavort as he had in his prime. Sartre had always enjoyed the luxury of being pampered; his life was a steady stream of companions, with caregivers replacing lovers as he aged. Somehow he managed to hang on until 1980. Beauvoir's liver was in equally bad shape when she followed him six years later.

In her 1996 monograph, *Simone de Beauvoir*, Mary Evans introduces her subject as follows: 'My subject is not one de Beauvoir but several, all of them inspired by the same actual person and the same social circumstances which inspired de Beauvoir herself. Thus just as "the other" was a central person in de Beauvoir's work, so the other de Beauvoirs are important here, "others" who have de Beauvoir's name, but who are often a long way removed from *the public person* whom de Beauvoir and feminism would like to record' (2–3; italics added). Beauvoir's predilection for the public sphere has been duly noted. Her insistence on working in cafés at the beginning of her writing career so that she could look up and remind herself that she was not alone, her silent, jagged crying bouts among circles of friends, and her penchant for travelling companions all have received their fair share of comment. The extent to which Beauvoir strove to create herself as a public person, however, is often underestimated. Even more so than in her fictional and philosophical output, Beauvoir was prolific autobiographically. Beginning in 1958 with *Mémoires d'une jeune fille rangée* (which appeared the following year in English as *Memoirs of a Dutiful Daughter*), there are four expansive volumes of official memoirs, ending with *Tout compte fait* in 1972 (*All Said and Done*, 1974), in addition to books on the deaths of her mother and Sartre. Beauvoir charts, at least in the first volume of her memoirs, a relatively smooth progression from ungainly though well-brought-up bourgeois daughter to critical, culturally acknowledged, intellectual woman: 'her conscience and self-awareness develop before the reader's eyes' (Francis and Gontier 1987, 276). Yet her structural principles allow her, like Lou

Andreas-Salomé, to exclude images that do not fit nicely into this frame: Simone the dutiful yet rebellious daughter, yes; Simone the world-renowned writer, certainly; Simone the lesbian lover, not a chance. Bair records that she once exclaimed with indignation: 'Well, you couldn't expect me to tell *everything*, could you?' (1990, 654, n30; italics in original). The public and private Simones can, and have, been read in a myriad of ways, the great majority of which, as in the case of Lou Andreas-Salomé, were initially virulently hostile and then increasingly feminist, which is not to say lacking in their own hostility.[12] The general trend in scholarship on Beauvoir's autobiographical writings can be discerned from the titles of the three 'Readings of the Autobiography' included in Elizabeth Fallaize's 1998 *Simone de Beauvoir: A Critical Reader*: Francis Jeanson's 'The Father in *Memoirs of a Dutiful Daughter*,' Alex Hughes's 'Murdering the Mother in *Memoirs of a Dutiful Daughter*,' and Elaine Marks's 'Encounters with Death in *A Very Easy Death* and the Body in Decline in *Adieux: A Farewell to Sartre*.'[13] In contrast to these feminist and often psychoanalytically tinged interpretations is the following reading, the focus of which is the dynamics of Beauvoir's relation to the French cultural establishment.

Simoniacal Simone

When the process of Beauvoir's self-construction as an anticipation of and response to cultural pressures is examined, what immediately strikes one is the chronology of her oeuvre. It was only after *The Mandarins* had won the prestigious Prix Goncourt in 1954, her first formal recognition in the beatifying world of French letters, that she set about her massive autobiographical undertaking; that is, it was only after, but also as soon as, she had come to occupy the long-cherished role of established French writer that she set about writing an official account of how she had achieved that goal. Her extraordinary speed in ensconcing herself as a recognized, distinguished French writer points to the importance the position held for her, as does the fact that she wrote no more monumental works of either fiction or philosophy after beginning her autobiographical project.[14] There has been a great deal of comment and conjecture about the highly autobiographical nature of Beauvoir's oeuvre, especially her tendency to write *romans-à-clef*. In a letter to Algren she 'complained with a certain degree of bitterness that no one gave her credit for having an imagination of her own' (Bair 1990, 449, 662, n57). Viewed against the chronology of her work, it seems as though Beauvoir had only been waiting to lift the veil of fiction and claim the life she had long aspired to: that her desire to write the stories of her experiences was constant, but she felt she had to wait to claim them until she could do so from the position of authority to which she aspired.[15] Given her notorious carelessness with respect to the detail and 'authenticity' of her memoirs, the only meaningful difference between the accounts she wrote, for example, of her relationship with Algren in the fictional *Mandarins* and the autobiographical *Force des choses* (*Force of Circumstance*), would seem to be the use of the pseudonyms Brogan and Anne in the former.[16] Certainly both infuriated Algren to the same degree and seemed to him the same breach of privacy; he considered both to belong to the scurrilous genre of 'autofiction.'[17] Her autobiographical writing is not, then, simply the 'core' of Beauvoir's oeuvre (Vintges 1996, 115), it is also its culmination.

Beauvoir began her autobiographical project at a pivotal point not only in her own career as a writer, but also in the existentialist movement just after it had crested, and she continued to write as though the position of authority of existentialists within French intellectual circles had not been eclipsed by first structuralists and then poststructuralists. '"It happened so fast," Beauvoir reflected in 1986. "One day we were the main attraction ... and the next day there was an entirely new way of looking at the world of politics and literature"' (Bair 1990, 522).[18] Consideration of Sartre's later works, especially the 1960 *Critique de la raison dialectique*, which renounces his earlier existentialist writing and is followed by a noticeably different style of auto/biographical work (*Saint Genet: comédien et martyr; Les mots; L'idiot de la famille, Gustave Flaubert de 1821–1857; Mallarmé: la lucidé et sa face d'ombre*), not to mention the Maoist turn in his political thought, throws a much different light on, especially, the second and third volumes of Beauvoir's memoirs, making them appear not a dialogue with Sartre (Evans 1996, 7) but rather a counterbalance to the writer he was becoming. As Bair astutely notes, 'her autobiography becomes in many instances an apologia for Sartre's life, a diatribe that scolds all those who ignored, reviled or disagreed with him'; one might add, in the light of Sartre's concomitant works, that her memoirs also scold Sartre himself. Given the time frame, Beauvoir can be seen to be recreating the Sartre that had barely defeated her to take first place in the *agrégation*, the Sartre with whom she had made the famous pacts, the Sartre whose existentialist principles she had helped to form and that served as her anchor – just as Sartre was in the process of intellectually as well as privately hoisting up that anchor and sailing away from her. In 1956, the year Beauvoir was immersed in the first volume of her memoirs and when the Algerian crisis was gathering momentum, Arlette Elkaim, then a seventeen-year-old Algerian student, later to become Sartre's adopted daughter and thus his literary heir, joined the Sartrean family and began quietly usurping Beauvoir's role in his life. Beauvoir's objections to Sartre's new blend of Marxian psychoanalysis which she could not follow – 'the *Critique of Dialectical Reason* went right over my head' – can in part explain his 'uncharacteristic indifference to her role as first reader, critic and editor of his work.' However, that 'more and more he wanted to do his writing at Arlette's apartment, which he claimed was most conducive to concentration and relaxation,' however, also points towards his having found more compliant ears elsewhere. It was on this threshold that Beauvoir found herself upon completing what she had intended to be the one and only volume of her memoirs. '"My last book, the story of my childhood, was fun to write and is selling very well, but I don't know what to write next in these upsetting times," she told Algren in her New Year's greetings of 1959,' without specifying how much of the upset should be attributed to the worsening political situation and how much to her worsening personal one. It did not take her long to decide to continue with her autobiographical project, not, as Bair would have it, despite the fact that it would mean writing the story of her relationship with Sartre and their life together, but precisely because it provided her with the opportunity to establish her Sartre (Bair 1990, 469, 516, 466, 495, 468).

In 1960, therefore, two very different Sartres were published, his and hers. Toril Moi finds the second and third volumes of Beauvoir's autobiography, published in 1960 and 1963, respectively, 'her most interesting works, not because they always offer the best plots or the most energetic writing, but because they are so profoundly contradictory in tone and style.' Moi attributes the dryness of Beauvoir's prose in writing about Sartre to her not being able to avow in writing the real nature of their relationship: 'it is not only Sartre's death that pains Beauvoir, it is also his lack of loyalty to her during their final years, his betrayal of what she took to be their common ideals, and his cavalier disregard for her feelings in his dealing with other women. The price she pays is an almost complete blockage of affect in her language' (1994, 251). As Beauvoir had so integrated a particular version of Sartre into her own autobiographical project that it became its dominant thread, one can hardly imagine her avowing the 'real' Sartre. What would her life look like without him, without their 'essential' love? Publically avowing Sartre's new political direction and accepting his rejection of his previous writings would have been tantamount to writing off both her emotional and intellectual investment in him and the philosophical underpinnings of her life-project. It would have meant re-imagining a future without him and the security their relationship provided her, because to avow his new writings would be to renounce her status as equal intellectual partner and become a faithful, non-thinking follower, while to publicly avow that any of his liaisons were anything more than 'contingent' would be to renounce her status as partner period. Beauvoir prided herself on the role she played in Sartre's formative, pre-1960 writing, which was substantial enough that scholarship has now begun to question just how much of it she actually was responsible for.[19] This pride is reflected in the prominent standing she chose to give Sartre in the second and third volumes of her autobiography: 'an informal, unscientific page count ... shows that she wrote as much about Sartre as about herself if not more, filtering the details of her life through his philosophy, political activity and travels' (Bair 1990, 469). The decision to do so, however, to interweave him and their existentialist philosophy into the very fabric of her autobiographical writings, had the serious consequence that after 1963 she could no longer renege on that philosophy without its threatening to unravel the very weave of her own life-project. Is it only an irony of fate that Beauvoir recreated her relationship with Sartre in writing just as it was falling apart? Or can this act not also be read as a sign of her lack of faith that he would live up to her dreams, which perhaps she suspected were doomed but nonetheless wanted to fulfil at least in writing?

Sartre's official adoption of Arlette on 25 January 1965, making her his legal heir, takes on more ominous overtones when situated in this chronology. More than simply a rude reminder of Beauvoir's age (something about which he knew her to be very sensitive, not surprisingly so), it was also an official expression of his breaking with her intellectually, by ensuring that she would not be able to posthumously publish his Nachlaß, such as the *Cahiers pour une morale*, which Arlette did publish in 1983. Even then, Sartre underestimated what their pact and their partnership meant to Beauvoir, the humiliations she was willing to bear: 'with her usual indomitable optimism, by March, when the adoption was final, she had not only stood as one of the sponsors (Lanzmann was the other), but was able to raise a glass of champagne to help the new father celebrate the joy of having a brand-new daughter' (Bair 1990, 496). It worked; Beauvoir was able to force her view of their relationship through. Francis and Gontier, in their biography, on which she collaborated, call *Force of Circumstance* 'a celebration of her extraordinary and singular understanding with Sartre.' One finds in it the following passage: 'In 1964 de Beauvoir and Sartre were as indivisible in the eyes of the public as they were in real life. "In more than thirty years, we have only once gone to sleep disunited," de Beauvoir wrote in the epilogue to *Force of Circumstance*' (1987, 302, 306); it is followed by a chronicle of their travels in the second half of the 1960s as politically engaged partners par excellence.[20]

In *Memoirs of a Dutiful Daughter*, Beauvoir predicts, 'my life would be a beautiful story come true, a story I would make up as I went along' (MDD 170);[21] in *The Prime of Life*, she describes her life as 'a lovely story that became true as I told it to myself' (1982, 363). In both cases it is the same story, a story for which she had a particular script in mind, an existentialist fairytale that, given the propensity in her correspondence with Algren towards what would now be considered most politically incorrect national slurs, could quite justifiably be entitled 'The Frog Prince.'[22] Vintges concludes her study of Beauvoir's philosophical project with a critique of Bair's biography: 'Deirde Bair wanted to write an intellectual biography of Simone de Beauvoir and to treat her life and work as interwoven elements ... Her enterprise stranded completely because her point of departure was that the life and work of Beauvoir had to be understood from Beauvoir's orientation on Sartre. Bair failed to see that Beauvoir *actually oriented herself on her orientation on Sartre*. Her work and life revolved around the problem of women's relative identity, and it is this theme that made it – and her – an original' (1996, 177; italics in original). While I would dispute the harshness of Vintges's judgment of Bair's work, it is a point well taken. If Bair's project 'stranded,' it was only insofar as her subject's story did. As many feminist writers have since concluded, it was an impossible, conflicted story upon which Beauvoir embarked, and the fact that she succeeded at all, that she managed to keep it as the foundation text for her entire life, only speaks to her indomitable will and courage. While it may be 'insufficient, and indeed damaging, to use de Beauvoir as an example to women, since in so many ways the paths which she followed were fraught with destructive possibilities' (Evans 1996, 119), North American feminists, especially, have made much of learning from her example, not because it was exemplary as much as instructive. Here, Beauvoir's fate overlaps that of Lou Andreas-Salomé. Both are admired for refusing to leave unconventional living arrangements for 'normal' marriage. Just as Lou Andreas-Salomé would not leave her husband and their open marriage for a noted Socialist politician with very traditional, patriarchal views, Beauvoir could not bring herself to leave Sartre in the 1950s and become a housewife in Chicago. That was not the course they had embarked on, the story they wanted to be able to tell about their lives. The difference is that Beauvoir felt her story required a hero, not one who would insist upon her doing the cooking and the housework, but rather one who would respect her independence and encourage her to be his equal partner – or at least would not object when she chose to write their relationship in such a light. Yes, Lou Andreas-Salomé's relationship with her husband was similar, but she did not choose, or have the need, to represent him as her story's overriding hero.

Stories, while integral to her development and very existence, had a serious drawback for Beauvoir. She felt they could not be realized alone: 'A partner was absolutely essential to me if I was to bring imaginary stories to life ... I owe a great debt to my sister for helping me to externalize many of my dreams in play ... What I appreciated most in our relationship was that I had a real hold over her' (MDD 44–5). Evans draws attention to the fact that it was this sense of control that provided the basis of Beauvoir's relationship with Sartre: 'For some thirty years de Beauvoir manages Sartre's emotional life; from a position of apparent detachment she guides him through the various complexities of his affairs and offers to him the comforting explanation that the reason why "other" women become upset is because they have deluded beliefs about heterosexual love' (1996, 103). Thus, the kind of relationships Beauvoir depicts herself in are far from those of either Lou Andreas-Salomé or Zarathustra and the tightrope-walker. The others she encounters are valued for what they can do for her as well as vice versa. It is not the case that Beauvoir feels responsible for her sister or for Sartre. Rather, she needs them to need her: 'As soon as I felt useful and loved, the horizon brightened and again I would begin to make fresh resolutions: "be loved, be admired, be necessary, be somebody"' (MDD 232). Karen Vintges derives from Beauvoir's need for admiration and love the ethical basis of her writing: 'She organized and guided herself through her writing and used it as self-practice within the framework of a "*souci de soi*." And for Beauvoir too, the self is something to be stylized on the surface rather than examined in depth. This basic approach would later culminate in the writing of an autobiography whose aim was to be useful for *others'* (1996, 91–2; italics in original). Because Vintges compares Beauvoir's project with that of Foucault, Beauvoir's ethics are found to be exemplary. Had she selected not Foucault but Lou Andreas-Salomé, her conclusions would have been less favourable. Lou Andreas-Salomé's serene, reverent acceptance of her lot in life is in marked contrast to Beauvoir's 'Writing of Depression,' her protracted, exhausting revisings of her life-story and its existential hero.[23] We have seen the way Lou Andreas-Salomé assumed responsibility for others in her autobiographical writing, the way she worried about abandoning even the characters in the stories she told as a child. In contrast, it is Beauvoir herself who is a character, who feels herself abandoned: 'The truth was that, separated from my family, deprived of those affections which assured me my personal worth, cut off from the familiar routine which defined my place in the world, I no longer knew who I was, nor what my purpose was here on earth.' Beauvoir's response to losing her belief in God is also markedly different from that of Lou Andreas-Salomé. Instead of feeling responsible for those who may not yet have made the discovery of this loss, Beauvoir's sole concern is to find an alternative source of affection: 'there was no longer any God to love me, but I should have the undying love of millions of hearts.' Beauvoir may have seen and written her life in terms of a search for her own values: 'We neither of us had any faith in conventional values; but I was determined to find some I could believe in, or else invent new ones' she may have claimed to aspire to the kind of life that Lou Andreas-Salomé fashioned for herself: 'That is why, when I got to know Herbaud, I had the feeling of finding myself: he was the shadow thrown by my future. He was neither a pillar of the Church, nor a book-worm, nor did he spend his time propping up bars; he provided by personal example that one can build from oneself, outside the accepted categories, a self-respecting, happy and responsible existence: exactly the sort of life I wanted for myself' (MDD 62, 143, 220, 317).

As we have seen, Beauvoir's ambitions for her writing compromised this desire for a self-respecting, happy, responsible existence. In choosing to write the story of her life as the Bildungsroman of an intellectual woman, Beauvoir made explicit the world view that motivated her struggles to attain the position of cultural prominence to which she aspired and that, at the time of writing, she felt herself to have achieved. This view could be a page out of Nietzsche: God is dead;

therefore, one must create oneself in one's own image. Unlike Lou Andreas-Salomé, however, Beauvoir did not feel herself enough a stranger to have an image unto herself. She needed others too much, was too much in their debt, to be able to take on responsibility for them in the way Lou Andreas-Salomé did. Beauvoir was willing to put up with satiny, gold-trimmed paper dresses, as long as they got her onto the literary dance floor she longed for. She made herself into a socially conscious, internationally respected writer, but the process left her 'writing depression.'

Part 2   Writing Back

NANAA: a Persian or Mesopotanian goddess whose temple treasures were confiscated in 164 BC by Antichus IV, who was then murdered by the priests.

Reclams Bibel Lexikon

Maitreyi Devi and Asja Lacis are not the cultural and feminist icons that Lou Andreas-Salomé and Simone de Beauvoir have become. Their writings can hardly be described as well known; indeed, they are rarely available in the west. Nor have they generated the tidal waves of critical words thrown up by the myriad of critical approaches that the subjects of Part 1 have. Yet in a strange way they have made their names or, rather, have found themselves made names through and on account of the writings of a disappointed love-interest. However, Mircea Eliade and Walter Benjamin are not usual flings. One might imagine that Eliade's and Benjamin's accounts of their short, fateful relationships to have piqued the curiosity of their acolytes, that being linked romantically with such popular yet enigmatic intellectuals would have guaranteed that their names would do more than surface periodically in the circles of their scholarship. That has not been the case. The whens and whys of the autobiographical writing of these two women remain unaddressed in the criticism. In the following two chapters I will trace the defiant wielding of the pens of these two women and detail how they provided a personal and cultural contextualization of their infamous involvements, so that they and their stories would live on as anti-myths to counter the inhuman creatures presented by others.

CHAPTER THREE

Maitreyi Devi

And if they learned to laugh from me, still it is not *my* laughter that they have learned. But what does it matter? They are old people: they have their own way of convalescing, their own way of laughing; my ears have suffered worse without becoming gruff. This day is a victory: it is already fading, it is fleeing, *the spirit of gravity,* my old archenemy! How good will this day end that began so badly and gravely!

'The Awakening,' *Zarathustra*[1]

Sreemati Maitreyi Devi was born in the coastal town of Chittagong in what was then known as East Bengal on 1 September 1914, just as retreating British troops were settling into their trenches in preparation for the First Battle of the Marne. European history was to have little effect on her, however. Although India sent more than a million troops in support of its colonial masters, the great majority were from the Punjab; Bengal's share was a mere 7,000. It was the European tradition of learning, not its history, that was to leave a more delible mark on Maitreyi.

Like Simone de Beauvoir, Maitreyi was the first born child in her family; like Ljolja von Salomé, she had five siblings and an ambitious, influential father with access to the highest echelons of society. Surendranath Dasgupta seems to have been of the type that pass directly from child prodigy to learned expert. Upon the completion of his MA degree in philosophy at age twenty-six, he was awarded a permanent professorship in Calcutta and the patronage of the Maharaja Sir Manindra Chandra Nandi of Kasimbazar.[2] With the Maharaja's encouragement and support, Dasgupta began what would become the five-volume *History of Indian Philosophy* and spent 1920–2 in Cambridge, studying and debating European philosophy. His paper on Croce at the 1924 International Congress of Philosophy in Naples prompted the latter's attendance and rebuttal, and his 1926 American lecture tour caused a similar international splash. Dasgupta thus had good reason to be a strong believer in the mutual benefit to be had in working with foreign scholars.

Maitreyi was fourteen when a self-confident Romanian student seven years her senior took the initiative in petitioning the Maharaja for a scholarship to study with Dasgupta in Calcutta, where since 1924 the latter had been head of the Philosophy Department. When Mircea Eliade's boat docked in November 1928, Dasgupta was there to extend him a hearty welcome. After several months, Dasgupta suggested that Eliade was acclimatized enough to move in with his family at their Bhowanipur residence. It would be misleading to assume that this invitation conveyed any particular favour. Devi recollects that 'Those were days when many foreigners visited us. Our house hummed with scholarly discussion on literary and philosophical problems' (DND 22).[3] The eminent historian of philosophy encouraged the two young people to exchange language lessons, Bengali for French, and to work together cataloguing his library. When they fell in love, however, not a particularly surprising turn of events given the circumstances,[4] the learned man seems to have been most taken aback, and, when confronted about the dalliance, his pupil even more so. Neither officer nor gentleman, Eliade took to his heels, fleeing first their home and then, after six months in a Himalayan retreat studying with Swami Shivananda, their country. As Eliade tells it, further paternal meddling was to blame:

> My father sensed that I was intending to stay in India for another three or four years, and he was afraid I might never return, that I might choose the solitude of the monastic life or marry an Indian girl. And I think his intuition was correct. So, since it was up to him to renew my exemption from military service, well, that year, January 1931, he simply did nothing about it. In the autumn he wrote saying that I must come back home. My father had been an army officer. He added: 'It would be a disgrace for me personally, and a great humiliation for the whole family, if my son became a deserter.' So I went home. I fully intended to return to India later on, to continue my research. Meanwhile, I presented my dissertation on Yoga, and the university committee in charge of these things asked me to work on a version for publication in French. (1982, 69)

However, the tides of academia and history were to sweep Eliade away; he never returned to India. After a period of de facto mourning, Maitreyi was married to an engineer fourteen years her senior, with whom she went to live in remote colonial circumstances near the Nepalese border in the Darjeeling district.

Upon arriving back in his native Romania, Eliade set about fictional-izing his Indian adventures in a *roman-à-clef* entitled *Maitreyi*. After its publication on 1 May 1933, a scant four months after Hitler's govern-ment was sworn into power in nearby Germany, *Maitreyi* quickly assumed the stature of a Romanian *Effi Briest* or *Anna Karenina*, and Eliade's reputation as a writer was made. When he began teaching at the university in Bucharest in November of that year, his lecture 'The Problem of Evil in the History of Religions' enjoyed unusually large crowds, the majority of whom, as he notes in his autobiography, 'had not come to learn what constituted the problem of evil and salvation, but to see and hear the author of *Maitreyi*' (1981, 270). Thus, when the fictional Sergui in Maitreyi Devi's own autobiographical novel, *It Does Not Die*, replies to the protagonist's question of 'Do you know me?' with 'Everyone in my country knows you. You are the heroine of a fairytale' (DND 12), he is not describing a fictional situation but stating a well-known fact in Romanian literary history.[5]

In the meantime, Maitreyi Devi was adjusting to life in the remote rural household she would run for the next twenty-two years before returning to Calcutta. While she did not find the pressures of the small colonial 'forest resort' particularly agreeable (DND 202), visits from her friend and mentor, the Nobel Prize-winning poet Rabindranath Tagore, strengthened her resolve. She did not allow her isolation to hinder her becoming as pre-eminent a poet and scholar in her own country as Eliade had been in his own pre-Soviet Romania. As the daughter of the learned Dasgupta and the 'lady-disciple of Rabin-dranth,' as she is referred to in the preface to *The Great Wanderer*, the volume in which she collected the reactions in the western press to Tagore's travels and lectures abroad to mark the Tagore Centenary of 1961, her cultural stature was guaranteed. Devi published extensively but not exclusively on Tagore. Her *Maung-pu te Rabindranth* (*With Tagore at Maung-pu*) was a Bengalese best-seller, and in her own English translation, *Tagore by Fireside*, it attained a measure of renown in England as well. She became a noted writer and social activist, founding boarding schools for destitute children and organizations such as the Promotion of Communal Harmony in 1964. She lectured on issues from social reform and philosophy to poetry and travel. A self-described 'globetrotter,' she received, like her father before her, numerous invitations to lecture abroad – in the Soviet Union, eastern and western Europe, and the United States. Her *Maha Soviet*, akin to Beauvoir's travel writings, received considerable attention and was important for sharing her impressions of life in Soviet Russia with Bengali readers.

By writing in his native language, Eliade successfully limited the readership of *Maitreyi*, preventing those with no knowledge of Romanian, such as Maitreyi Devi and her family, from having access to his text. Thirty years later, in 1963, when he returned to the events in India in his autobiography, Eliade once again chose to write in Romanian, even though by that time he had already served for six years at the University of Chicago as chairman of the History of Religions Department and had published scholarly work in both English and French. It was in French that Eliade's autobiographical work first appeared. In 1950 *La nuit bengali*, a translation by Alain Guillermou, was published by Gallimard. Then, in 1973, Gallimard published *Fragments d'un journal*, the journal Eliade kept in French, in which he recorded, among other things, the experience of writing his autobiography. The entry for 5 April 1963, for example, reads: 'I'm beginning the second volume of my autobiography. I will try to summarize my years spent in India by emphasizing certain events exclusively and by omitting all the others. I must keep certain secrets for myself. Moreover, I've written about India so many times that I no longer have any desire to return to the subject' (1977, 183). The last of these efforts to write about his experiences in India and his later rewritings – the journal – was the first work to be translated into English, by Fred H. Johnson Jr; in 1977 it appeared as *No Souvenirs: Journal, 1957–1969*. The autobiography was translated from the Romanian into English by Mac Linscott Ricketts, one of his former students at the University of Chicago; it was published in 1981 as *Autobiography*, vol. 1, *Journey East, Journey West, 1907–1937*.

In 1972, before any of Eliade's autobiographical writings were available in English, the only European language in which Maitreyi Devi was proficient, a Romanian visitor confronted her with details from Eliade's *Maitreyi*. This event compelled her, first, to become familiar with the book's contents, then to visit Eliade at the University of Chicago and, finally, to answer the 1933 novel that bore her name with one of her own. *Na Hanyate* appeared first in Bengali in

1974 and then two years later with an Indian publisher, P. Lal, as *It Does Not Die: A Romance* in Maitreyi's own English translation. It was not until 1994, however, after the deaths of both protagonists – Eliade in 1986 and Maitreyi Devi in 1991 – that their stories appeared for the first time together in the same language, English, and for the same press, the University of Chicago.[6] As publication occurred shortly after Maitreyi's death, it does not seem untoward to assume that Eliade acted to hinder an English version of his novel from appearing in her lifetime.[7]

It seems appropriate that two of the articles in English devoted solely to Eliade's *Maitreyi* should be by a Romanian male and an Indian female. Coincidently, both were written for special collections by noted scholars: Mihai Spariosu's 'Orientalist Fictions in Eliade's *Maitreyi*' is a contribution to a 1978 conference at UCLA, 'Fiction and Drama in Eastern and Southeastern Europe'; Meenakshi Mukherjee's 'Mircea Eliade and India: A Reading of *Maitreyi*' is an expanded version of a book review, prepared for the 1995 Festschrift for Professor M. Sivaramakrishna, *Framing Literature*. Spariosu is interested in revealing the ways in which both Eliade's and Devi's tales are ideologically bound: 'If Maitreyi revolves around certain Orientalist fictions, *It Does Not Die* predictably reveals certain preconceptions and simplistic generalizations about the Western world' (357). He draws attention to the myths typical to their respective cultures on which the works are based: Eliade's narrative is 'nothing but the reenactment of a most common Christian myth: the story of the Fall of Man' (356), while Devi's 'is built around the myth of the immortality of the soul, (and the confrontation between the atemporal and the historical results in a not uncommon fictional form)' (358). Eliade's Maitreyi is an 'unpredictable, cruel sex-goddess who is beyond the Western moral code' (357); Devi's Mircea is 'a cold-blooded, rational Westerner who spends his life (and his passion) buried in books' (357). Both demonstrate 'the typical attitude of a traveller who reads his [*sic*] own ideological biases into a foreign culture' (354). Thus, just as Maitreyi becomes Eliade's passage to India, he kindles for her a bonfire of the vanities. Mukherjee's more recent article (1995) covers much the same ground, considering 'the more fascinating aspect ... the gaps in cultural comprehension which underlie their relationship' (91), but she takes a more literary focus. She finds Devi's work 'far superior to Bengali Nights [*sic*], its complexity and maturity is perhaps due to the fact that it is emotion recollected' (93).

A Passage to the Vanities

These gaps in cultural comprehension, these orientalist and occidental-
ist fictions, manifest themselves in striking images of their male and
female protagonists. The exotic, orientalizing representation of the
character of Maitreyi at the beginning of Eliade's eponymous novel,
however, quickly descends from the mythic to the melodramatic. Eliade's Maitreyi is not a conventional beauty but rather is 'so disturbing
and so unfeminine' that 'On catching sight of her, a strange tremor
went through me, accompanied by a curious feeling of contempt. I
thought her ugly, with eyes that were too large and too black, thick and
curling lips and the powerful chest of a Bengali maiden who had
developed too quickly' (1994, 2, 1). Not only is Maitreyi portrayed as
lacking in beauty, the poor thing is not even allowed to be mortal. Her
eyes are 'absent, inhuman'; her 'too black' hair, 'too large' eyes and 'too
red' lips have the effect of 'inhabit[ing] this veiled body with a life that
was somehow inhuman, miraculous and hardly real': 'it was the flesh
of a goddess or a painted image rather than a human' (25, 7, 2). Fur-
thermore, goddesses, unlike other, merely female, mortals, tend to
have a certain effect on men. Maitreyi's 'quaint and formal, somewhat
scholarly' English is found to be 'like the calls of a siren'; her 'irresistible, contagious' laugh is that of 'both a woman and a child. It gripped
my heart, and I shivered. I leaned out of the window and beheld,
stretched out across two steps of the courtyard stairs, Maitreyi, almost
naked, her hair in her eyes, her arms clasped over her chest. I saw her
move her legs, quite shaken with laughter, and then, with a brisk jerk
of her ankles, throw off her two slippers against the wall opposite. I
stood transfixed, unable to avert my eyes.' (7, 9)

Why should it be these otherworldly aspects of the ugly goddess-
like creature that attract Alain, Eliade's protagonist, and set the tale on
its fatal course? Alain's ability to recognize the magical qualities inherent in this girl, this hierophany, this revelation of the sacred in everyday experience, proves his inherent superiority over both the Indians,
who are primitives and barbarians, and the Anglo-Indians, whom he
considers 'idiots and fanatics' (1994, 2). Unlike the Anglo-Indians, Eliade's hero is enchanted with India. He knows better than to fall for one
of the Anglo-Indian girls he and his Anglo-Indian friend Harold take
out, girls that 'come too cheaply to love' (13). Neither English nor Bengali, freed by fate from the dilemma of being either master or slave,
Alain boasts of being 'very proud of my [Romanian] nationality and

my continental origins' (2),[8] and proud, too, of the offer to live in his host's house, to live 'this new life that no white man, to my knowledge, had ever experienced at source, the life which Lucien's research had revealed to me as magical and which Maitreyi's presence would render more fascinating and mysterious than a medieval legend' (23–4).[9]

Eliade's memories can take on their bittersweet quality, however, only within a tragic framework, and thus the tale follows a very unfairytale-like course. First, the unique, memorable nature of the passion generated is emphasized: 'Maitreyi squeezed my legs between hers as though she wanted to break them, expressing in that embrace all her final passion and terror. Then, with a gentleness I had never known in her before, her warm skin rubbed softly against mine. Her last caress infused me with a warmth and a passion that I will never forget, separated though we are in time and in distance' (1994, 131). Then Maitreyi's father 'suggests' that their guest is tired and should leave immediately for the mountains, and Eliade's protagonist understands that he is being evicted. The effect is immediate and violent: 'The engineer left and I collapsed into sobs, pulling my hair and biting my knuckles like a madman. I threw myself onto the chair, obliterated, almost suffocating from a pain for which I had no name. It was neither frustrated love nor sorrow but rather a feeling of total dissolution. I had suddenly woken up alone in a cemetery, with no one to hear my woes or comfort me. I had been broken into a thousand pieces, my body nothing but a gaping wound, my soul destroyed' (135). So his story ends, after an interlude in the mountains where a love affair with a Jewish woman from Finland serves to confirm his love for Maitreyi: 'It was Maitreyi whom I loved, Maitreyi alone! I had had to grit my teeth as I invented all sorts of caresses that made the innocent Jenny swoon with delight – but which only excited my rage, because they did not numb my pain, or efface from the lively memory of my senses the other, the only one, Maitreyi' (171). Maitreyi is thus reduced to a memory, albeit lively, no more to him than a pang of conscience: 'I would like to be able to look Maitreyi in the eyes,' and 'I wish she would forget me, that she were not suffering. Our love is over' (176, 173).

As the title of Maitreyi Devi's 'romance' indicates, however, it was not over. It did not die, but rather it modulated from minor to major key. Devi chose not to structure her story around the tragic encounter: 'Such episodes are aplenty. They have happened in the past and will happen in the future. Many writers have written about the sad ending of first love, with pens much more powerful than mine' (DND 245).

Rather, she concentrates on the unique way the experience unfolded: 'I am writing to record the episode that happened forty-two years later, because it is astounding and probably without precedence' (DND 245). By choosing thus to interweave past and present, she thickens her story from a soupy romance into a veritable historical stew, with a decidedly philosophical and theological tang replacing the syrupy seasonings Eliade preferred. Like Eliade, Devi does not set herself up as the hero of her tale: 'this is not my biography, this is just a story in which Mircea is the hero' (DND 168). However, her hero is given a less than godlike demeanour. Whereas Eliade's Maitreyi is a siren, Devi's Mircea is so unassuming that he does not attract her immediate attention: 'during this time Mircea used to visit father. But I had not noticed him' (DND 30). It is only after they are introduced that he makes a certain, by no means unfavourable, impression: 'Mircea stood up. I noticed he wore spectacles with thick lenses, his hair was thin, he had a square face, broad forehead, high cheek bones and very sensitive lips. I like this habit of Westerners – they stand up to greet a woman' (DND 31). It is not Mircea himself but rather his European-ness that registers favourably. These European manners are one of first memories of Mircea she recounts:

> Our first car was a Chevrolet – comfortable and high, no one wants that kind now – but to us it was a beauty. Mircea would offer his arm to help me out of the car.
> 'Do I need help to get down from this little height?'
> 'Our custom. One must help a lady out of the car and must kiss her hand while greeting or taking leave.'
> 'Custom?'
> 'Yes. One would be considered uncivilised if one failed to do so. Have you no such custom?'
> 'No.' (DND 19)

Mircea's heroic status is further undercut by the figures of her husband and her mentor, Tagore. It is Tagore who makes her 'twenty-two years of ... solitary confinement in a forest life' bearable; it is her husband without whom she is incomplete (DND 175, 168). Mircea is 'just a tool, ... someone else who is using his name, changing my whole personality, my inner being' (DND 225).

In contrast to Mircea's generic qualities, her own prismatic figure is decisive and courageous. The forty-two years that separate their meetings are both a disruptive and a uniting element in her life: 'And I have entered eternity, I have no future or past. I stand with one foot in 1972 and another in 1930' (DND 10). Even split, Maitreyi's protagonist is a more imposing figure than her 'hero.' In her final conversation with Mircea, which ensues upon her showing up unannounced in his office at the University of Chicago, she emphasizes the courage the decision to visit him required:

'It has not been an easy task, ignoring the frowns of society round me. Before my family, relatives and even before my own children, I have fallen from the high pedestal of honour. Some must think me senile. What will people think if they come to know of this? You know our country – they will spit at me. Is it easy to come to see you after forty-two years?'
'Not at all. I could have never done it. How many times have I had invitations from my dreamland India, but I have never gone.' (DND 254)

Not only does she have greater intestinal fortitude than Mircea, she also comes out on top during a conflict with her English neighbours in her mountainous, far from postcolonial retreat: 'A clash is imminent over the issue of drinking alcohol. I am not going to be defeated. I am not the person to yield to pressure and gradually follow in their footsteps. They say a person is known by the company he keeps. I am a different bird; I will not flock with them' (DND 179). This different bird never finds a situation in which she can belong. Upon moving back to Calcutta in 1954, she notes that 'when I left this city twenty-two years ago the ethos of the literary world was different,' and, as she did in the mountains, here too she feels: 'estranged, I am a stranger here' (DND 202). Like Lou Andreas-Salomé, Maitreyi's sense of strangeness coexists with a personal ethos based on agency: 'I was thrown into a world where I did not belong. I watched them just as a clean person watches the unclean, the awakened the sleeping, and the emancipated the person in bondage' (DND 181). She, with her courage found in difference, is emancipated; the conformity of the others condemns them to bondage.

Eliade's journal indicates that he mistook this courage for freedom: '26 January 1961: I think that my interest in Hindu philosophy and ascesis can be explained as follows: India has been obsessed by *freedom*, by absolute autonomy. Not in any naïve, superficial way, but with full regard to the numberless forms of conditioning to which man is subject, studying them objectively, experimentally (Yoga), and striving to find the tool that will make it possible to abolish or transcend them.

Even more than Christianity, Hindu spirituality has the merit of introducing Freedom into the Cosmos. A *jivanmukta*'s mode of being is not *given* in the Cosmos; on the contrary, in a universe dominated by laws, absolute freedom is unthinkable. India has the merit of having added a new dimension to the universe: that of free existence' (1982, 63–4; italics in original). While his Maitreyi is lacking in transcendence and driven mad by the chains of duty, Maitreyi's own writing both substantiates and refines his claim. As in the case of Lou Andreas-Salomé, Maitreyi expects women to be strong and free. Lou Andreas-Salomé's disappointment in Malwida's conventionality is matched by Maitreyi's feeling about her mother: 'Before, mother was in full command of the house; now her voice is ignored ... I feel ashamed of her weakness,' and, 'I constantly ask myself, How can I be free? Mother was never properly free, she has to steal money or persuade father for her constant need of helping poor relatives ... I used to wonder how those who love freedom could want to keep others in chains' (DND 154, 157). Maitreyi realizes her freedom, as does Lou Andreas-Salomé, through the exercise of a strong sense of agency within the framework of an open marriage: 'The emptiness I felt at the time of my marriage did not disrupt my world. My desire to be free had been fulfilled. The moment I entered my husband's home, my shackles fell off. I realize that from then I would be able to do what I felt was right. Freedom of course does not correspond to irresponsibility. I hope I have never used my unlimited freedom in a way that is unworthy of me' (DND 168).[10] The use she makes of her freedom is what allows her to answer for herself. Because it is 'worthy,' she feels herself in a position to judge, beginning with herself: 'I judge myself severely – I do not condone any weakness' (DND 13).

At the same time as she trumpets female agency, Maitreyi acknowledges, as Lou Andreas-Salomé did before her, her helplessness and the facticity of her situation. She therefore makes much of the fact that she chose for many long years to remain in ignorance about Eliade's book. Her protagonist tells the Romanian visitor who finally sparks her interest in the past that she knows of Eliade's book only from hearsay: 'It is today fortytwo years since Mircea left; off and on I have heard about the book, named after me, but I never asked anyone about the contents of that book. Is it a story, or a book of poems, or a dissertation? I never cared to enquire. Today I ask you, tell me, what is in that book?' (DND 12). She later conveys her earlier impression of the book's content in a way that makes intelligible her lack of curiosity:

As far as I can remember that was in 1938. Father told me in Calcutta, 'Mircea has dedicated a book to you and he has sought your forgiveness in the dedication.' ... After a few minutes he said, 'He has been jailed for writing pornography.' My English was poor, I did not know what the word pornography meant. I had no desire to ask father. I knew it could not be anything excellent if it had sent the writer to prison. I walked away silently. I was astounded to look up the meaning in the dictionary – how ugly – perverse – is the book he dedicated to me the same one? ... I felt no curiosity about the book because my mind shrank in disgust. I shivered to think that at one time I had come so close to such an awful man. I tried to forget the whole affair. With a firm determination I rolled down a boulder of repugnance and closed the opening of that cave which lay in abysmal depth, illuminated by the colours of memory. It would be wrong to say I did it. It just happened that way. (DND 175)

Her account aims at mirroring the confusion she felt in the face of Eliade's text, first claiming to have deliberately tried to close off access to her memories of that time and then that 'it just happened' without any wilful act on her part. It would not have been impossible for Devi to have come across a copy of the French translation. She tells of later trips she made to France both with her husband and alone, the first in 1953, three years after the appearance of *La nuit bengali*, during which she met with Romanians who knew her as Eliade's 'first flame' (DND 199). She even mentions an opportunity to meet Eliade, which she could not bring herself to take advantage of. It was not to be. She preferred to see the situation, as Lou Andreas-Salomé did, as beyond her control, as a 'conspiracy of destiny,' the 'conspiracy of eternal time,' that 'fate has conspired to tell me all now,' that is, in 1972 (DND 227, 234). It was not until 1972 that she was finally confronted with that which she had hitherto been able to avoid – the form of things that 'do not die.' The problem was that 'the book is alive. I can see that it has an unusual longevity ... I tell my friends, "Look at the prank fate has played on me. The family I have raised, the events of my long life, my husband and children – they will be wiped away in time. This, my real life, will become a shadow, but someone who is nobody to me, whom I met for a brief while in the long journey of life, he will remain – someone who is nowhere in my life – my name shall remain tied with that total stranger, even after death. Social relations, even blood relations end with death, but the tie he has created is unbreakable"' (DND 215). Devi's disappointment with Eliade's text is not with its immortality as such. Like Lou Andreas-Salomé's writing that life 'lives us, it composes us ... we are works of art – but we are not the artist,' Maitreyi Devi's view of life is also recounted in the passive voice. Eliade's book is part of the game of life, which she admits 'is someone else's game we are playing. We are marionettes in his hands' (DND 225). She, too, sees life in artistic terms: 'As I try to write the story of my life I can very well see that there is no story at all. How can there be? Stories emerge from contact with life. The contact and conflict of human experience and variety of efforts give colour to our life's picture. What story can nature evolve? Many incidents occur that are fierce but one cannot make stories out of them' (DND 187). Her problem with Eliade's *Maitreyi* is not that it is a story but rather that it is an unethical one, that 'it wears a mask of truth,' and that lies can be as immortal as truths (DND 226, 216). Devi's disappointment with Eliade is that he chose not to share her truth, that he chose the wrong form of immortality for her soul: 'I lay wondering why he destroyed this love, a gift of God. What did it matter if he had to go? If in ten years we could have exchanged even a single letter, that would have been enough. With that one letter we would have bridged the oceans and continents of separation and could have become "ardhanariswar." Our two-selves could have acquired a completeness ... I can see myself again in his arms, framed with a door. He is whispering, "Not your body, Amrita. I want to touch your soul." This is the truth, truly the truth. The body perishes, the soul is immortal' (DND 217–18). Her immortal soul, however, was not touched as she wished, but textualized – and misrepresented into the bargain. She may have wanted, may have set out, to meet the truth: 'So I say, 'Uncover your face, O Truth, I want to meet you,' but her encounter was with 'eyes turned into stone' – blind, mute surfaces capable only of reflection (DND 226).

CHAPTER IV

Asja Lacis

Companions the creator sought once and children of his hope: and behold, he
found that he couldn't find them, unless he created them himself first. Thus I
am in the middle of my work, going to my children and returning from them:
for his children's sake, Zarathustra must fully realize himself. For one loves
completely only one's child and one's work; and where there is great love for
oneself, there is pregnancy emblematic: that's what I have found.

'Of Involuntary Bliss,' *Zarathustra*[1]

Anna Ernestovna Lacis was born on a country estate in Latvia on
19 October 1891, the same year as three of the individuals we will
encounter in the third part of this study: Romola and Bronislava
Nijinsky and Osip Mandel'shtam. The circumstances into which Lacis
was born, however, were considerably humbler; in fact, they were by
far the humblest of any in this study. Her mother wove and dyed
blankets, gardened, sang sad hymns, and suffered, while her father
was off repairing the gentry's furs and saddles. The progressive
socialist proclivities of the latter ensured that his only daughter
received an upper-class schooling and moral, if not financial, support
to continue with her studies. The Bekhterev Psychoneurological
Research Institute in St Petersburg was one of the few of the day that
accepted women, and so it was there that Lacis went, in pursuit of a
course of study to complement her interest in the theatre, since she
had caught the theatre bug at school. Studying in St Petersburg in
1913–14 and then in Moscow at Fyodor Komisarevsky's theatre studio in 1917, she soon found herself caught up in the political ful-
minations of the times and quickly became active in pedagogically

oriented revolutionary theatrical circles. When events dictated her presence in Orel during the civil war, she set about organizing a theatre school for *bezprizorniki* (war orphans) and other young war refugees in the villa that once had served as the setting for Turgenev's *A Nest of the Gentry* and is now a Turgenev museum. In 1922 her interest in expressionist theatre took her to Berlin, where she met her second husband, the director Bernhard Reich. (While still in Riga, she had married, had a child with, and divorced Julijs Lacis, and also had had a relationship with one of the leading Latvian revolutionary poets, Lainards Laicens, whose volume of love poetry dedicated to her, *Ho-Tai*, is among the classics of Latvian literature.) When Reich and his younger colleague, Bertold Brecht, were appointed to the Munich Residenztheater, she moved to the city with them and, at Brecht's insistence, was hired on as an assistant director despite the initial refusal of the bourgeois Bavarian management to have a foreign communist on their premises. During a 1924 trip she and Reich made to Capri to aid her daughter's recovery from a serious bout of pneumonia, they took the opportunity to visit, among others, Maxim Gorky and the famed Futurist Filippo Marinetti. It was also in Capri that she met and decisively intervened in the fate of Walter Benjamin, encouraging his Marxist leanings, his *Einbahn-strasse* (*One-Way Street*), which is dedicated to her, and his trip to her sanitorium bedside in Moscow in the winter of 1926–7 which resulted in his *Moskauer Tagebuch* (*Moscow Diary*).[2] Upon recovering her health, she worked with Lenin's widow, Nadezhda Krupskaya, to establish a children's cinema in a movie theatre near the crowded, chaotic Sukharevky market in Moscow. In 1928 she was appointed cultural attaché to the Soviet trade commission in Berlin, where she again had the opportunity to visit with her good friends Benjamin and Brecht and where she set about furthering the cause of Soviet film in general and Vertov's Kinoglaz (kino-eye) in particular. In 1930 she returned to Stalinist Russia, first working with Erwin Piscator during the filming of Anna Seghers's novella, *The Revolt of the Fishers from St Barbara*, and then embarking on doctoral studies in theatre in Moscow. Like so many good communists, she was arrested in 1937. Unlike so many good communists, she survived ten years in the gulag in Khazakhstan, something she would later attribute to the fact that she had been allowed to organize her fellow prisoners into an amateur theatre troupe.[3] She returned to her native Latvia in 1948 and began re-establishing herself as a director and theoretician of the theatre, first in

Valmiera and then in Riga, where she was a prominent member of the Soviet Latvian cultural scene until her death in 1979.

During this last period of her life, Anna Lacis composed two volumes of memoirs.[4] The first volume is the German *Revolutionär im Beruf* (*A Revolutionary by Profession*), the subtitle of which – *Berichte über proletarisches Theater, über Meyerhold, Brecht, Benjamin und Piscator* – is an accurate overview of its contents. Lacis recounts its genesis as follows: 'In the mid-1960s I received a letter from the chief editor of the West German journal *Alternative*, Hildegard Brenner, with the request that I send copies of my correspondence with Walter. Unfortunately, that correspondence had been destroyed, but I offered some of my recollections in their place. My story was printed in *Alternative*, and later, in the April 1968 issue, my article on the children's theatre of aesthetic education [in Orel] appeared with Benjamin's program' (RC 133).[5] One has the impression that Brenner was pleasantly surprised to have come across such a wide-ranging source of information. Her initial request resulted not only in the *Alternative* selections but also in *A Revolutionary by Profession*, which was published in 1971 to coincide with Lacis's eightieth birthday. For Brenner, Lacis was an important link in reconstructing the circumstances of intellectual life in the Weimar Republic in general and of the proletarian worker's movement in particular, as well as affording an opportunity to point out how conservative postwar scholarship had operated to ignore or delete valuable voices of the 'wrong,' that is, Marxist, ideology. Brenner was interested in what Lacis was able to add to knowledge about well-known, left-leaning, male cultural figures, as indicated by the subtitle of the volume, and she thus solicited Lacis's recollections on these particular figures. Both Lacis's personal circumstances and her theatrical connection are downplayed; for example: 'A decisive stage for me was working in Riga. (Personal circumstances had brought me back)' (RP 32).[6] Those circumstances involved a frustrating, unsuccessful attempt to cross civil-war-torn Latvia in time to be with her dying mother. When the German memoir was reprinted in 1976, scaled back by ten pages, it was these areas – Lacis's childhood reminiscences, her descriptions of relatives, and the final excerpt from her book *Revolutionary Theatre in Germany* – which were shortened, and the title of the first chapter correspondingly changed from 'Latvia: In the Village/Riga' to 'St Petersburg, Moscow, 1913/17,' originally the title of chapter 2. Lacis was thus introduced to the west in the guise of an impersonal Marxist functionary, a *mulier sovietica* who, as is emphasized in the collection

Russen in Berlin, 'had a decisive influence on [Benjamin's] entire existence' (Mierau 1991, 352). It was in this guise she was to remain; her other memoir, *Krasnaia Gvozdika* (*The Red Carnation*), was posthumously published in 1984 in Riga and has garnered no attention west of the former Iron Curtain.

Anna Lacis died in 1979. In 1980 Walter Benjamin's *Moscow Diary* was published by Suhrkamp. The timing is not a coincidence. As the editor of the English translation, Gary Smith, informs us, Benjamin's diary was not produced earlier, 'for two reasons. First, the publishing house decided not to issue the diary during the lifetime of Asja Lacis. Secondly, the diary was scheduled for publication in the sixth volume of Benjamin's *Gesammelte Schriften*, which contains all of his extant autobiographical writings and fragments' (1986, 145). It is unfortunate that Lacis was thus deprived of the opportunity to respond to Benjamin's portrayal of her. As pointed out in both Gershom Scholem's preface and Gary Smith's afterword, Lacis is the diary's catalyst and ostensible heroine in the same way that Maitreyi is in Eliade's 'homage.' The diary begins with Benjamin's arrival in Moscow, on 6 December 1926, where he immediately displaces his rival, Bernhard Reich: 'We had only been underway a few minutes ... when Asja waved to us from the side of the street, Reich got out and walked the short remaining distance to the hotel, we took the sleigh' (1986, 9). When Benjamin leaves Moscow on 1 February 1927, the narrative breaks off not with his actual departure from the city but with his final farewell from Asja: 'I asked her to hail a sleigh. As I was about to get in, having said goodbye to her one more time, I invited her to ride to the corner of Tverskaia with me. I dropped her off there, and as the sleigh was already pulling away, I once again drew her hand to my lips, right in the middle of the street. She stood there a long time, waving. I waved back from the sleigh. At first she seemed to turn around as she walked away, then I lost sight of her. Holding my large suitcase on my knees, I rode through the twilit streets to the station in tears' (1986, 121). In addition, most of the initial entries begin with a reference to her: 8 December: 'Asja dropped by in the morning' (12); 9 December: 'Asja again came by in the morning' (14); 10 December: 'We went to see Asja in the morning' (16); 12 December: 'Reich took a walk with Asja in the morning' (19); 14 December (written on the 15th): 'I shall not see Asja today' (21); 15 December: 'Reich stepped out briefly after he got up and I hoped I would be able to greet Asja in private. But she didn't turn up' (25); 16 December: 'I was writing my diary and had given up hope that Asja would stop by. Then she knocked. As she entered the room, I wanted to kiss her. As usual, it proved unsuccessful' (27). There can be no mistaking that Asja was the primary motivation in Benjamin's coming to Moscow, that she did not reciprocate his feelings, and that she has been subsequently vilified in German scholarship because of it.[7]

Moscow Believes in Tears

There are striking similarities between the representations of the figures in the *Maitreyi* saga and those of Walter Benjamin and Asja Lacis in their albeit less duelling autobiographical writings. Just as Eliade's first description of Maitreyi is rather unflattering, emphasizing her ugliness and lack of femininity, when Benjamin first catches sight of the object of his affections, he notes that 'Asja did not look beautiful, wild beneath her Russian fur hat, her face somewhat puffy from all the time she had spent bedridden' (1986, 9). In the sketch he makes of their relationship on 20 December, Benjamin admits that 'on three or four occasions, I directly or indirectly avoided sharing a future with her' because of a 'fear of those hostile elements in her which only now do I feel I can confront' (1986, 35). His conclusion, that he has 'no idea whether I could even now bear living with her, given her astonishing hardness and, despite all her sweetness, her lovelessness,' which, in the light of the fact the sketch begins with the dejected statement, 'I find myself facing an almost impregnable fortress' (1986, 35, 34), takes on a self-justifying air, as if to say 'I can't have her but she's not really worth having anyway.' As in the case of Eliade's protagonist, there is a curious discrepancy between Benjamin's rather unflattering portrayal of his alleged object of desire and the passions she is claimed to inflame. In both cases, the protagonists make much of the unique quality of this passion. Not only does Benjamin get 'a great deal of pleasure out of the way she was unpacking my suitcases and tidying up my things,' he 'cannot remember a woman granting gazes or kisses this long'; he goes on to describe the way Asja 'grabbed hold of me violently and ran her hands though my hair' (1986, 19, 35). Benjamin's tale is given similarly tragic dimensions within a similar framework of an educational voyage.[8] Just as Eliade must leave India, so, too, must Benjamin leave Moscow, and he responds to the cruelty of the fates in the same way, with a passionate outburst, as though despair and tears offered proof of the sincerity and the strength of their feelings. In contrast to Alain's histrionics, however, Benjamin's tears as he rides 'through the twilit streets to the station' (1986, 121) are tastefully understated. Thus, despite differences in genre and circumstance, Eliade and Benjamin construct their female love-interests and the nature and course of their relationships in a remarkably similar fashion.

While Eliade and Benjamin write about voyages of discovery, during which the self emerges from necessarily short-lived, intense, and doomed contact with a mythical goddess-type creature, Lacis and Devi also chart courses similar in bend, bank, and current. More specifically, Devi's *It Does Not Die* resembles the Russian memoir that Lacis put together and reworked herself, rather than the German *A Revolutionary by Profession* assembled by Brenner, since it is the former that reflects Lacis's own priorities.[9] *The Red Carnation*, unlike *A Revolutionary by Profession* but like *It Does Not Die*, is the literary endeavour of an intellectual woman and radiates scholarly interest. Just as Devi follows and includes details about Eliade's later career in the west, Lacis reports on the archives in Potsdam and Frankfurt devoted to Benjamin's writings and includes one of the poems Brecht wrote in memory of Benjamin's suicide at the Franco-Spanish border during his flight from the Nazis. The following statement by Devi could be attributed to either of them: 'I am very conscious of my name and fame. If someone tells me, "I read a report of your speech," I at once get the paper to have a look at it. If any paper criticizes me, I am very upset' (DND 216).[10]

When these intellectual women come to write their own stories, similar shapes and figures emerge. Just as Maitreyi's Mircea does not attract her attention until they are introduced, Lacis recounts that it is not she who notices Benjamin but vice versa: 'For around two weeks now I've been watching this woman in a long white dress and her long-legged daughter in her green one: you don't walk across the piazza, you float!' (RC 84). Just as Mircea makes a favourable impression on the heroine of Maitreyi's tale as a well-mannered western intellectual, so, too, does Benjamin impress Lacis: '[H]e explained to the shopkeeper what I wanted. I bought up most of the small packages and the stranger didn't leave. He had very thick, dark hair, and thick glasses with golden rims that flashed with his every movement, sparkling in the sun. "Permit me to introduce myself: Dr Walter Benjamin." I gave my name and he offered to carry my packages home, but they immediately fell out of his hands. We both began to laugh. Benjamin looked elegant, he was wearing expensive striped trousers. "Probably from a rich bourgeois family," I decided. We walked, and enjoyed a lively discussion' (RC 83).[11] The role that husbands and lovers play in these two women's lives is also similar. Both women find great support and happiness in old age with their husbands, and both pay homage to these men in their texts. Lacis dedicates *The Red Carnation* to Reich, and Devi writes: 'in order to complete the story I have to say something about my husband too, because I am incomplete without him' (DND 168). Despite these strong bonds, both women are also captured by their memories of previous involvements with European scholars, Devi admittedly more so than Lacis. Unlike Devi's 'story of two young people ... [t]he sudden and abrupt ending of an early love' (DND 245), Lacis offers the anecdote of two people, both married with children, who enjoy a holiday romance and develop a friendship based on common intellectual and ideological pursuits. Lacis can praise Benjamin as 'elegant' and admire his 'exceptional knowledge of contemporary French literature and of French, of which he was no less a master than of German' (RC 84), but she never refers to the possibility of a serious relationship with him. Devi, on the other hand, did have such expectations and thus tries to condemn Eliade. However, even the reference to Eliade's morally questionable behaviour during the war, which she is careful to include, is marred by the wistful confession of her desire to hear from him: '"He has not actually died, but he is dead to us. He had gone over to the fascists." "Has he?" I chuckled. I could see him standing there, with a butterfly moustache like Hitler's, opening the gas-chamber. It suited him well. He is certainly competent in the job. Has he not sent me there repeatedly by refusing steadfastly to respond to my call?' (DND 202). If Devi's Mircea is, as Sparioso claims, 'a cold-blooded, rational Westerner who spends his life (and his passion) buried in books' (1980, 357), it is perhaps not only a reflection of Devi's reading her own ideological biases into a foreign culture. Lacis comes from a different culture and should be projecting different biases into her text; yet her portrayal of Benjamin bears a remarkable resemblance to Devi's depiction of Mircea, with the important exceptions that she felt herself neither jilted nor subsequently vilified, since she did not have access to Benjamin's written account of his visit to her.

The motor driving these two autobiographical projects also revs along on similar fuel: the evolving relation of text and truth against the background of a broken family. As young girls, both Devi and Lacis assume with pride the ideological burdens their well-intentioned fathers inflict on them, incorporating them as the cornerstone of their identities. Both describe the way in which as children they were encouraged to learn, that their fathers not only provided them with books but also supported their efforts at acquiring an education.[12] Lacis mentions her father's role in both of her memoirs: 'Although ours was a difficult life, Father felt that I needed to receive a good education. Mama was against it, but he insisted' (RC 17). 'Father took care that I studied and absorbed knowledge. Once he drove to Ligatne, to a relative whose sons had university educations. Father wanted to know which secondary school in Riga was the best. They recommended – Kenins. I remember my father placing a book on my desk, *Woman and Socialism*, by August Bebel: "Read it, it's a useful book"' (RP 13).[13] Devi's father also had educational ambitions for his daughter: 'Father saw such philosophic ideas reflected in my poems that he was certain in due time I would be either a great philosopher or a great poet' (DND 23). She reports his telling her mother that their daughter 'will have to go out in the world – she must learn to mix with people. She will not stay at home like you. Why, if she exerts herself a little, she will one day become another Sarojini Naidu' (DND 29).[14] Both sets of parents are described as having 'different' (RP 9), 'opposite' (DND 22) characters. Just as both fathers are progressive and learned, both mothers are beautiful, talented, and subservient. Lacis writes: 'Mother embodied her day's conception of female beauty – of medium height, dainty hands and feet, a face of milk and blood, large blue eyes and the long, luxurious, greenish blond hair of a mermaid ... Actually Mother was very talented. She had a beautiful voice, a high soprano. She liked to sing folksongs, as well as church hymns: "A Mighty Fortress Is Our God," "Oh Head, Full of Blood and Wounds." Developing her voice – that was out of the question, and even singing in the choir was almost impossible; we lived far away' (RP 10–11). Devi's mother is described as 'exquisitely beautiful in 1930; tall and erect, she moved like a shaft of moonbeam in our house ... [and] carried in her heart kindness and love like a bowl full of nectar' (DND 22). She is 'like that spreading tree. She had spread a cool shadow over my father's path, to take away his fatigue. She wanted nothing for herself, she kept him encircled by the warmth of her love, untiring service and constant sacrifice of all personal comforts' (DND 55). Neither marriage is reported as being particularly happy. Lacis's father is 'not home often. But when he was, there were often fights and tears,' while her mother 'suffered her bitter fate in silence, as that was what she thought life was – a valley of darkness, of suffering and hardships. The worse one's lot on this sinful earth, the better the one which awaited us in heaven. When I directed

Ibsen's *Ghosts* in Valmiera, Mrs Alving's opinions and errors before her enlightenment were very familiar to me' (RP 11). Both marriages end in divorce, the children staying with their mothers. While Lacis refers to the events only briefly in the German memoir and obliquely in the Russian, Devi describes the trauma of the break: 'Exactly eleven years after Rama came to us, that is twelve years after Mircea's departure, my mother's life became a shambles. The decay that started ten years ago slowly and steadily undermined the edifice on which a family is built ... In spite of her unwavering loyalty to her husband, her constant endeavour to cover up his faults, she could only postpone the ultimate collapse that happened in 1941. Father left her with her four minor children to fend for herself. Our beautiful home that had floated on the crest of poetry and philosophy crashed on the rugged rocks of a mundane world' (DND 196). Both daughters also refer to the sorry states in which their mothers die. Devi's mother is 'crushed in body and mind' (DND 207); Lacis's mother is 'helpless, alone' (RC 50).

Against the rather bleak backdrop of these dutiful, suffering, undesired female role models, the daughters turn for inspiration and strength to the texts with which their fathers found satisfaction. These familial constellations account for the otherwise puzzling struggles that give shape to both their lives and their texts. Why did it take Devi forty-two years to be able to read Eliade's story? What was the attraction of the communist ideology for Lacis, and why was she seemingly blind to the system's obvious inequities, inefficiencies, and cruelties? The answer in both cases can be located in a crisis in textuality.

Just as Devi is horrified when she finally brings herself to discover the 'mask of truth' worn by Eliade's story, Lacis also sets out to equate texts with truth, to be revered, venerated, and worshipped, and she too runs up against an equally cold, reflective, brick wall of alterity. She becomes just as caught up and bogged down in her relationship with communist doctrine as Devi does with Eliade's story. It is the sociocultural aspects of revolutionary activities that attract Lacis; she sees them as part and parcel of western philosophy and culture: 'Being friends with Leons Paegles and his friends opened my eyes to much. I gradually became a politically engaged member of their circle. It was from Daige, a man of wide-ranging education, that I first heard the name of Vladimir Soloviev and other philosophers. Daige was very nice to me, gave me literature to teach. Thanks to his friendship with the well-known collector Tshukin, I had the opportunity to become acquainted with his valuable collection of Western European art: the paintings of Gauguin, Van Gogh, Picasso' (RC 36). This first reference in the Russian memoir to the political tenets that were to become her guiding principles demonstrates the way Lacis associates communist engagement with learning and art. At the time, Lacis was in her twenties, studying abroad in Russia and experiencing the revolution first hand. She formulates the choice she saw facing her at that time as follows: 'The students from Komisarevsky's studio were also divided into two groups: one for the Soviets, the other – against. The former insisted on an immediate change in repertoire, concentrating on new plays which were close to the masses and which they could understand, representing the interests of the revolution; the others – that a change wasn't necessary, that the revolution, so they said, would soon be over. We, the *believers* in the Soviet government, went to factories, handing out free tickets to shows, organized circles and workers' clubs' (RC 43; italics added). The granddaughter of serfs and daughter of a staunch socialist, Lacis was innately aware of the injustices of the imperial class system, an awareness that was fostered further in her theatre circle. That she formulates her relation to the Soviet government in terms of 'belief' is noteworthy. It served the function of a religion, providing her with a way of giving life meaning and purpose: 'People committed to the revolution, who gave their own lives for the happiness of the people, became my examples, my ideal' (RC 43). Her early condemnation of Christian hypocrisy lies not in the fact that it demands suffering, but rather that it offers no material prospects for that suffering, that it occupies a power base that acts against the simple folk: 'The protestant religion held great sway over the consciences of simple Latvians, especially the women. This opium also poisoned my mother. Her life was tepid and monotonous' (RP 10). Religion is her mother's 'last joy and hope' (RP 11), a function Lacis judges harshly. Its utopian vision is otherworldly, useless; it serves only to encourage and protract her mother's tepid and monotonous existence. God, for Lacis, is decidedly dead: 'As a high school student, I wanted to "reeducate" Mother. If she sang one of her endlessly long church hymns, I would say, "Why do you sing those songs and pray? God doesn't exist, He isn't in Heaven." And I made an effort to explain to her the origin of the world' (RP 11). The new gods are to be of the *homines sovietici*, the new Soviet people.[15]

Lacis's writings offer us an opportunity to reflect on the role of textual models in the negotiation of personal and state ideology. How was it possible to have lived in what has come to be recognized as one of history's most brutal dictatorships without experiencing it as such, without traces of critique or disillusionment seeping in through the cracks of one's memoir, especially if that memoir was being published in the west? As will be discussed in the next chapter, Nadezhda Mandel'shtam composed her memoirs at approximately the same time as Lacis did – *Hope Against Hope* appeared in 1970 in Paris, *A Revolutionary by Profession* in 1971 in Munich. If Lacis had been so inclined, the time was ripe for stories about 'how it had really been' to emerge. Yet Lacis was not so inclined. Like the diary of Stepan Podlubnyj, the son of a Ukrainian kulak who came to Moscow in 1931 to become a New Soviet Man, Lacis's memoirs reveal how the tenets of the communist ideology could positively affect identity formation. In Lacis's case, they even act as a crutch with which to hobble through totalitarian perversion of that ideology.

In his introduction to Podlubnyj's diary (1996), Jochen Hellbeck compares it with contemporary articles from *Pravda* and identifies aspects of the Soviet ideology that appear in both, that is, that Podlubnyj had made his own.[16] Extending this comparison to Lacis's memoirs draws attention to the Soviet-specific ideals that are also present or implicit in her writing and that Hellbeck identifies as encouraging the participation and loyalty of a certain profile of young people. Becoming a *homo sovieticus* involved both 'working on oneself and for society' (1996, 37); that is, it implied a certain dissatisfaction with both oneself and one's surroundings, a certain conviction that change is both necessary and possible.[17] Both Podlubnyj and Lacis shared a respect and reverence for the kind of learning and culture that aim at self-improvement, not only for themselves but for the 'simple folk,' the workers, and so on. Lacis's priority was didactic in this sense: 'we strove to find a way to the hearts of the people in order to bring them closer to the revolution, to an understanding of how complicated the world we lived in was' (RC 101). In his capacity as 'Brigadier' of a section of printers and Komsomol representative, Podlubnyj was also convinced that he must educate his subordinates, to get them to realize 'that work went more smoothly when it was carried out in the proper spirit' (1996, 37). Both Podlubnyj and Lacis turned to texts in their search for examples and motivation and judged texts and art in general by their ability to educate, to provide answers. Lacis saw the function of the theatre in these terms: 'People came to study and comprehend life' (RC 44); Podlubnyj looked to literature, museums, and theatre 'once again seeking guidance for his thinking' (1996, 39), and expressed disappointment in Gorky's *The Life of Klim Samgin* when it did not provide him with a clear direction for his own thinking. Both he and Lacis dreamed of completing higher studies – Podlubnyj in medicine, Lacis in the theatre – and, like the state, both kept scrupulous track of their progress towards to these goals. Just as 'Stepan's own yearly reports contain a critical review of his work at the factory and his private studies, as well as his "cultural growth"' (1996, 41), Lacis offered summaries such as 'The year I'd spent in Riga hadn't been a waste. It had been very rewarding creatively: discussions and debates about the workers' theatre, appearances in the press, shows for adults, founding the children's section ... And the most important task – the political enlightenment of the workers – which I fulfilled with all my strength' (RC 110). One can thus see that the ideal expressed in both Podlubnyj's and Lacis's writing is 'an ideal of human development: the New Soviet Person, who through "cultural" work works for the state and at the same time towards their own emancipation' (1996, 41).

Podlubnyj was eventually forced to confront the senseless reality of Soviet terror when his mother was arrested in 1937. While there is little in Lacis's writing to indicate that she similarly assimilated the extent of Soviet brutality, there are indications that censorship, whether by her Soviet editors, herself, or both, was likely a factor. The name Stalin is singularly lacking in her memoirs – not mentioned once in either text – and it is not a coincidence that the years glossed in her writing are precisely those of his tenure. Further, there is an identifiable turning point in *The Red Carnation* with respect to Lacis's relation with the Soviet state. In the late 1920s, when the RAPP (Proletarian Writers Union) board of directors and the members of its theatre section, to which she belonged, diverged: 'a majority of the members of the theatre section left RAPP, forming a new section for proletarian theatre' (RC 123), and bitter infighting resulted. The RAPP decision marked the end of Lacis's overtly political engagement. She turned her attention to film, accepted an assignment in Berlin as Soviet cultural attaché, and, when she returned to Moscow, was interested only in aiding German refugees fleeing the fascists. After the war she distanced herself completely from earlier propaganda work and immersed herself in provincial theatre.

A different interpretation of her silence is provoked by a notable irregularity in the numbering of the chapters. Chapter 14 ends with an anecdote illustrating the favour her work had found with Lunacharsky: 'In 1933, I was lucky enough to become acquainted with Anatoly Vasilievich Lunacharsky ... In those years the newspaper *Proletarian*

Revolution appeared, which sometimes carried my articles. Somehow Anatoly Vasilievich was given my sketch 'Differentiations among the German Intelligentsia' to review. "Article discussed. Fit to print. A. Lunacharsky" he wrote in a corner. The article was published' (RC 150). Chapter 15 begins some fifteen years later: 'In January 1948, I was offered the position of director at the Russian Theatre in Karaganda. But I wasn't to work there long: an unexpected letter arrived from Riga from Daga, asking me to come to her' (RC 154). Between 14 and 15 is a chapter numbered '22,' in which the events of the intervening years are summarized in a little over four pages (150–4). Its tone and emphasis hint at an inner break that Lacis made with those administering the Soviet system. Usually, Lacis portrays herself as being convinced, and convincing others, of the necessity of new assignments. 'I returned to Latvia [in 1925] more convinced than ever of the rightness of my revolutionary convictions, in the necessity of founding a political theatre in my home country' (RC 96) is a comment typical of the pre–Second-World-War years. In chapter 22, however, Lacis makes a point of emphasizing that she had no choice but to accept the two positions she was offered. First, she was approached by the Central Committee of the party: ' "We have a huge request: help us build up the Latvian Theatre 'Skatuve' [Scene]." Although I was swamped at the time – family, work in MORT [the International Union of Revolutionary Theatres], doctoral studies at GITIS [the State Institute of Theatre Arts in Moscow], it wasn't possible to refuse' (RC 150). Her reaction to being 'offered' the position of artistic director in a Latvian collective theatre by the Russian Soviet Socialist Republic's Narkompros (Commissariat for Education) is similar: 'The seat of the theatre was Smolensk. But I also had work and obligations in Moscow, so I declined. "But you don't necessarily have to live in Smolensk the entire time," they told me. "Put together the repertoire for the season, appoint an assistant and drop in from time to time to make sure your concept is being carried out. And, of course, attend the dress rehearsal." I had to agree' (RC 152). Then: '1937. Reich and I were separated for a long time. For the term of ten years I led an amateur group in Khazakhstan ... In the summer of 1941, I lost touch with Reich' (RC 153–4). One is left to speculate whether chapters 15–21 originally covered this critical time in more depth and, if so, what became of them. In the chapter 15 included in *The Red Carnation*, the final chapter, which begins in 1948 and ends with Reich's death in 1972, Lacis's life returned to its 'normal' course on conviction:

Before my return to Karaganda I was walking along some street, sunk in my own thoughts. Unexpectedly a tall man barred my way.
'Anna Lacis?'
'Yes.'
In front of me stood Andrejs Upits.
'You're alive?'
'As you can see,' I smiled sadly. 'I'm just about to leave for Karaganda where I'm working as a director.'
'Not under any circumstances!' he protested. 'We need our directors here. Come to my dacha tomorrow.'
So there I was in Yurmal. Upits tore off a clean sheet of paper: 'Sit down and write an official request: You want to stay in Latvia and work here.' He spoke in a tone that brooked no objections.
'What are you talking about! I've already agreed to work in Karaganda. I've stayed here too long as it is.'
Upits set about convincing me to stay, for so long and with such fervour that I stayed. (RC 155)

The emphasis in the last chapter on her private and theatrical accomplishments as well as the irregularity in chapter numbering point to a subtle but pronounced shift in her allegiance, which is also a subtle but pronounced critique of what became of Soviet ideology.

Soviet doctrine thus proved as disappointing to Lacis as Devi found Eliade's novel to be when she could finally bring herself to read it. Youthful infatuation gave way in both cases to disillusion with later deeds done by the paramour. Lacis was attracted to the early Soviet tenets. In her opinion, Marx, Engels, and Lenin wrote with wisdom and astuteness; there was much to be learned from them. Anyone recognizing the values of these texts, such as Reich, was worthy of admiration: 'Reich knew the classical works of Marxist-Leninism backwards and forwards' (RC 112); those who did not know them, the doubters, such as Benjamin, came in for heavy debate. Although Devi enjoyed the luxury of being able to object to the crassness with which Eliade portrayed what had been for her a beautiful reality, it nevertheless took her a long time to be able to do so. Lacis's silence and her directorial activity are the only indication we have that she experienced the reality resulting from the implementation of her beautiful texts, the classics of Marxist-Leninism, as anything less than ideal.

Part 3   Writing Up

ATALIA: the widow of a king could also gain power. The daughter of King Ahab of Israel, married to Joram of Judea. She tried to introduce the cult of the tyrannical Baal in Jerusalem. After her son Ahasia fell, she seized power and ordered all Davidinians killed. Only her grandson Joash escaped, and six years later (840 BC) toppled her (2 Kings: 11).

Reclams Bibel Lexikon

Is black an appropriate colour for literary widows? Some literary biographers have tended to think so, those who have maligned or satirized women like Florence Hardy and Sonya Tolstoy, making them look ridiculous for their 'willingness to be attached, Nora Barnacle-like, to the underside of an author's career; and then, when the career is over, to submit herself to the unrewarded task of preserving that career in the public imagination' (Rifkind 1990, 532). However, there are also literary widows who have been painted in much brighter hues. In the case of Soviet Russia, in particular, where, as Nadezhda Mandel'shtam noted, people could 'be killed for poetry – a sign of unparalleled respect – because they are still capable of living by it' (HA 23),[1] the inclination, Beth Holmgren and Sarah Pratt have argued, was for women to function and be revered as guardians of the domestic and literary spheres, as 'angels in the Stalinist house.' In the following two chapters I look at two such angels, one from each side of the former Iron Curtain, both known for their authoritative biographies of husbands they portray as tragic heroes. Not merely 'a widow to culture' (Brodsky 1986, 154), Nadexhda Mandel'shtam has been hailed as 'the most heroic literary widow in modern history' (Rifkind 1990, 544) for saving her husband's poetry from almost certain destruction by acting as a living library through the dark years of Stalinism and then transcribing it when possible, if not safe, to do so. The efforts, literary and otherwise, of another notable eastern European widow, the Hungarian-born Romola Nijinsky, to engage in the sorry fate of her schizophrenic husband, Vaslav, the meteoric star of the Ballets Russes in the first decades of this century, may have been comparably heroic, but in the international beau monde of the ballet they have been decidedly less well received. As in the previous two parts, it is instructive to compare the mythologizing means by which these two women create themselves and their significant others, in this case as part of cultural couples.

CHAPTER FIVE

Nadezhda Mandel'shtam

This providence lies over my destiny, that I must be without caution.

And whoever does not want to fade away while among people must learn to drink out of all cups; and whoever would stay clean while among people must know how to wash even with dirty water.

And thus I often comforted myself, 'Well then, old heart! You have experienced a misfortune; enjoy it as your – good fortune!'

'Of Human Prudence,' *Zarathustra*[1]

Nadezhda Iakovlevna Khazina and Osip Emilovich Mandel'shtam met on May Day 1919, in the Junk Shop, the artsy drinking establishment in civil-war-torn Kiev that the nineteen-year-old Nadezhda and her avant-garde painting companions habitually frequented. The poet, eight years her senior, was passing through town on his way to the Crimea, and the two, as Nadezhda Mandel'shtam tells it, 'at once took up with each other as though it were the most natural thing in the world' (HA 28). And why not? They had much in common. Both came from pampered, Jewish bourgeois backgrounds. Osip's father had been so successful a leather merchant that he was able, soon after Osip's birth (on 15 January 1891), to move the family from Warsaw to St Petersburg; his mother was a cultured lady who taught piano. Nadezhda's father had 'completed a degree in mathematics ... finished law school in several months ... staggering his professors with his brilliance' (KT 81; cited in Holmgren 1992a, 92) and moved the family from Saratov to Kiev; her mother was among the first wave of Russian women doctors. Both Osip and Nadezhda were equally well versed in European mores, history, and languages from their education and youthful travels. Nadezhda's family had made several trips to Europe, and she had been sent to a girls' school 'with a "male" (that is, implicitly more difficult) curriculum that required such impressive subjects as Latin' (Holmgren 1993a, 89); even as an octogenarian, she remained fluent in English, German, and French. Osip also knew Europe well, having studied in Paris in 1908 and in Heidelberg the following year and then travelled through Italy before returning to studies in Romance and German philology in St Petersburg. In 1913 Osip's first collection of poetry, *Kamen'* (*Stone*) appeared in *Appolon*, 'one of the elegant journals of art and literature that adorned the revival of Russian taste around the turn of the century' (O. Mandel'shtam 1965, xi). *Appolon* was the forum of a group of young poets who called themselves Acmeists to reflect their constructively classicist aspirations and their rejection of Symbolist mysticism, on the one hand, and the revolutionary, experimental pyrotechnics of Mayakovsky's Futurists, on the other. Led by Nikolei Gumilev and his wife, Anna Akhmatova, their apolitical, historical stance was to prove untimely. Gumilev was shot by the Cheka in 1921; Akhmatova was first 'unofficially' forced into 'inner exile' and later openly denounced in the 1946 *Zhdanov Report*, but she was nonetheless permitted to expire naturally, which she did in 1966. Osip was less fortunate.

Nadezhda Mandel'shtam attributes the naturalness of her spontaneous connection with Osip to their 'lightheadedness and a sense of doom' (HA 28), a shared sensibility that made it possible for them not only to survive but to enjoy their togetherness through the next two decades of chaos and destruction. During these years they travelled to all but the far corners of the Soviet Union, scrambling to maintain the dignity of their existence as the Stalinist hammer and sickle descended: 'We used to think of arriving in a new town as a kind of game. We had passed through Moscow, Rostov, Baku, Batumi, and Tiflis, and now, going in the reverse direction, Novorosslisk, Rostov, and Kharkov. We seemed to spend all our lives coming to strange cities, and I went on doing it without M. – but then it was no longer a game' (HA 95). Although their relationship began in May 1919, they had only a short time together before Osip had to leave. Nadezhda 'promised him I would come down to the Crimea with the Ehrenburgs, but with all the bloodshed in the streets outside I just couldn't bring myself to move' (HA 35). It was not until a year and a half later, after the end of the civil war, that Osip was able to return to Kiev to seek her out and take her away with him, thus beginning their great 'wander years,' as Maitreyi

Devi might have called them had she been called on to chronicle their fate rather than that of Tagore. At some point during the following eighteen and a half years, the Soviet bureaucracy required a marriage certificate of them, as it had of Asja Lacis and Bernard Reich, and so they too acquired one: 'Before buying a ticket for a "special" coach ... we had to pay a visit to the Register Office to obtain a marriage certificate. As soon as we arrived in Moscow we lost it. I am not even sure, in fact, that we got it on that particular occasion' (HA 97). They attached as little importance to marriage as Lacis and Reich did, considering themselves bound by greater forces, forces that whisked them about like autumnal leaves in a forest of nightmares.

March 1921: After a brief stay in Moscow, Nadezhda and Osip set off on an extended trip to the Caucasus that lasted a little over a year. Upon their return to Moscow during the next summer, Osip's second book of poetry, *Tristia*, was published and they were granted a room in Herzen House, the infamous headquarters of the Writers' Union on Tverskoi Boulevard where those currying the regime's favour (and those under surveillance) were housed. They spent the summer on the Crimea, where Osip wrote the autobiographical *Shum Vremeni* (*The Noise of Time*). As intrigues against Osip multiplied, they moved to Leningrad and tried to support themselves with odd jobs translating and editing. Clarence Brown surmises that, as in the case of Beauvoir and Sartre, Nadezhda provided more assistance to Osip than can ever be ascertained: 'She translated and edited numerous books – probably, I should think, under a pseudonym. At any rate, it would be impossible to determine what she translated, for those chores were no sooner finished than forgotten. She even collaborated with Mandelstam on many of the works, including those in verse, that carried his name as translator ... It must surely have been Nadezhda Yakovlevna who was mainly responsible for translating things like Upton Sinclair's *Machine* or editing the novels of Captain Mayne Reid for she knew English far better than her husband, but when I asked her this she waved the question away with a gesture of distaste: "Who knows? What *didn't* we translate?"' (O. Mandel'shtam 1965, vii; italics in original). Only in 1926, when Nadezhda contracted tuberculosis and spent the winter in Yalta, did Osip have to work on translations on his own, to pay for the sanatorium. The year Stalin assumed power, 1928, marked the pinnacle of Osip's commercial success in the Soviet Union. Thanks to the patronage of Bukharin, his second autobiographical story, *Egipskaya Marka* (*Egyptian Stamp*) appeared, as did a collected edition of his poems, a volume of collected essays, *On Poetry*, and, more important, several not unfavourable reviews. In 1930 Mayakovsky, the yellow-coated flame of the revolution, snuffed himself – or was snuffed – out, and Osip and Nadezhda went on a six-month journey to Armenia, which resulted in a poetry collection that he later was pressured to denounce. Upon their return, Osip's poems took on a more politically critical tone. In 1933, after returning from a summer of feeling assaulted by the starvation on the Crimea, he wrote the infamous poem his widow referred to as 'Kremlin's Mountaineer' and, whether carelessly or defiantly, recited it in the presence of 'friends':

We live, deaf to the land beneath us,
Ten steps away no one hears our speeches

But where there's so much as half a conversation
The Kremlin's mountaineer will get his mention.
[an earlier version reads: All we hear is the Kremlin mountaineer,
The murderer and peasant-slayer.]

His fingers are fat as grubs
And the words, final as lead weights, fall from his lips,

His cockroach whiskers leer
And his boottops gleam.

Around him a rabble of thin-necked leaders -
fawning half-men for him to play with.

They whinny, purr or whine
As he prates and points a finger,

One by one forging his laws, to be flung
Like horseshoes at the head, eye or groin.

And every killing is a treat
For the broad-chested Ossete.   (HAH 13)

In 1934, the year of the First Congress of Soviet Writers and the assassination of Kirov, Osip was arrested for the first time. Thanks to Bukharin's intervention, he was saved and released into three years of exile in Voronezh, after which they returned to Moscow to beg for work and lodgings. In April 1938 they were offered a place in a rest-home for writers by the secretary of the Writers' Union, and it is from there that Osip was arrested for a second time; he was sent to a Siberian grave, thus putting an end to at least his nightmares.

For the first two dozen of her subsequent years alone, Nadezhda kept her politically suspect self alive through the purges, the Great Patriotic War, and the pestilent post-war years, vigilantly maintaining the low profile of a provincial speck of dust in order to survive long enough to transcribe her husband's entire oeuvre from memory. She supported herself by teaching English at various teachers' colleges and in 1956 completed a doctorate in English philology under Zhirmunsky; her dissertation was titled 'Functions of the Accusative Case on the Basis of Materials Drawn from Anglo-Saxon Poetic Monuments.' In 1964 she was granted permission to live in Moscow, where she remained until her death in 1980, providing her with the long-awaited opportunity to finally realize her life's task of 'tell[ing] the story of what happened to us' (HA 15). *Vospominania* (*A Memoir*) and *Vtoraia Kniga* (*Second Book*) were smuggled to the west, where they were published by the YMCA Press in 1970 and 1972, and immediately translated into English as *Hope against Hope* (1970) and *Hope Abandoned* (1974).

Nadezhda's sharp wit and acidic, irreverent style initially raised the ire of many in the Soviet literary establishment used to hagiography. As Carl Proffer notes in his 1987 *Widows of Russia*, in the Russian tradition of memoir-writing: 'there is little of the rough and tumble of Western memoirs and diaries; a Russian Anais Nin would cause cramps; Harry Truman's bluntness and language would be totally unacceptable. Art is mentally capitalized, sex does not exist. And unpleasant historical events are glossed over or not mentioned' (35). Typical is the following account offered by a close friend of the Mandel'shtams in their final years together: 'Surely it is rare to find such a marriage, such understanding, such spiritual kinship. Nadezhda Iakovlevna was equal to her husband in intelligence, education, and her enormous spiritual strength. I never heard her complain, I never saw her irritated or depressed. She was always even-tempered, outwardly calm. Without a doubt she was Osip Emil'evitch's moral support ... His difficult, tragic fate became hers. She took this cross on herself as if there were no other way' (Shtempel' 1987, 230).

Nadezhda Iakovlevna herself was much harsher in accounts of her contemporaries. Unseemly comments in her memoirs about Russian literary icons such as her close friend, the regal and respected Anna Akhmatova, created a furore. Instead of offering appropriately humble worship, Nadezhda saw fit to use her memoirs to bluntly correct and criticize Akhmatova: 'Akhmatova is wrong when she says that this was said about [the well-known critic, translator, and author of children's books] Kornei Chukovski – M. would never have wasted such a splendid quip on him' (HA 389). Akhmatova's cultivation of feminine 'cults' and wiles comes under heavy criticism: 'What Akhmatova has to say is also not completely reliable, given her cult of love' (HA 290); as does her temperament in her later years: 'In her old age she was impervious to argument and would simply take refuge in her own authority, brooking no challenge to it: "What are you trying to tell me? I know." The slightest attempt to contradict provoked a storm of furious indignation. "Annush, you're like an angry cat," I used to say to her, whereupon she would erupt in resounding fury, and there was nothing to do but give in ... In her last years Akhmatova "put on her phonograph record" for each visitor, that is, told him or her the story of Acmeism and her own life, hoping they would commit it to memory and pass it on in the only permissible version – her own' (HA 499, 511). Appreciative as they might have been of the fact that she had preserved her husband's poetry,[2] many within the Soviet literary community initially found it difficult to forgive Nadezhda these scathing comments and inappropriate characterizations. Anti-memoirs, such as those of Lidiia Chukovskaia, an influential literary critic and daughter of the above-mentioned Kornei, were published in an unsuccessful attempt to throw her unconscionably brash assertions into disrepute. With time and glasnost, however, the rancour has subsided. Not only do Nadezdha Mandel'shtam's memoirs now receive universal high praise for what they convey about her husband (Althaus-Schönbucher 1981) and the plight of women in Stalinist Russia (Holmgren 1993; Pratt 1996), not only has the romance of the relationship as she described it become part of literary legend (Rifkind 1990; Margolina 1993), Nadezhda Mandel'shtam has also begun to receive attention and praise as a writer in her own right (Griffiths and Rabinowitz 1994; Isenberg 1986, 1987; Robey 1998). In the increasing number of works and collections devoted to Russian women writers since Barbara Heldt's influential *Terrible Perfection: Women and Russian Literature* (1987) and to twentieth-century Russian documentary writing, such as the 1990 collection *Autobiographical Statements in Twentieth-Century*

Russian Literature edited by Jane Gary Harris, and the special volume of *a/b Autobiography Studies* (Fall 1996) devoted to Russian autobiography, it is rare for her memoirs to go without mention. Parallel to this inexorable rise to canonical status in Slavic women studies is the increasing amount of international attention Nadezhda is garnering, as evidenced by the inclusion of the Mandel'shtams among the sixteen couples in the 1989 collection *Liebespaare* (*Couples*), which features the stories of Lou Andreas-Salomé and Rilke and Beauvoir and Sartre, among others.[3] As the following reading will attest, this status and the manner in which their relationship is now represented are due in no small part to Nadezhda's own efforts.

We

Beth Holmgren, who has written the only book-length study of Nadezhda Mandel'shtam that I know of, alludes to the fact that the Nadezhda in these memoirs is a construct, a literary creation.[4] She also reiterates Charles Isenberg's comparison of the Mandel'shtams' relationship with that of Sartre and Beauvoir. Isenberg supports his comparison with the following details of the 'extraordinary' nature of the Mandel'shtam's relationship: 'There is the casually undertaken commitment, the testing through extramarital affair, the refusal of children, the long separation with their letters and telegrams, the perpetual homelessness, the wrenching poverty and constant, grinding scutwork, the utter subservience of Nadezhda to Osip's gift – and then decades later the revelation of her own gift, and finally, the will evident in Mandel'shtam's prose to make the marriage, in retrospect, both a counter society and a laboratory for understanding the spouses' own social formation' (1990, 195). As far as it goes, Isenberg's comparison stands. However, it does not address the related issues of cultural context and relational representation, as the following reading does. While both Beauvoir and Mandel'shtam wrote their memoirs within contested cultural spaces, the nature of those frays and the aim or target of their writing was very different. Sartre was still alive when Beauvoir wrote each of the four volumes of her memoirs, and in writing them, as shown in chapter 2 of this study, she was trying to resurrect what Sartre had once been and what they had once shared. Mandel'shtam's resurrection could proceed more smoothly, since she did not have to battle the resurrected's resistance at every turn. Like Lou Andreas-Salomé, Maitreyi Devi, Asja Lacis, but not Simone de Beauvoir,

Nadezhda Mandel'shtam wrote her memoirs at the end, not in the prime, of her life. Unlike them, but like Romola Nijinsky, who will be discussed next, she wrote as a widow and witness to the western tradition of high culture. Like Maitreyi Devi, but not like Beauvoir, Mandel'shtam used her autobiographical writing as a counterbalance to what she knew to be the false testimonies of others and the silence of those with less courage. Like both Lou Andreas-Salomé and Maitreyi Devi, Mandel'shtam wrote out of a deeply spiritual sense of rightness, whereas Beauvoir's and Lacis's writings, as we have seen, were essentially hampered by a lack in this area.

What separates Nadezhda Mandel'shtam from the rest, however, is her finessing of the act of mutual creation. Mandel'shtam 'repeatedly invokes the life story her husband imagined for her' (Holmgren 1993a, 87).[5] She repeatedly represents herself as 'the work of his own hands,' his 'Europa,' the wild horse and foolish young thing he tames (HA 218, 139, 146, 298). She never lets the reader forget her husband's influence on the formation of her thoughts and values, creating the impression that she has been more of a disciple than a wife: 'From what M. told me I know that Tsygalski was quite exceptionally kind – a quality M. taught me to value above all others' (HA 107).[6] This meekness in her attitude towards her husband is accentuated by her refusal to subordinate herself to or conform with any implicit literary and social contracts, such as those of genre and gender: refusing to write an hagiographic biography and flying in the face of the societal constraints on women.[7] Osip commands her respect because of the world view he imparts to her, because of the meaning with which he imbues her existence: 'M. was perhaps the only person I knew who pondered the meaning of events, as opposed to their immediate consequence – the only concern of the older generation – or the garish manifestations of the "new," which was all the young thought about' (HA 33). Without him, she would have been only one of many: 'The only restraining influence on me came not from Dostoyevsky, but from M. It was he who stopped me from drifting with the current and aping the latest fashion of our cruel and tawdry age' (HA 305). Just as her life 'really began when I met M.,' when he dies, she, too, ceases to exist and comes back to life again only when writing her 'other self' (HA 211, 23): 'In writing my first book, I excluded myself. This happened quite spontaneously, without any conscious intention: it was simply that I still did not exist. I came back to life only when my main task was at an end' (HA 24). In 'her' memoirs, Nadezhda makes much of her task 'to preserve M.'s verse and tell the story of what happened to us' (HA 3) and of her goal 'to justify M.'s life by means of preserving what constituted its meaning' (103). From beginning to end, the focus is ostensibly Osip. As critics do not tire of pointing out, however, she is included in this focus, since she is, as she entitles one of the chapters of *Hope against Hope*, his 'Archive and Voice.' She would not tolerate anyone else's editing Osip's poems and has rather harsh words for those who interfered, such as her 'devoted friend' Nikolai Ivanovich Khardzhiev (Holmgren, 1993b, 139), whom she accuses of destroying rough drafts and variants of Mandel'shtam's poetry so that his editing would be consistent: 'Future editors please note: the cycle to Bely is no longer to be found in the "Codex Vaticanus" manuscript because it was ripped out and destroyed by Khardzhiev, the first "well-wisher" to work on M's poetry ... He did nonetheless return the bulk of the manuscripts, keeping a few items for his "collection" and destroying things on which he wished to change the date or replace with some other text not considered the final one by M. – as in the case of "January 10" ... I am myself to blame, of course, for entrusting the papers to someone who is mentally ill, but who except madmen ever did anything about the work of forbidden poets? I must say, too, that I have suffered less from Khardzhiev than from Rudakov, whose widow returned nothing at all' (HA 447).

In the 1960s, when Osip had not yet been rehabilitated, 'both Russian and non-Russian specialists made their way to Mandel'shtam and other widows as they were writing their essays and dissertations' (Proffer 1987, 28) and Mandel'shtam 'vigorously developed this instruction on her own, providing introductions for those few verses that were being published, writing out textual commentaries for at least one M. scholar, and, in general, dispensing all the information she could about M. and his work' (Holmgren 1993, 140). It is also to be noted that while she was quick to help, she was equally quick to criticize the way in which her M. was interpreted. As the following examples illustrate, Mandel'shtam set herself up as the final authority on his work. It was her domain and her word on him was final: 'It is preposterous to suggest, as somebody does, that he was talking about himself in the line: "ashamed, strange fellow, of his poverty/Yevgeni breathes in petrol fumes and curses fate" ... [N]ever, for one second, could M. have thought of saying about himself that he "cursed fate." Together we went through all kinds of ordeals and endured terrible disasters. It sometimes happened that I cursed life and fate, and everything under the sun. But it was I who did so, not he. I never once heard him say such things ... I would like to dispel another legend, the one put about by Ehrenburg to the effect that it was Voloshin who saved M. from Wrangel's jail. What actually happened was the following' (HA 91, 106).[8] These repeated assertions of unique authority are supported by her first-hand knowledge of the production of the entire oeuvre, since she had been its stenographer: 'The final versions were generally taken down by me to his dictation. As he dictated, he always grumbled because I could not at once memorize the whole poem at first hearing' (HA 536). In offering details of the circumstances in which the dictation took place, not only is she substantiating her claims to authorial sovereignty, but she is drawing attention away from the process of double creation at work in the memoirs, because it is a story that is being told, characters that are being created, and memories that are being recreated. While she claims to be his creation, she is creating herself and her life philosophy in telling his story and the story of his poetry.

The Osip in Mandel'shtam's memoirs has become the 'canonical image of the poet' (Freidin 1987, 250). It is a believable, realistically human image, heroic in its humaneness. Mandel'shtam's 'M.' has a concrete, consistent, many-sided character, one 'full of energy, wiry, high-spirited, and talkative, reacting to the slightest thing,' one whose 'blithe good spirits' never desert him, one whose 'chirpy, free and easy self' closes his eyes to the future (HA 111, 128, 383). This free spirit is given completely human dimensions and passions: 'There was nothing at all of the ascetic about M., and no end to the things he was fond of, or would have liked to have. He was always hankering after the south; he loved large rooms with plenty of light, a bottle of dry wine for dinner, a well-made suit (and not some monstrosity produced by the Moscow Tailoring Combine); and most of all, he loved well-baked bread rolls, something we always particularly longed for after our first experience of hunger' (HA 159). He is sociable, within limits: 'He generally got on well with people – unless they were lackeys, hangers-on, or the sort of writers who, as he put it, produce "things solved in advance" and "help the judges to visit punishment on the doomed"' (289). Not able to answer both his own conscience and the demands put on him by others, Mandel'shtam represents him as opting repeatedly for the former, paying heed to no one else, neither his wife nor Soviet societal standards: 'M. had a knack for making enemies by a blunt outspokenness which was quite needless in situations of this kind' (HA 142); 'I never had the slightest influence on M., and he would have thrown me over rather than his city' (HA 118); 'Everybody knows from his letters that he loved me, but he was infinitely exacting (yet indulgent at the same time) towards his "you," and if I had not agreed to become his shadow, ready to partake in his sense of joy, he would have had no difficulty in giving me up as well' (HA 291). His actions are decisive, vehement and always of his own accord: 'Just as a few hours previously M. had been quite oblivious to me, he was now totally unmoved by Olga and her tears ... I am still surprised even now at the ruthless way he chose between us and at the decisiveness with which he acted' (HA 244); 'M. tackled him [Berdiayev] with all the vehemence of his Jewish temperament ... I wasn't actually present at this scene, but I had more than once borne the brunt of M.'s fury (sometimes for good cause, sometimes unjustly), and I can imagine how it must have frightened the unsuspecting Berdiayev. M. told me himself that he had never seen Berdiayev have such a bad attack of his tic as during this conversation' (HA 113). Besides being decisive and of his own mind, Mandel'shtam's M. is also decidedly despotic: 'Nothing would have induced him to set foot in the place in the evening. Nor would he let me go anywhere by myself, so I never got to know the Moscow salons in those early days of the new imperial epoch then beginning' (HA 141). He is also misunderstood: 'Even Akhmatova did not completely understand him ... Nobody was closer to us than Akhmatova, and if she failed to grasp the forces that shaped M., then there is no point in expecting others to' (HA 152–3). An important consequence of M.'s uniquely multi-sided character is that it marks him, identifies him as unassimilable, sets him apart: 'In the crowd of braggarts M. stood out like the proverbial white raven' (HA 273).[9] He is heroic precisely in the strength of his individuality and in the tragic impossibility of being anything else, both unique and one of millions who suffered for it.

In portraying her own character, Mandel'shtam adopts a similar strategy, alternating in her emphasis on the one and the many. There are many 'we's of which she feels part, which she uses to establish her identity as an intellectual woman, a Russian Jew, and, most important, the wife of a great poet.[10] Her first, most general 'we' refers to her feminine side: 'I remember the wretched things I hankered after, in common with all the women of my generation: a little place to call my own or, rather, a room in a communal apartment; a wad of rubles, at least enough to last the week through, a pair of shoes and some nice stockings. All of *us*, whether housewives or secretaries, were obsessed about stockings. Made out of real, but slightly spoiled silk, they never lasted for more than a day and, swallowing our tears, *we* all learned to mend ladders. And there was not one of *us* who did not weep real tears when the high heel – a legacy from a very different life – broke on her beloved only pair of those foolish shoes which had once been designed for stepping from one's gracious residence into a waiting carriage, and no farther.' (139–40, italics added). Second, she belongs to a certain Russian class: the intelligentsia: 'To appreciate M.'s poem about meeting again in Petersburg, one has to understand the situation that had arisen for people like *us* who belonged to the intelligentsia by birth and had grown up in an atmosphere of *our own* intimate small talk, bound together by common interests' (HA 76; italics added); 'At the present day – in 1970 – the little differences between *our* government and the handful of intellectuals who as a result of them land up in forced labour camps really spring from only one thing: *we* are forbidden to let out "state secrets"' (HA 102; italics added). The Russian intelligentsia was, and to a great extent remains, a class one is born into, and it is the world she was born into: 'The doctors who came to see my parents were intellectuals in the true sense of the word, as one could tell from the conversation at table and the books they took away with them to their homes deep in the country' (HA 114–15). As in the cases of Maitreyi Devi and Asja Lacis, discussed in Part 2, it is Mandel'shtam's father who is given credit in her writing with having provided the initial impetus to her studies: 'It was my father who once taught me to read by asking me a seemingly quite casual question: What kind of material was Chichikov's frock coat made of? For my father, as for the author, this was a telling detail which put the stamp of the age on Chichikov and showed him up quite precisely, in an analytical way, for what he was: a semidandy who displayed his soul in his dress' (HA 615); 'I shall never forget the hush that fell on the audience when he [V. Ivanov] ascended the rostrum (this I once witnessed as a young girl when my father took me to hear his lecture on Scriabin, or Medtner)' (HA 454). Although a member of the Russian intelligentsia, Mandel'shtam does not identify herself as a Russian national. She does not write of 'we Russians' but rather both compares herself to and sets herself apart from them: 'I too was always ready to drop from weariness, but because I simply did not dare, I managed to preserve my strength. I have all the staying power of the Russians – it developed during my years of waiting. For half a century it was all that kept people going here and has become a weakness with them' (HA 213). Her ties are determined not nationally but linguistically, to a socio-historical entity distinguished clearly from the Soviet state in which she lived: 'If, for one single moment, I had started speaking in my own language instead of in prescribed official jargon, none of them would have hesitated to ensure that I spend the rest of my life felling timber' (HA 626); 'All the same I am glad that my capital is Moscow, not Kiev – my native language, after all, is Russian, and if the Jews are going to be slaughtered in both places, better it happen to me in Moscow. In Moscow there will always be some kindly soul who will try to stop the mob with a few good-humoured oaths: "Don't you touch this one," she will say, "you so-and-so sons of bitches!" It will be easier to die to the familiar sound of Russian swearing' (HA 96).

This self-confessed 'Jewish girl' (HA 31) for whom the Orthodox religion became increasingly important as her life neared its end, is clear about which 'we' has the most importance to her. At the beginning of the second book, Mandel'shtam introduces herself as follows: 'Like any other wife of a prisoner, like any other *stopiatnitsa* or exiled person, I thought only about the times I lived in ... The fact is that there was nothing exceptional about my case. There were untold numbers of women like myself roaming the country – mute, cowed creatures' (HA 3). However much she may have resembled other women, Mandel'shtam was also aware that hers was a special case: 'I would eventually, before I died, have a sealed bottled with a message to cast upon the waves, [while they have] only empty bottles' (HA 4), that is, the kind you take back for money. She is a poet's wife, wondering: 'How many of *us* are there spending sleepless nights repeating the words of our dead husbands?' (HA 276; italics added). She feels kin, not to every poet's wife, though, but to a select group: 'those who would name "accomplices" only under torture, never voluntarily, at the first invitation. As long as there are people who try to overcome their instinct for self-preservation, hope is not lost and life may continue' (HA 652). It is to those who preserve themselves in preserving others, who prefer to endure rather than inflict suffering, that she feels bound, those for whom life's meaning is found in their connections with others. She writes at length about the importance of feeling connected to a special group of others that she terms a 'we': 'We witnessed the disintegration of a society which was as imperfect as any other, but which concealed and curbed its wickedness and harboured small groups of people who were truly entitled to refer to themselves as "we." I am quite convinced that without such a "we," there can be no proper fulfilment of even the most ordinary "I," that is, of the personality. To find its fulfilment, the "I" needs at least two complementary dimensions: "we" and – if it is fortunate – "you"' (HA 39). In this description, one becomes aware of the exact dimensions that unity assumes for Mandel'shtam. She is both of the multitude and unique, because her self, as she perceives it, came into being, that is, took on meaning, only through others: 'If my life had any meaning at all, it was only because I shared all the tribulations of Akhmatova and M. and eventually found myself, my own true self, through my closeness to them' (HA 266). She is aware, and wants the reader to be aware, of the extraordinary nature of her accomplishment: 'Surkov's first question was about M.'s papers and literary remains. He could hardly believe his ears when I said I had preserved it all – a small part he could have understood, but *all* of it!' (HA 656; italics in original); and of the feisty nature of her personality, hence the 'salty' language, sexual candour, and forthright opinions (cf. Holmgren 1993a, 109; Proffer 1987, 17, 22–5). Yet more important is that the reader understand how this strength of character came about, that in her view it is a gift of others, one to which it is imperative to be open.

This phenomenon of existing by, through, and for others is the basis of the cohesive ethical program laid out by Mandel'shtam in her memoirs. In the words of Max Hayward, her English translator, she endeavours in *Hope Abandoned* 'to complete on [M.'s] behalf something he did not himself have time to do before his life was cut short, namely, to set forth a system of values and beliefs that run quite counter to the dominant ones of the age we live in, whether in the East or the West' (7). The most salient tenet of the Mandel'shtam philosophy as it is found in the pages of Mandel'shtam's memoirs is the question of answerability.[11] It is placed by Mandel'shtam on the side of poetry and freedom and distinguished from the duplicity inherent in totalitarian life, which she likens to acting: 'Like actors, everybody lived a double life – with the difference that for an actor his duality, the wearing of a mask, is essential to his art, whereas for Tynianov's contemporaries it was more in the nature of a protective device' (HA 373). She then contrasts actors with poets: 'it is no good for an actor to try to be like a poet. These are quite different types of activity: one in a mask and the other without' (HA 373). The difference between them is a fundamental one and lies in taking responsibility for one's words: 'The actor's personal contribution can be made only jointly, as it were, with the character he plays and whose words he speaks. Having to represent someone else, he becomes a dual personality who does not play in his own right, any more than he answers for the words he learns by heart: they have been put into his mouth on behalf of the character whose identity he assumes on the stage. But the poet answers for everything' (HA 365).

In digressions juxtaposing freedom with licence and fear with cowardice, Mandel'shtam expounds on the necessity of maintaining an inner freedom by doing not what one wants but what one is willing to answer for. For Mandel'shtam the poet is an exemplar of such a person; he or she can maintain links with a special 'we,' that is, express in verse not the platitudes forced upon him or her from outside but those ideas which he or she believes in and has assimilated into a special communal individuality. It is 'a capacity to select and define the components of one's own inner world' (HA 112) that sets each person apart. Finding one's own voice implies freeing oneself from external influence: 'The one thing a poet – or indeed any man – must not do is give up his freedom, become like everybody else, merge with his surroundings, and speak in the current language of the day' (HA 303–4). Verse has the potential to liberate, for both the reader and the poet: 'In full consciousness of being a slave, I repeated to myself: "For free is the slave who has overcome fear." I could not really, of course, overcome fear, but verse gave inner freedom, showed that man was capable of higher and better things' (HA 201). She encourages people to be not atomized individuals but rather interconnected yet unique personalities sensitive to all of creation, asking why is it 'that in this country the individual, the particular, is never seen as a token or a symbol of the world as a whole?' (HA 395). Personalities such as her husband, who remained connected with others and with history, are an important countervailing force to the disconnected, destructive evil against which her writing is directed. She elaborates such an ideal at length because it is for her the only answer to the calamitous events she has experienced: 'A person possessed of inner freedom, memory, and a sense of fear is the blade of grass or wood chip that can alter the course of the swift-flowing stream' (HA 206).

CHAPTER SIX

Romola Nijinsky

I would believe only in a god who can dance ... I learned to walk: ever since I let myself run. I learned to fly: ever since I don't want a push-start. Now I am light, now I fly, now I see myself beneath me, now a god dances through me.

'Of Reading and Writing,' *Zarathustra*[1]

In the history of the ballet, the figure of Vaslav Nijinsky makes the impression of the kind of blade of grass or wood chip that Nadezhda Mandel'shtam would have had great empathy for – carried along by a turbulent stream but nonetheless engaged in a struggle to maintain internal freedom and in doing so perceptibly altering the ballet world. Generally regarded as one of the greatest male ballet dancers of all time, the tragic piquancy of Nijinsky's fall into madness subsequent to being dismissed from Diaghilev's Ballets Russes guaranteed his legendary status. It is not owing to his spectacular jumps and unique interpretations per se that the figure of Nijinsky enjoys a special standing in the history of the ballet. Although the technology was available at the time, the phenomenon of Nijinsky's dancing was never captured on film, and the faded photographs of him that have come down to us are, for the most part, studio portraits that only hint at the electricity with which his dancing ignited audiences. Rather, it is as an English-language literary creation that the 'God of the Dance' has become an integral part of balletomania, which resulted from an intricate series of cross-cultural mediations and translations and was primarily of his Hungarian wife Romola's making. Her role both in his dismissal and in legend-making after his illness has received critical attention in the scholarship on Nijinsky and in ballet circles where memoirs are habitually written by artists, their relatives, friends, and patrons.[2] In this chapter I focus on Romola's efforts at becoming a Nijinsky and at writing Nijinsky and on how those efforts have been received. After doing so, I highlight the similarities and differences between her heroic creation and accomplishments and those of Nadezhda Mandel'shtam, particularly with respect to the important, contrasting role that Russia played in both lives.

Romoalda (Romola) Flavia Ludowika Polyxena Consuelo Marie de la Consolation de Pulszky first saw the great Nijinsky dance in Budapest in March of 1912.[3] One of the many questionable facts in Romola's story is her age at the time of this first encounter. Although she claims 'that I was already seventeen years of age' (N 21)[4] when she was allowed to study with the Ballets Russes's Cecchetti at Christmas of that year (that is, a good nine months later), according to her mother's prayer book she was born 'in the year 1891 on the 19th February at dawn 3:45 am' (N&R 1; see also Reiss 1960, 139; Ostwald 1991, 80), which would have her pushing twenty-two at the time. In the panache evidenced by this sleight of hand, Romola displays the single-minded determination of a Zarathustrian sibling. While she may not have been as young as she claimed, Romola still was two years younger than the genius she saw on the stage that spring night,[5] who so captured her imagination that she promptly took advantage of her family's prominent cultural standing to insinuate herself into the circles of Diaghilev's Ballets Russes. Her mother, Emilia Markus, was the foremost Hungarian actress of her day, the 'Blonde Wonder,' whose talents were considered by many to outstrip those of Sarah Bernhardt and Elenore Duse, while her father, Count Karoly de Pulszky, was a member of Parliament and director of the Hungarian National Gallery of Art.[6] Romola does not fail to draw attention to the advantage she took of her familial connections: 'But why was my godfather head of the Imperial Family's archives and the confidant of Franz Joseph? To help me. And why was my brother-in-law [Eric Schmede, the husband of her sister, Tessa] the first Wagnerian star of his day? To serve me, of course' (N 23). It worked, as Romola was confident it would: 'I was neither awed nor embarrassed when we went to see Diaghileff. I was determined to obtain my point, and, when my mind was definitely set, nothing and nobody mattered' (N 24).

Diaghilev gave his permission, and Romola was allowed to accompany the Ballets Russes on their 1913 season from London, to Monte Carlo, Paris, back to London, and then, because so many of the regular dancers refused to go, to South America. The latter leg of the journey was to prove fatal. Diaghilev remained in Europe pleading seasickness and Nijinsky was unaccompanied for the first time since Romola had begun travelling with the troupe. By the time the boat docked in Buenos Aires on 6 September 1913, the two were engaged and on their way to the first suitable altar. Diaghilev's dismissal of his protégé and his lover upon getting wind of the hasty wedding was a matter of course. Further work in America, England, Spain, and South America was marred by contractual squabbles and Nijinsky's inability to attend to the business of running, not simply dancing and choreographing for, a ballet company, as well as by the first historical glitch to derail Romola's arduously laid plans: the First World War. By the time the Nijinskys had found a safe haven for themselves and their three-year-old daughter, Kyra, in Switzerland in December 1917, Vaslav was fit more for its sanitaria than a cosy chalet in St Moritz. Indeed, it was not long before his increasingly bizarre antics landed him in the Bellevue Sanitarium in Kreuzlingen. The diagnosis of 'schizophrenia' was first articulated by the psychiatrist Eugene Bleuler in 1911. Romola was quick to seek out Bleuler's expert services in nearby Zurich, and he in turn was quick to see in Vaslav a manifestation of this newly defined malady of the soul. Romola reports that the Professor told her: 'Now, my dear, be very brave. You have to take your child away; you have to get a divorce. Unfortunately, I am helpless. Your husband is incurably insane' (410).[7] Kreplin, Ferenczy, Freud, and Jung all would later confirm the diagnosis.

The following decades were not easy for Romola. For periods of time, she would try to reincorporate Vaslav, together with a trained male attendant, into her household, but his fits of violence would force her to readmit him to a nearby sanitarium. In 1921 Vaslav's sister, Bronislava, and their mother escaped from the same carnivalesque Kiev that Osip and Nadezhda Mandel'shtam were also then departing, in order to rejuvenate him with their presence. But by the time they made the trek to Vienna where Romola had moved during the previous summer to give birth to their second daughter,[8] Vaslav's condition had deteriorated to the point that he no longer recognized them. In 1923 Romola moved her family to Paris, as her younger daughter claims, in yet another attempt to bring her husband around: 'She nourished the implicit belief that Paris, the city of his greatest triumphs, would awaken at least the dimmest spark of recollection in her Watza. People have told me in later years how hard she tried, taking him to the theatre, the ballet, to the haunts he had frequented in happier days, long strolls through the Bois de Boulogne, motor tours of the environs. All to no avail' (N&R 215). Romola became increasingly overwhelmed at the task of providing for nine mouths (N&R 222), with no stable source of income and no marketable skills.[9] She disbanded the household in 1925 to pursue opportunities in the United States, leaving Vaslav in the care of her sister and sending Kyra to a boarding school in Switzerland and Tamara to her grandparents in Hungary. By the time of Diaghilev's death, appropriately enough in Venice, on 19 August 1929, a few months before Black Friday created chaos on international stock markets, Romola had given up on script-writing in Hollywood. It had occurred to her that it was 'both necessary and desirable, for the history of art and of genius, and to help preserve the memory of the greatest and kindest human being [she] had ever known' (LYN 419)[10] that her husband's story appear in print. In a letter to her mother marking the end of 1931, she conveyed her new resolutions: 'Now I will aim at establishing the Bayreuth of Dance and win the Nobel Prize of Literature; with God's help ... this is my humble ambition for the time being' (N&R 242). With Lincoln Kirstein acting as 'a kind of supervisor cum ghostwriter' (Kirstein 1991, 130), her *Nijinsky* was completed and published in 1933. She then set about culling the notebooks in which Vaslav had been madly scribbling during the six weeks leading up to his hospitalization for non-incriminating selections, which were published under her editorship in 1936 as *The Diary of Vaslav Nijinsky*. Following his death on Easter Saturday 1950, Romola felt motivated to tell the world about *The Last Years of Nijinsky* (1952), chronicling their adventures and experiences with mental institutions before, during and after the Second World War. As Peter Ostwald tells it: 'Romola lived for another 28 years [after Vaslav's death]. She travelled widely, usually with Paul Bohus (her distant relative and companion since WWII), visited Russia – where she had an amusing interview with Krushchev[11] – and Japan, where she fell in love with a transvestite actress who remarkably resembled the young Nijinsky. Romola died in 1978 in Paul Bohus's arms in a Paris hotel. She too lies in the Montmartre Cemetery, but not close to her husband (1991, 341).[12]

Romola presents a daunting interpretive challenge to those writing about Nijinsky, whether in the form of documentary writing, biography, or artistic production. Beginning in 1937 with Anatole Bourman, one of the six boys in Vaslav's first class at the Imperial School of Ballet in St Petersburg in 1898, who 'would survive to write a bad book about his great school-fellow for the bafflement of future biographers' (Buckle 1971, 4),[13] Nijinsky scholarship has been hard pressed to avoid the versions of the Nijinsky saga that Romola so actively promulgated. Even those works that adhere strictly to Vaslav's artistic accomplishments and avoid his personal life, such as Kirstein's elegant picture book *Nijinsky Dancing*, cannot but perpetuate the highly stylized way that life has come down to us, something that drove a reviewer, even in 1938, to complain that 'because of the way in which his misfortunes have been flaunted and commercialized, one cannot help but ask the question – Is Vaslav Nijinsky fact or fiction?' (Ware 1938, 39). It is a question Romola's younger daughter would echo some fifty years later: 'Did she know when she crossed the borderline between fact and fiction?' (N&R 33).

On the question of how Romola was received, a striking tendency is immediately apparent: rarely neutral, it is usually either very much for her or very much against her.[14] Among the harshest condemnations of Romola for her culpability in her husband's fate, her attempts to capitalize on it after the fact, and her general disregard for matters of fact in her biography, are by those associated with Diaghilev. Serge Lifar heads this group. Originally a pupil of Bronislava Nijinska in Kiev, he became one of Diaghilev's protégés and later the driving force of the Paris Opera Ballet, where he was responsible for moving Nijinsky's body to the Montmartre Cemetery in June 1953 so that it might rest beside Auguste Vestris, the male dancing legend of the nineteenth century. Lifar repeatedly castigates Romola for inaccuracies in her depiction of Diaghilev and uses them as an excuse to throw her entire project into question: 'Unfortunately in her biography, interesting and rich with material as it is, there are so many unchecked and deliberately falsified facts [for example, about Diaghilev's life] that it is difficult to make use of it' (1994, 177). Misia Sert, a patron of the Parisian avant-garde art scene and a close friend of Diaghilev and his ballet, also concentrates on the negative aspects of Romola's involvement with the ballet, describing the Nijinskys' marriage as 'one of the first tragedies to shake the Russian Ballet' and blaming Romola for the lack of a reconciliation afterwards: 'many times both men were on the verge of reconciling. But Romola stopped at nothing to prevent this. God only knows whether Nijinsky wouldn't have enjoyed many more years of fame if he hadn't met this woman who drove him so quickly into the mad-house' (1953, 89, 93).

These accounts are tempered by those of Romola supporters, in the first instance Vaslav's younger sister, Bronislava, a noted dancer and choreographer in her own right.[15] In *Early Memoirs*, Bronislava draws on her insider's knowledge of the situation and contextualizes her brother's decision to get married in terms of tensions surrounding the Ballets Russes, Diaghilev's constant struggle for patronage, and the reinstatement of Fokine, whose condition for rehire was that he replace Vaslav as the company's choreographer (1992, 475). She reports that the news of her brother's marriage brought her 'great joy' and that she was positively predisposed towards her 'pretty' sister-in-law on first meeting her in Paris in 1914, not least because both she and Romola were pregnant at the time (1992, 478, 494). The only hint that their relations were anything less than harmonious appears in the descriptions of the preparations for the London 'Saison Nijinsky': 'I had strongly advised Vaslav that he should present his Faune in the first programme, but Romola and one of her influential London society friends insisted on Les Sylphides. They both tried to persuade Vaslav to return to the classical dance and perform ballets that were more appealing to the general public, rather than continue on the way of Sacre. They disapproved of both Jeux and Faune, though Vaslav did plan to include them in the Saison Nijinsky' (1992, 498). Here, it is clear that the reason Bronislava resented this 'outside' influence of high society was that it went against what she felt to be her brother's integrity as an innovative artist. In general, however, one is given the impression that she was kindly disposed towards Romola when she felt that she was acting in her brother's interests and respecting the ways of the ballet world.

A comparison of the two most substantial English-language Nijinsky scholars on the question of Romola's always precarious financial situation further demonstrates the dichotomous tendency in her reception. The fact that publication of Romola's books was intended primarily as a money-making enterprise is not in dispute. Romola relates being questioned by the invading Soviet forces at the end of the Second World War:

'What is your profession?'
'I haven't one. I was brought up as most other society girls, a general edu-cation, chiefly the arts and music.'
'So how did you provide for both of you?'
'At first I used the funds my husband gave me which he earned while he was dancing. Later, when I saw that the doctors' fees, treatments and

nursing homes would swallow all our savings, I began to write, lecture and work for film.' (LYN 513)

The presentation of these circumstances, however, is a matter very much open to scholarly interpretation. Richard Buckle belongs to the inner circle of English ballet aficionados. He was one of the pall-bearers at Nijinsky's funeral, and his 'definitive' 1971 biography of Nijinsky was approved by both Romola and her grand-niece Irina. Buckle characterizes Romola as 'courageous,' 'dauntless,' and 'indomitable'; he emphasizes that she had been Vaslav's wife for thirty-seven years and his breadwinner for thirty of those years; and he casts a noble light on Romola's literary endeavours: 'one of the tasks Romola undertook in order to earn money to keep Vaslav and herself was to write her husband's life' (1971, 501, 507, 519, 537). Buckle's respect and admiration for Romola seep into his description of the challenge she faced upon Nijinsky's being diagnosed as hopelessly insane: 'Now began for Romola Nijinsky thirty years of hope, despair, struggle, poverty and heroism ... Romola was advised to make use of her American visa and to leave Vaslav in a Swiss State Asylum ... Rather than risk cancelling all the good Vaslav's treatment had done him, she renounced comfort and security for herself in America and resolved to stay beside him. This was perhaps her most unselfish and heroic decision' (1971, 501, 521). Peter Ostwald, in contrast, is decidedly less enamoured with Romola. His interest in Nijinsky is that of a sensitive, cultured psychiatrist, and his 1991 account of Nijinsky's illness, *Vaslav Nijinsky: A Leap into Madness*, received the support of Romola's daughters, although they did express reservations about the less than glorious nature of the project. Instead of emphasizing Romola's heroism, Ostwald focuses on the unrelenting trail of debts resulting from her insistently lavish lifestyle: '(As can be surmised from Mme Nijinsky usually staying in the best and most expensive hotels, she was not as destitute as she often claimed. However, she was notably negligent in paying her bills.)' (1991, 283). Ostwald's research disclosed correspondence such as: '"It was a considerable disappointment to us," writes the bank manager [of Barclays], "to learn that you had gone [back to Austria] without making any arrangement for the repayment of our advance"' (1991, 329). He also includes what he thought were the pertinent parts of the records kept of Vaslav's stays in sanitaria: '"*A visit from his wife!*" reports his psychiatrist, Dr Kroll, on 4 April 1934. Having been away for four years, Romola created quite a stir at Bellevue.

"Generous as always," writes Dr Kroll sarcastically, "she brings with her many presents, for which the hospital is expected to pay customs duty and freight charges. But at least she buys some clothes and laundry for the patient, who smiles at everything" ... Regarding the non-payment of his hospital bill, Romola explained that her daughter Kyra is "extraordinarily gifted and will be ready to contribute to her father's support in just a few years"' (1991, 287; italics in original).

This tendency to be either for or against Romola is also reflected in the artistic productions of the phenomenon that was Nijinsky.[16] They generally take as their lead either Romola's biographies or Vaslav's diary, with those based on the biographies tending towards a more sympathetic portrayal of Romola and those based on the diary either paying her no or limited but negative heed. The publication of an unexpurgated version of the diary in French in 1995, the same year that Romola's version first appeared in Russian, has been accompanied by a comparatively large number of productions that take their material from, or are in some way based on, the diary.[17] Because Romola's role, first in withholding and then in heavily editing the original version of the diary, has been roundly condemned, one can detect a perceptible shift towards more negative portrayals of her in these more recent works. Time has not been as kind to Romola Nijinsky as it has to Nadezhda Mandel'shtam; in the majority of artistic as well as scholarly productions one is left to choose between her and Diaghilev as the greater of two evils.

In Search of a Motherland

Before exploring the problems inherent in the husband and wife representations in Romola's writing and comparing them with those of Nadezhda Mandel'shtam, attention should be drawn to the fact that the less than flattering portrayal of Romola as a manipulative, power-hungry, scheming, and conniving vixen answerable for the unhappy fate of her husband, is not simply one contrived by mean-spirited historians, biographers, and dramatists, but rather is one mostly of her own creation. Romola herself describes her pursuit of Nijinsky in terms of 'ha[ving] succeeded in fooling such an inconceivably clever man as Diaghilev' (N 21) into allowing her to travel with the company. As soon as she can communicate with her new husband somewhat in pidgin French and Russian, she relates, 'I began to rave about all the Callot dresses, Reboux hats, and Cartier jewels, and of all the mondaine life I was going to lead in the future' (N 208). She reports that upon seeing smoke coming out of the closet in their bedroom, she thought, 'I might save the money, jewels, furs, and passports,' and she flies into a panic thinking her jewels had been stolen during a train ride to Paris (N 264, 316–17). She frequently admits to less than gracious or harmonious behaviour. She is 'very unhappy' that her first born is a girl, not the desired male (N 219). By her own accounts she does not seem to have been a very good-humoured companion: 'He had many little tricks of driving that I disliked intensely'; 'I was so angry that I sat silent'; 'I was really angry with him this time'; 'for two days I was disagreeable,' 'I really got angry, and walked home with Kyra'; 'I lost my temper' (N 267, 287, 206, 332, 333). Further, she makes good on a threat to walk out on her husband if he does not comply with her demand to drop Tolstean friends she regards as an evil influence (N 300–1).[18] Thus, Romola did nothing to counteract the prevailing opinion that she was a pampered, status-conscious socialite, either before their marriage, when the presence in the ballet troupe of a girl who insisted on travelling first class with a maid and whose connections were more evident than her talent was viewed with general derision and cynicism, or after Vaslav's institutionalization, when she travelled back and forth across the Atlantic writing letters to the likes of both Eleanor Roosevelt and the Queen Mother (Ostwald 1991, 332–3), and Presidents Nixon and Giscard d'Estaing (N&R 479, 494) for help in getting treatment for her husband.

What lies behind this deliberately provocative self-representation? Romola's younger daughter attributes it to upbringing: 'It was inevitable that the Pulszky daughters were to be strongly influenced by their environment. Throughout their lives, neither could quench her thirst for luxury and a high life style. Both had absorbed a craving for the finest fashion, and money was to run through their fingers like grains of sand' (N&R 10).[19] In this respect, one cannot overlook the fact that their father was 'highly educated ... could boast degrees from the Universities of London, Turin and Leipzig ... spoke eleven languages ... was an avid reader of the classics,' and named his younger daughter after the heroine of a George Eliot novel which he had translated into Hungarian (and published under a pseudonym) so that his wife might read it (N&R 5).[20] However, there is a further consideration. Romola conspicuously sets herself up as an outsider to her husband's world: 'Bronia was untiring too. She spoke only Russian and Polish, but I soon noticed that she did not like me; she seemed to resent everything that happened and blame it on me. I was the intruder in the Russian Ballet, in the family. She isolated herself behind a screen of ice which I could never penetrate' (N 212). In the light of Bronislava's positive reaction to her brother's marriage (she 'deeply wanted to share this happiness with Vaslav' (1992, 478)), Romola's feelings of exclusion seem to have much less to do with the sister than with the brother. Not only did Romola suddenly have to share Vaslav's attentions with someone else for the first time since their marriage, but she found herself facing competition for his attentions with a rival enjoying a distinct home-field advantage: 'At Laroux's, or at Jiel's, I used to await them for lunch sometimes until four or five o'clock in the afternoon. But they worked and danced all the time' (N 212). Her reaction to Diaghilev when they met in New York was similar: 'But Sergey Pavlovitch was beyond forgiveness. I could see that he still loved Vaslav and deeply resented my existence' (N 262). One further instance of Romola's alienation, as shown in the following description of her eldest daughter, offers an important clue to the mechanism behind it: 'It was remarkable how the child changed the moment Vaslav entered the room. It seemed almost as though they had been one person split apart, and constantly wishing to be reunited. Sometimes I almost felt as if I was intruding on them. They were both essentially and fundamentally Russian – something we Europeans can never, never penetrate' (N 317). These words echo exactly those she put into the mouth of the Ballets Russes's venerable ballet master, Cecchetti, a dozen pages earlier: 'These Russians are a strange lot. For thirty-five years I have taught and studied them. They are my friends, I love them, but there is something about them that we Europeans can never, never penetrate' (N 305). Despite the fact that Vaslav was Polish,[21] Romola continually draws attention to his 'Russianness,' that 'he carried in his heart an eternal love for Russian soil,' that he 'loved Russia with every fibre of his being' (N 30, 97). She also raised their first born to be a Russian. During the First World War, while interned with her husband and young daughter at her mother's house, she writes that she was: 'reproached with teaching Kyra only Russian, and forbidding her to learn Hungarian. But I said, "She is only sixteen months old. *Of course* she will be learning Russian, but she is too small to speak any language yet"' (N 235; italics added).[22] Romola presents it as a matter of course that she will place her daughter in the world she herself has failed to enter. Romola's identification with and glorification of Russia are unmistakable. When arrested in Spain, she says with pride, 'you have no right to arrest me; I am a Russian citizen, and not a member of the Russian Ballet,' and when she learns that 'the power in Russia had been seized by the local soviets, and Lenin and Trotsky, repatriated three days ago, had formed a Government,' her comment is 'We neither of us knew what this really meant for *our* country and the world' (N 303, 316, italics added). Describing the Stravinskys, she comments: 'The wife was a real Russian woman, a devoted wife and mother; in her great simplicity there was the strength of one who devoted herself – her life and personality – to the genius of another. She was the ideal wife for a great artist ... Madame Stravinsky was a real artist in handicraft. She embroidered, knitted, and painted beautifully. I always tried to please Vaslav by emulating these Russian women, but with little success' (N 253).

The reason behind this emulation can be revealed by relating it to Romola's attitude towards her nationality and her mother. When their boat was searched by English officers during the First World War on the way back to Europe from South America, Romola reports herself as panicking and throwing overboard the Jesus of Prague picture that Vaslav had given her as a present:

> I became frantic. 'Vaslav, they will arrest me, take me off the boat.'
> 'But what for, femmka?'
> 'Because I was born Hungarian.'
> 'Now, femmka, tu es bête. The English are sensible people, they will not do anything to you.' (315)

Hungary is the country where they were interned during not only one but both world wars.[23] Upon finding herself a prisoner for a second time with her husband in her mother's house, Romola comments: 'I deeply worried, realizing the great mistake I had made in bringing him to my family's home where he had suffered so deeply in the past. It was an error with far-reaching consequences to place him here in this antagonistic atmosphere, charged with discord and suspicion, especially after the insulin shock treatment. Vaslav needed now to be surrounded with sympathetic understanding and kindly people' (LYN 456). In a word, he needed Russians, who, when they finally arrived four years later, are recorded as understanding intuitively how to deal with the 'patient': 'For the first time since 1919 people did not stare at him, did not shrink from him because he had suffered from a mental illness. They [the Russian soldiers] spoke to him in the same nonchalant manner as they did to us. At first I warned them: "Leave Vaslav

Fomitch alone, don't talk to him. He might get annoyed and impatient, he is afraid." But they just laughed. "He won't be afraid of us," they said. "Let him alone to do what he wants" ... As the days and weeks passed, I noticed that the primitive Russian soldiers had a better method of treating him than we had, in spite of all the doctors and nurses of the last twenty-six years' (LYN 516–17).

It is the Hungarians, not the Russians, who were their tormentors. Throughout the text they are consistently portrayed as less than pristine figures. Not only does the 'kinsman,' called only Don de B., whose acquaintance they make on their second trip to South America, turn out to be an extortionist (N 308–12), her mother is portrayed as an inveterate schemer and autocratic terror.[24] Perhaps the most graphic display of the antipathy Romola feels for her mother is her account of a distasteful incident during their first internment in which her mother unjustly accuses Vaslav of killing her pet cat, after which Romola 'could not stand this any longer. Next day I went to our Chief of Police and begged him to send us to a concentration camp' (N 232).[25] Her godfather, at the time one of the five members of the Austro-Hungarian War Council, explains that the root of her mother's difficult nature is her nationality: 'Your mother, the great artist, was chained to Hungary all her life. Her success never passed the frontiers, because she played in Hungarian. Your husband's art is universal. He is known and admired everywhere' (N 234). The last thing Romola wanted was to be chained to Hungary, or to her mother. In becoming Vaslav's femmka, she attempted to distance herself from her past and join the Russian cultural aristocracy. Just as Nadezhda Mandel'shtam left behind her 'small herd of painters' (N 26) to accompany Osip on his life-journey, so, too, was Romola trying through marriage to escape. However, she was not to have the same success. The Soviet powers that provided for the arduous atmosphere in which Nadezhda persevered, first as girlfriend and then as literary widow, closed off the escape route that Romola had assumed would be open to her when she married the God of Dance in 1913: 'I'd always wanted to visit Russia,' she confessed in an interview; 'Nijinsky and I had planned a journey in 1913, but then he became ill' (Stevenson 1965, 10). The regal aspirations of the elder de Pulszky daughter were to be foiled, time and again, by historical circumstance.[26] After the birth of their daughter Kyra in Vienna on 19 June 1914, nine days before the assassination of the Austrian archduke and duchess in Sarajevo, the Nijinskys intended to travel to Russia: 'We decided to return to St Petersburg as soon as I was allowed to travel,' writes Romola in her autobiography, betraying with the word 'return' the strong affinity she felt for the country she had never visited. Their week's stop in Budapest in July 1914, however, before they proceeded to Russia – 'to allow a rest for Kyra and myself' (N 223) – was to turn into a year and a half's internment, until January 1916, at which point historical, diplomatic, and cultural intervention had determined a much different destination: New York. It was not in Russia but in America, in the New York based beau monde of the ballet, that Romola would be feted, particularly after her husband's death, as the cultural aristocrat (or, translated into American, celebrity) she believed herself to be.[27] According to Stevenson, 'Among holiday visitors to New York was one whose connection with Ballet is both legendary and real. She is Madame Romola Nijinska, widow of Vaslav Nijinsky and author of the primary source book of his career. But she is also very much a part of the real world of today, especially as she recently emerged victorious in a lengthy legal battle over screen rights to her book, long tied up in the estate of the late King Vidor. This, in fact, was the reason both for her visit and its brevity. She was passing through New York en route to Hollywood and conferences with several contesting bidders for production rights to the Nijinsky saga' (1965, 10). It was to be in pre- and post-war America that Romola found she could make a 'career' of being Nijinsky's wife, as in the newspaper article with the headline, 'Being the Wife of a Dancer – It Is an Arduous Career!'[28] An announcement for a lecture series Romola gave in New York in 1952–3 indicates that after Vaslav's death in 1950 there was ample cultural space available in the United States for her to occupy in the role of widow to culture and that she wasted little time in assuming functions in this capacity. Like Nadezhda Mandel'shtam, Romola attempted through her marriage to imbue her life with both meaning and a future.[29] When her first attempt, through marriage, did not succeed in the way that she had hoped, Romola resorted to another means that Nadezhda would well have understood: writing her husband into legend.

Another Giant Leap

Romola's portrayal of her husband as martyred hero and the techniques with which she sketches his character and career and their relationship bear noteworthy similarities to those of Nadezhda Mandel'shtam. M.'s 'blithe good spirits' and 'chirpy, free and easy self' were a match for Vaslav's, who 'was gay, laughing, mischievous, like a boy always trying to play some prank' (N 203). Just as Nadezhda mentions that M. 'liked order and would always put things back in their proper place after I had scattered them around the room' (HA 159), even the insane Vaslav was 'neat, and as orderly as ever' (N 341).[30] Both men shunned adoration and praise. If Nadezhda 'happened to blurt out some word of praise to him (which was against our rules), [M.] was sincerely taken aback' (HA 273), whereas 'Vaslav was thoughtful, modest, not in the least conceited, and so embarrassed if anybody complimented him' (N 225). Both are represented as uncompromising and highly principled. M's 'deep bedrock of principles' (HA 160) finds its match in Romola's Vaslav, who 'was always just and correct, even to his enemies,' and never led astray by temptation: 'The news of Vaslav's dismissal was known in a few days through-out the world. Offers were showered upon him, from impresarios, theatres, with incredibly high salaries. But Vaslav refused. The agents came personally to Budapest to win him over. The fee rose higher and higher, but Vaslav shook his head, and asked the secretary of the Russian Consulate, who was constantly with us: "Please tell them I cannot do anything inartistic. I must first have the right ballets, artists to appear with me. I must think, create, and, under no circumstances will I appear in a vaudeville house. I cannot be unfaithful to my art." No money could tempt him' (N 251, 210). The trajectory that the wives of Messrs Mandel'shtam and Nijinsky recount also is very similar. Both men enjoyed early renown and fame as part of a new artistic movement, Osip with Gumilev's Acmeists, Vaslav with Diaghilev's Ballets Russes. Just as Osip went through a period of silence and adjustment in the 1920s – 'The austere person I now found myself living with in Herzen House was completely different from the carefree one I had met during the Kiev carnival' (HA 141) – only to regain his equilibrium and rediscover his voice after their journey to Armenia, so too did Vaslav suffer greatly in the chaotic historical circumstances, and so too was he able to regain his equilibrium, at least briefly during their first internment in Hungary, through art: 'Where and when this ballet [*Til Eulenspiegel*] could be produced was a mystery, but we did not think of it. Vaslav was a changed person. He became mischievous again, and I saw his face light up with joy' (N 231). Just as Osip's tragic fate is attributed by his wife to his principles and is presented as a choice on his part, a choice of death over spiritual compromise, Romola's Vaslav also refused to remain in a world that prevented his living an artistically principled existence and chose to 'withdr[a]w from this world' (N 341).

These artists of principle offered their wives new visions and endowed their lives with meaning. Just as Nadezhda emphasizes the new vistas that her husband opened to her, so too does Romola: 'Vaslav inspired and influenced me, in my feelings and outlook on life and art. He opened to me an unlimited vista of humanity, and gave me constantly new ideas from the undrainable richness of his thoughts' (N 236).[31] Like Nadezhda, Romola is only too eager to take on this new vision and to become her husband's disciple: 'I was brought up to believe that this [the high life] was what marriage meant, and Vaslav, to whom all this was strange, perhaps, for a second, felt a little tired of it all; he had yet to teach me' (N 208); 'He developed the theory of the dance. Every day, as a test, to see if it would be practical for general use, he taught me the system of notation' (N 231). The nature of both relationships was similar and special, second only to art. In her commentary to Sandoz's vignettes, Romola writes: 'It is true, as Mr. Sandoz quotes, that our "marriage was perfectly happy and that my husband loved me more than anything in the world" *except dancing* and that, I am convinced, he would not have sacrificed for anybody's sake' (N 11; italics in original). Each relationship was uniquely shaped by the isolation imposed on the couple: 'When a man was isolated – at first by his own wish and later thanks to the official disfavour still in force today – it was natural that he should look for someone to whom he could say "thou," and M. stubbornly tried to make a wife out of me, a wretched girl he had found quite by chance' (HA 163). 'During those long months of our internment, when we were thrown utterly on each other's company, we gained a knowledge of each other's character which under different circumstances would have hardly been possible ... In our great isolation we talked over many subjects' (N 236). Both wives made a point of choosing to share their husbands' fates, a point that has been duly noted and credited in the scholarship:

> Of the two [her and her husband], Nadezhda Iakovlevna seemed to have the better chance for escape; she might have spared herself much grief if she had divorced Mandel'shtam and recanted her association. But she chose, again and again, the noble, tragic role of sharing his life and persecution, of working for him and even begging with him and they staved off his inevitable doom. (Holmgren 1993, 97)

Now [after Nijinsky's being diagnosed hopelessly insane] began for Romola Nijinsky thirty years of hope, despair, struggle, poverty and heroism ... Romola was advised to make use of her American visa and to leave Vaslav in a Swiss State Asylum ... Rather than risk cancelling all the good Vaslav's treatment had done him, she renounced comfort and security for herself in America and resolved to stay beside him. This was perhaps her most unselfish and heroic decision. (Buckle 1971, 501, 521)[32]

Neither wife neglects to mention how firmly rooted the relationship was in the physical. Nadezhda made no secret of the fact that she had slept with Osip on the night they met and had briefly engaged in a ménage-à-trois with the one woman who posed a serious threat to their relationship (Proffer 1987, 23); Romola's recounting is more decorous: 'Our intimate life was ideally happy. Sometimes the strangest feeling would come over me, and I felt that the women of mythology may have felt as I did when a God came to love them. There was the exhilarating and inexpressible feeling that Vaslav was more than a human being. The ecstasy that he could create in love as in art had a purifying quality, and yet there was something intangible in his being that one could never reach' (N 300). Neither woman took up with another man after the loss of her husband. Although Nadezhda seems to have remained celibate, Kyra recalls finding her mother with another woman: 'Mother told me she had given up on men. "The only man in this world I will ever love is Vaslav"' (cited in Ostwald 1991, 285).

While both Nadezhda and Romola imbued their lives with meaning by writing their husbands' lives, there is a crucial difference in their attitudes towards locating themselves and their husbands within a larger artistic tradition. Nadezhda portrays herself as motivated only by her faith in her husband's poetry, the worth of which she does not see as in any way related to his current favour: 'In the years when we [she and Akhmatova] preserved M.'s verse, we scarcely dared hope, but we never ceased to believe in its rebirth. It was only this faith that kept us going ... Now that this [his poetry's being read by others] has come to pass, what happens in the future is out of our hands. All we can do is believe and hope. I never ceased to believe in M.'s and Akhmatova's poetry' (HA 21). One must not mistake her concern about whether others will read her husband's work for a willingness to allow those others to dictate to her the worth of that work. On the contrary, she is rather harsh in her pronouncements about them: 'I would love to know who these readers are. I have no great faith in their quality, since they were brought up on a rationalist pap which has impaired their capacity to think logically – every idea is mulled over for them in a thousand ways before it actually reaches them' (HA 22). Romola, on the other hand, considers the collective consensus on the Ballets Russes and her future husband as a measure of their worth. She is impressed by the 'fantastic tales of the great heights of artistic achievement' that precede the company to Budapest and describes Nijinsky as 'the marvellous apparition the whole world had learned to admire' (N 11, 15). She happily accepts the terms of membership into the Ballet and assumes rather than condemns its ruthless mores (N 22). Whereas Romola and her characters occupy a largely aesthetic space ruled by matters of taste and inveterate scheming, in Nadezhda's world situations repeatedly arise in which the characters choose not between staging arrangements, costumes, or the like, but between life and death: 'With the best will in the world, N.N. could not bring herself to name five "accomplices." It was an act of free choice, a truly human gesture, and this is why she remains so human and has such a zest for life' (HA 650). The question of responsibility resounds throughout Nadezhda's writing: 'Poor, trembling creatures – we don't know what meaning is; it has vanished from a world in which there is no room any more for the Logos. It will return only if and when people come to their senses and recall that man must answer for everything, particularly for his own soul' (HA 23); 'Everyone of us, to some degree or another, had a share in what happened, and there is no point in trying to disclaim responsibility' (HA 191). While one would search Romola's writing in vain for a similar passage, and come away with the impression that she had the scruples of a Mme de Merceuil and the self-reflectivity of a fruit fly, her description of continuing with a second volume of memoirs is strikingly similar to that of Nadezhda in terms of necessity and a sense of mission: '[It seemed] both *necessary* and desirable, for the history of art and of genius, and to help preserve the memory of the greatest and kindest human being I had ever known' (LYN 419, italics added); 'if the verse I have preserved is of some use to people, then my life has not been wasted and I have done what I *had to do* both for the man who was my other self and for all those people whose humane, that is, human instincts are roused by poetry' (HA 23; italics added). While their differing receptions would lead one to believe that the writings of these two women are incomparable, this analysis, which focuses on their sense of obligation and duty as well as their mythologizing tendencies, would suggest otherwise.

Autobiographical Writing and the Postmodern

Do you have courage, o my brethren? Are you hearty? Not courage before wit-
nesses, but anchorite and eagle courage, which not even a God any longer
regards? ... They have heart who know fear but vanquish it; who see the abyss,
but with pride. They who see the abyss but with eagle's eyes – who with eagle
talons grasp the abyss: they have courage.

'Of the Higher Person,' 2/4, *Zarathustra*[1]

In the previous chapters I have explored a form of documentary
self-representation that proceeds, and understands itself, as cultural
engagement. I have read the autobiographical texts of women who
have intervened into their surrounding literary culture by textualizing as true a life-story that both was and was not their own. The subjects of the first part, Lou Andreas-Salomé and Simone de Beauvoir,
wrote to entrench themselves as established, iconoclastic writers; the
second pair, Maitreyi Devi and Asja Lacis, have been written as
women responding to situations of portrayal turned betrayal; and
finally, Nadezhda Mandel'shtam and Romola Nijinsky wrote as
wives guaranteeing their husbands' artistic inheritances. The readings concentrate on the subtle mythologizing of the lives in question
and, more specifically, on the conjunction of these lives and those of
the culturally prominent others with whom they were intimately
involved.[2] The readings demonstrate how these autobiographical
writings turn the intimate relationships in which their authors were
involved into masks, albeit masks with unusual, generative, herme-
neutic properties, masks that serve to recoup a sense of otherness so
crucial in going beyond a strictly formal ethics. It is this relation to
alterity that imbues individual ethics of personality with whatever

moral substance they possess. John Caputo's Dionysus maintains a trace of the rabbinical; Agnes Heller's Nietzsche is 'Parsifalized' or 'Levinasized.' This alteric gesture is enacted to varying degrees in these autobiographical texts, and the differences noted between the two subjects of each part can be and in the second section of this conclusion will be ascribed to it. Before dealing with these differences, however, I should summarily restate the theoretical underpinnings on which their similarity rests.

What unites these women writers is a common tenor in the relational nature of their self-representation: fiercely independent, unshakeably intransigent, all at the same time belie a definite interdependence. Will-filled statements may seem to evidence a strong sense of personal autonomy, yet that autonomy is unconventional, continually called into question, and undermined by unabashed admissions of specific subservience vis-à-vis the men with whom they chose to remain in long-term relationships, since these relationships provided them the kind of freedom their strong characters insisted upon.[3] When they tapped into the modern zeitgeist, the sap that these women extracted had a similarly distinctive, yet ambiguous, autonomous flavour. That sap now needs to be poured onto the sullied snows of the postmodern debate in order to discern from the resulting frozen configurations its relevance for the increasingly autobiographical tendencies in the academy. In identifying the ambiguously autonomous agency of my writing subjects, I am not downplaying the objectifying forces inherent in either the process of textualizing one's life or the cultures in which we all live. Rather, as will be accounted for in the opening section of the conclusion, my argument is intended as a parry to those forces; that is, it reflects and refracts that which I claim is enacted in the six texts. Let me then, in the concluding chapter of this project, first isolate the issue of autonomy by relating it to the model of modern art, and then revisit the texts in question with an eye towards pulling, if not tying, together the threads relevant to ethics and postmodern scholarship. Targeting the potentiality and slipperiness of the Munchhausenesque proclivities residing in the Zarathustrian spirit of these autobiographical texts will prove to be the study's coup de grâce.

Portrait of the Artwork as an Old Woman

'But how does this happen?' I asked myself. What convinces the living one to obey and command and commanding still practice obedience?

'On the Self-Overcoming,' *Zarathustra*[4]

'Not the artist,' writes Agnes Heller in *An Ethics of Personality*, 'but the artwork (more precisely, the modern artwork) will stand for the model of Nietzsche's ethics of personality' (1996, 81). The key feature of the model, which it shares with modern artwork, is a problematic sense of autonomy: 'In modernist arts, the achievement of the autonomy of the object is a problem – the artistic problem. Autonomy is no longer provided by the conventions of an art, for the modernist artist has continually to question the conventions upon which his art had depended; nor is it furthered by any position the artist can adopt towards anything but his art' (Cavell 1976, 116).[5] The historical antecedents for this state are not applicable or relevant only to art, as the following description illustrates: 'Autonomous art, art whose forms are no longer underwritten by or derived from myth or religion, metaphysics or tradition, whose forms are internal to each artistic domain itself (literary forms, musical forms, etc.), this art has become problematic because autonomization makes the question of its sense, meaning, point, telos without any but an external, relative and contingent answer' (Osborne 1989, 50). Uprooted and adrift, the modern condition entails a continual search for the 'sense, meaning, point, telos' previously to be found in tradition, and the continual creation of new myths and traditions, or revival of old ones. Similarly, as Heller so tirelessly repeats, 'the modern person is a *contingent* person' (1990, 5; italics in original) and must continually imbue his/her existence with the 'sense, meaning, point, telos' that were a given in premodern times. In order for life to become meaningful and for 'the disengaged, particular [modern] self, whose identity is constituted in memory ... [to] find an identity,' that life, pace Charles Taylor in *Sources of the Self*, must be lived like a story (1989, 288–9).

The women in this study, however, go beyond living life simply like a story à la Taylor and Ricoeur.[6] They live modernist lives, composing them as stories lived out in words and mythologies. In other words, they work to cross the life/art divide as Bürger suggests avant-garde art does. Just as avant-garde artists, such as the Dadaists with their readymades or Marcel Duchamp with his objets trouvés, sought to overcome the insular world of autonomous aesthetic practice in art by drawing attention to its real world components, these women sought to overcome the equally insular and aesthetic practice of bourgeois life by recreating them autobiographically. As we have seen, the query made about Romola – 'Did she know when she crossed the borderline between fact and fiction?' (N&R 33) – is applicable to all of the others with the exception of Lacis, whose life was bound up in the theatre and acted out. The epigraph at the beginning of Lou Andreas-Salomé's memoirs reads:

'Human life – indeed all life – is poetry. It's we who live it, unconsciously day by day, like scenes in a play, yet in its inviolable wholeness It lives us, It composes us. This is something far different from the old cliché "Turn your life into a work of art": we are works of art – but we are not the artist' (LRB). Maitreyi Devi writes: 'As I try to write the story of my life I can very well see that there is no story at all. How can there be? Stories emerge from contact with life. The contact and conflict of human experience and variety of efforts give colour to our life's picture. What story can nature evolve? Many incidents occur that are fierce but one cannot make stories out of them' (DND 187). Nadezhda Mandel'shtam writes: 'The fact that I have begun to ponder whether I had a task, and how well I have acquitted myself, is a sure sign that I have begun to recover my "self." In writing my first book, I excluded myself. This happened quite spontaneously, without any conscious intention: it was simply that I still did not exist. I came back to life only when my main task was at an end' (HA 24). Simone de Beauvoir writes: 'I was particularly anxious to arouse the interests of the men: I tried to attract their attention by fidgeting and playing the ingenue, waiting for the word that would snatch me out of my childhood limbo and really make me exist in their world' (MDD 8); 'But I do not feel a gap between the intention that incited me to write books and the books that I have written ... I wanted to make myself exist for others by conveying, as directly as I could, the taste of my own life' (ASD 463). Nehamas notes that Nietzsche himself heeds Zarathustra's counsel to become who one is: 'Characteristically, he [Nietzsche] follows it [Zarathustra's counsel] by making it the object of his writing as well as the goal of his life' (1985, 169). Seen in this light, realizing the desire to become 'the poets of our life' (Nagl 1989, 747), this desire to write oneself into history (Nehamas 1985, 234) means not only moving beyond the general good and the general evil; it means doing so by linking life to an addressee,[7] to the inherently shared and thus ethical medium of words, and struggling to create out of them, and to express, the values one wants to share.

Ecce Mulieres Modernae

'You call yourself free? I want to hear your ruling idea, and not that you have escaped from a yoke.'

'Of the Creator's Way,' *Zarathustra*[8]

While all six women complicate their sense of autonomy, and the textually oriented of them explicitly acknowledge the literary means of their existence, they do not handle or resolve the tensions inherent in their autonomy in the same way. Returning by way of summary to the texts, one cannot avoid the observation that the question of control neatly cleaves the group in two. Nijinsky, Lacis, and Beauvoir make a point of their preference for situations in which they were needed and that offered them the opportunity to control and shape others. As we have seen, Lacis's Russian memoir overflows with instances in which her expertise and usefulness are called upon. Time and again she mentions the way someone convinces her to accept a position organizing some revolutionary theatrical endeavour or another. Lacis was well aware of the Zarathustrian potential of her profession – to give children the self-confidence and the support to become who they are. However, it is not an entirely innocent, altruistic project. The hands of the director do not shape only herself; they also shape her charges: 'I divided the plot into parts according to its main ideas and we began to act out scenes. The children didn't sense any interference from the director, any guiding hands. The improvisation was a fun game for them, an exciting adventure' (RC 12). Her charges were not trusted to shape themselves; after all, they might make the wrong choice and become, God forbid, Mensheviks or fascists. This is the same unobtrusively guiding directorial role Evans identifies Beauvoir as playing in Sartre's life: 'For some thirty years de Beauvoir manages Sartre's emotional life; from a position of apparent detachment she guides him through the various complexities of his affairs and offers to him the comforting explanation that the reason why "other" women become upset is because they have deluded beliefs about heterosexual love' (1996, 103). Algren accused her of playing such a role in directing their visits so as to create better material for her memoirs. In fact, it is a common enough charge to be considered a trope. In *The Groves of Academe*, Mary McCarthy refers to it as the 'Potter's Hand,' or, more specifically, 'the insidious egotism of the Potter's Hand, the desire to shape and mold the better-than-common clay and breathe one's own ghostly life into it – the teacher's besetting temptation' (1951, 75). It is not the veracity of these charges that is at issue here, but rather the question of whether and how the women themselves responded to these kinds of issues in their autobiographical writing. As we have seen, Lacis not only admitted but took pride in the guiding, shaping nature of her work. Beauvoir, too, readily confessed to the satisfaction to be had from exerting her influence: 'When I started to change ignorance into knowledge, when I started to impress truths upon a virgin mind, I felt I was at last creating something real' (MDD 45). Romola also seems to have taken such exertions in stride: 'But Cambo assured us that Diaghilev would have to grant Vaslav the terms he asked. So he drew up a contract, that Vaslav was willing to go to South America, and that his salary was to be the same as in the U.S.A., payable, in gold dollars, one hour before the curtain rose at every performance. *I insisted* on such a clause' (N 303; italics added). Lou Andreas-Salomé, on the other hand, represents herself as exceedingly laissez-faire and even helpless in her dealings. Rilke himself was captivated by Russia; she merely enhanced and provided the frame in which these longings could be expressed: 'But the greatest part of his energies he – who had been deeply involved with Russian literature *for a long time* [i.e., independent of her] – now dedicated to the study of the Russian language and national customs, since we were seriously planning for our grand voyage there. For a time this was tied to my husband's plan to take a trip through Transcaucasia into Persia, which, however, never materialized. Around Easter of 1899, we three left together to visit my family in Petersburg and then to Moscow' (LRB 116–17/70; italics added).[9] Similarly, Nadezhda Mandel'shtam claimed to have had no illusions about influencing either her husband or her circumstances: 'We were silent. There was no point in objecting: he knew what he was doing'; 'we knew too well there was no escaping anywhere ... We used to tell an anecdote comparing our existence to life aboard ship: limitless ocean all around, but nowhere to go' (HA 332, 613). Maitreyi Devi, too, writes of being helpless in the face of a merciless 'conspiracy of destiny' (DND 227).

Concomitant with an insistence on agency in the texts of the women discussed in the second chapter of each of the three parts of this study – Beauvoir, Lacis, and Nijinsky – is a ceding of responsibility. Expressed conversely, a deference to the agency of others in the texts of the women in the opening half of each section is accompanied by an assumption of responsibility. While Lou Andreas-Salomé, Maitreyi Devi, and Nadezhda Mandel'shtam lade themselves with this heaviest of burdens, their counterparts do not do so. One could ask of them, as Nadezhda Mandel'shtam does of the young woman she holds up as a shining example of 'Surviving with Honour' towards the end of the second volume of her memoirs: 'What is the source of N.N.'s independence and inner freedom? Being a true child of her times she believes in nothing, and talk about immutable values just makes her laugh. For her these are pure fictions, and good and evil are abstract categories to which she has never given a moment's thought – they simply have no place in her matter-of-fact mind. When I asked her: "Why is it you behave well and not badly?" she replied without pausing to reflect: "Because I want to." By such licence I am quite disarmed' (HA 647). One is equally disarmed by the way she, Devi, and Lou Andreas-Salomé all spontaneously express the same type of desire to 'do the right thing.' One could ask, reiterating the question of the ethical, how they know how to live, why it is that their answers to this fundamental question are of a piece. What is it that makes Maitreyi Devi express the following sentiment: 'Freedom of course does not correspond to irresponsibility. I hope I have never used my unlimited freedom in a way that is unworthy of me' (DND 168)? What is it that makes Lou Andreas-Salomé both have and write of nightmares in which 'I saw a multitude of characters from my stories whom I had abandoned without food or shelter. No one else could tell them apart, nothing could bring them home from wherever they were in their perplexing journey, to return them to that protective custody in which I imagined them all securely resting' (LRB 18/7)? I can offer no answer, only a curious coincidence with respect to the seemingly obverse relation between agency and responsibility.

Where controlling efforts are acknowledged, or even boasted of, these efforts in each case generate such strong resentment in at least one family member that a hostile 'anti-memoir' results. In the case of Beauvoir, the posthumous publication of her correspondence with Sartre, which revealed the 'Dangerous Liaisons' nature of their ménage-à-trois machinations, prompted Bianca Lamblin's 1993 *Memoires d'une jeune fille dérangée* (*A Disgraceful Affair*, trans. 1996), in which she tells of how being involved with Beauvoir and Sartre eventually drove her to seek therapy from Jacques Lacan. Lacis's daughter, Dagmara Kimele, wrote a similarly scathing chronicling of her childhood in the 1996 *Asja: Rezisores Annas Laces dekaina dzive*, while Romola's youngest daughter, Tamara Nijinsky, offers a somewhat less harsh condemnation of her mother in her 1991 *Nijinsky and Romola*. The form of critique offered in these 'Mommie Dearest memoirs' is of a much different, more intimate nature than the scholarly attacks to which these women have also been subjected. They speak not only to the public stature of their targets but to the increasingly intimate nature of the discourse on public figures.[10] In our post-Auschwitzian reality, it is perhaps inevitable that the matter of morally questionable conduct will raise its shorn head, and this is an important way in which the women in this project can be seen as precursors of a particular skein of the postmodern: not of the pop-culture postmodern for which they will first be shown to be an antidote but rather of an inter-disciplinary, increasingly autobiographically oriented, academic post-modern.

Precursors to the Postmodern: Encounters Artistic, Academic, and Otherwise

I taught them ... to create and carry together into one what in human beings is fragment and riddle and dreadful accident; as creator, guesser of riddles and redeemer of chance, I taught them to work on the future and to redeem with their creation all that *has been*.

'On Old and New Tablets,' 3, *Zarathustra*[11]

Hope against Representation

A preliminary point should be made regarding the overcoming of autonomy evidenced in these autobiographical texts, since it antici-pates the argument to be made about modernist and postmodernist art in this section. This hallmark of Bürger's avant-garde evidences a cer-tain commonality with the postmodern critique of representation and the subject.[12] In 'Adorno, Poststructuralism and the Critique of Iden-tity,' Peter Dews outlines the convivial symbolic that Borges's fish story, 'The Fauna of Mirrors,' provides Lyotard for his critique of mod-ern subjectivity in his 1973 essay on the painter Jacques Monory: 'Borges imagines these beings [these fish] as forces, and this bar [between representation and the represented] as a barrier; he imagines that the Emperor, the Despot in general, can only maintain his position on condition that he represses the monsters and keeps them on the other side of the transparent wall. The existence of the subject depends on this wall, on the enslavement of the fluid and lethal powers repressed on the other side, on the function of representing them' (cited in Dews 1989, 4). This protest at the coercive unification implied by the notion of a self-conscious, self-identical subject is, as Dews reminds us, one of the central themes of poststructuralism. In the importance in their own self-representation that they grant to others, the six subjects of this study similarly register a protest at such coercive unification and render inoperative the notion of a self-identical subject, which is in keeping with the relational nature of both women's writing and women's subjectivity: 'feminist critics have explicitly rejected accounts of the "birth" of human consciousness in the originary moments of Western individualism, often turning to psychoanalytic theories to explore psychic identity and models of intersubjectivity in autobiographical texts, including the concept of "relational" selves proposed by theorists such as Nancy Chodorow' (Marcus 1994, 220).[13] As we have seen, however, the women in this study offer a twist to this general tendency: they take the fact of their relationality as a keystone, and play upon it. Strong, sleek fish – not dangerous ones like the moray eels associated with the biblical Salome in fin-de-siècle art, but spirited, intelligent fish, like porpoises – these six were satisfied with neither attaining complete autonomy nor remaining subserviently relegated to the station in life to which their gender tried to condemn them. They swam purposively in and against the cultural current, jumping purposively back and forth, cross-fertilizing the streams of life and art.

No matter the direction, it seems to be the motion of a paradoxical non-crossing or impermanent crossing of the life/art divide that is a precondition, though not a guarantor, of critical potential. To reiterate, the stuff of these women's existences bears a striking resemblance to modernist art, 'the sort of art for which the existence, the meaning of art is a question, and that question is posed by art's autonomy' (Bernstein 1989, 64). In a more recent essay on Adorno's aesthetics, Jay Bernstein draws a parallel similar to the one I am making here: 'What Ibsen discovered, and what remains a central ingredient in Adorno's aesthetics, is the isomorphism or homology between the position of women in society and the position of art and art works in society' (1997, 170). My parallel is not with any *pauschal* notion of modernist art but rather is with one particular stream of it. The analysis of the relation between the Surrealists and other historical avant-garde movements that Richard Wolin offers in 'Kulchur Wars: The Modernism/Postmodernism Controversy Revisited' is helpful in understanding how the women in this study act to counter, to albeit different but nonetheless substantial degrees, the non-auric, simulacric, postmodern sense of non-identities that continues to amass pop-cultural capital.[14] Just as the Surrealists found a way to critique the public sphere of art while still remaining art, so too did these women find a way to critique public stricture of personal identity without surrendering their own ethics of personality.[15] As Richard Wolin so ably recapitulates, the Surrealists found a third way, that of 'de-aestheti-cized autonomous art': 'This category suggests that surrealism's uniqueness lies in its having simultaneously negated the aura of affir-mation characteristic of art for art's sake, while nevertheless refusing to abandon the modern requirement of aesthetic autonomy ... [Theirs is] a still aesthetic attack on bourgeois aestheticism. It consciously divests itself of the beautiful illusion, the aura of reconciliation, pro-jected by art for art's sake, while refusing to overstep the boundaries of aesthetic autonomy, beyond which art degenerates to the status of merely a thing among things' (1995, 21). The historical avant-garde and its provocations, on the other hand, in desperately seeking to avoid being works of art, ironically found their socio-critical program quickly assimilated by the commercializing pressures of the bour-geois art world. The same fate awaited post-war, postmodernist art, which 'behaves as if the radical transformation of material life sought by the avant-garde has already been achieved. But since this is not in fact the case, what results instead is merely the false sublation of autonomous art' (1995, 23). In other words, instead of resulting in a potentially productive, critical sublation, modernism's dialectical anxi-ety of being and non-being devolves into postmodernist simulacra. In again drawing a parallel with the life side of the life/art divide, we find the development of postmodern pop-cultural models of identity. Like Wolin, I am less inclined to view popular culture as 'a repository of spontaneous dissent and refusal' and would also insist that 'one must seriously question whether the proliferation of clone-like "wanna-bes," more firmly than ever ensconced in a consumer-ori-ented cultural identity, furthers the type of critical individuation that the notion of empowerment suggests' (1995, 29). The contrast the women in this study provide to such models is where the antidotal properties to which I referred reside. Just as the Surrealists 'proffered fragmentary works of art that are nonetheless still works' (1995, 21), these women offer hope in proffering fragmentary, ambiguously autonomous identities that are nonetheless still, and perhaps all the more so, identities.

Hope über Alles

Wake and hark, you lonely ones! From the future come winds with a secret flapping of wings; and good tidings go out to delicate ears.

'Of Gift-Giving Virtue,' 2, *Zarathustra*[16]

The value of the women in this project, however, is beyond the anti-dotal. In their parallels with the Surrealists, they also provide a hith-erto missing link in understanding at least one aspect of postmodern cultural production. In 'Feminism and Postmodernism,' Joanna Hodge succinctly diagnoses a major pitfall of many scholarly exegeses of the modern/postmodern condition: the relation of cultural formations to socio-historical conditions. Her work, on the other hand, clearly

> presupposes that Benjamin, in his study *Baudelaire: Lyric Poet of High Capi-talism*, has shown how modernism as developed by Baudelaire is a response to and articulation of the condition of modernity. Furthermore, it supposes that Adorno's cultural Marxism is a development of Benjamin's analysis of modern cultural production as the articulation of the modern age, although the precise nature of their agreements and disagreements remains to be clarified. Their work establishes a connection of some kind between the condition of modernity and the cultural formation called 'modernism.' No such connection has been established between a condi-tion called 'postmodern' and a cultural practice called 'postmodernism.' Habermas's paper ['Modernity: An Incomplete Project'] suffers from its presupposition that both connections have been established, when there is only an established connection between modernity and modernism. (1989, 90)

In the remainder of this conclusion, I would like to suggest such a link. Instead of proceeding from Walter Benjamin's writings on Baudelaire, I would like to call on his essay on the Surrealists and suggest that their postmodern equivalent is a specific kind of writerly academic practice to which the women in this study are precursors.

Benjamin's Surrealism essay is subtitled 'The Last Snapshot of the European Intelligentsia.'[17] Originally published in *Die Literarische Welt* in 1929, it identifies the task of the intelligentsia as one of overcoming the opiates of the people with the opiate of critique, or, as Benjamin termed it, profane illumination: 'the true overcoming of religious illu-mination certainly does not lie in narcotics. It resides in a *profane illumi-nation*, a materialistic, anthropological inspiration, to which hashish, opium, or whatever else can give an introductory lesson' (1978, 179, italics in original). Fast-forward seventy years and one finds a prepon-derance of technological opiates, various forms of mind candy that have not replaced the old ones but rather added to and considerably fortified their ranks. If one were to screen a 'Last Video of the Global

Academic,' one would find the task of literary criticism has not changed as much as mortified even further.[18] 'To live in a glass house is a revolutionary virtue par excellence. It is also an intoxication, a moral exhibitionism that we badly need. Discretion concerning one's own existence, once an aristocratic virtue, has become more and more an affair of petit-bourgeois parvenus' (1978, 180). Benjamin wrote these words without dreaming of the glass houses that would be created by future technological developments and the nostalgia for discretion they would, in turn, generate. Our simulacric glass houses are entwined in nets of images and webs of intrigue. The last academic video seems in danger of mimicking its socio-political counterpart caught in automatic loop mode, stuck on a never-ending roller coaster of scandal and destruction.[19] In the final remarks that follow, the concept of auto-biographical writing will be reiterated as an interrogatory light to be shone on the autobiographical element in the postmodern academy.

Because of Beauvoir's status as 'mother' of feminism, however problematic such a designation may be,[20] it behoves us to question what exactly she is supposed to have given birth to. The superficial answer of 'feminism and women's studies' does not capture the full scope of the changes that Beauvoir's writing helped to inaugurate. Beauvoir herself signals the direction, in 'point[ing] out the fact that her autobiography generated a great response from women who, like her, practiced an intellectual profession: "In contrast, other readers are women of my own age who have had to go through the same struggle in order to lead the life of an intellectual. I have received many letters from women working in education"' (Vintges 1996, 118). Here is the final paragraph of Moi's monograph on Beauvoir, slightly truncated:

Simone de Beauvoir now belongs to a past generation. Her pioneering example has opened the way for women to be taken seriously – and loved – as intellectuals and as women. On the threshold of the twenty-first century, she still makes it easier for us to live our lives as we wish, without regard to patriarchal conventions. My awareness of the complexities and contradictions of her life has added depth to my admiration for Simone de Beauvoir ... Reading her autobiography, I am struck at once by her strength, energy and vitality, and by her helplessness and fragility. When I realize how hard it was for her to gain a sense of autonomy and independence, I find her achievements all the more admirable. To admire, however, is not to worship. We do not need to be perfect, Simone de Beauvoir teaches us, we simply need never to give up. To me, that is both a comforting and an utterly daunting project. (1994, 256–7)

This warm, personal, very moving conclusion evidences more than Beauvoir's influence. It also exemplifies the kind of scholarship increasingly being produced. Going against the grain of what pseudo-scientific prose was once supposed to sound like in its ample use of personal pronouns and emotive language, Moi's text presents difficulties in genre classification similar to those of its object of study. Moi problematizes her book's methodological stance in the introduction, asking 'what I am to call this thing I have written?' (1994, 7). Because it goes beyond the traditional categories of biography and literary criticism to 'contain reception studies, sociology of culture, philosophical analysis, psychoanalytic inquiry and feminist theory,' she eventually settles for 'personal genealogy,' at which point she footnotes Biddy Martin as sharing her impatience with generic limitations (1994, 7). Shoshana Felman goes a deconstructive step further in *What Does a Woman Want?* by suggesting that 'we might be able to engender, or to access, our story only indirectly – by conjugating literature, theory, and autobiography together through the act of reading and by reading, thus, into the texts of culture, at once our sexual difference and our autobiography as missing' ... 'If the critical suggestion I am making in this book is that people tell their stories (which they do not know or cannot speak) through the others' stories, then the very force of insight of this critical suggestion was at once borne out and actively enacted, put in motion, by the process of my writing which was driven, in effect, by the ways in which I was precisely missing my own implication in the texts before me' (1993, 14, 18). Upon finishing Moi's and Felman's books, one cannot but feel a sense of admiration for them similar to that which Moi professes for Beauvoir. Theirs is engaged, passionate writing, writing that encourages the reader by example, by the sense that the writing process has led the writer to some kind of personal realization.[21] Could we not call theirs autobiographical writing and, if so, what is its relation to or place in the postmodern?

At the onset of this study, autobiographical writing was introduced as involving the intervention into one's surrounding written culture based on one's own lived experience and its realization into writing. Nietzsche's *Ecce Homo*, despite, or on account of, its flamboyantly, ironically euphoric style and copious citations from the decidedly fictional *Thus Spake Zarathustra*, can thus be read as Nietzsche documenting his intervention into his surrounding written culture. Moi's work and that of Felman et al. are not substantially different, except for the important distinction that they do not take their own lives as the object of study but subtly weave them through their theoretical explorations. Two trends in recent academic writing show how blurred this boundary is becoming: the increasing number of minority scholars (referred to in the Introduction as the 'counter-postmodern,' that is, not necessarily heterosexual WASP males) who are forging new, increasingly personal styles of scholarship and the increasing number of autobiographies written by 'intellectuals' in general.[22] Where inroads are being made, however, is within the former grouping of 'personal criticism,' which, as Nancy Miller elucidates, 'entails an explicitly autobiographical performance within the art of criticism' (1991, x). Works such as Christine Overall's *A Feminist I: Reflections from Academia* and Tania Modleski's *Old Wives' Tales and Other Women's Stories* as well as collections such as *The Intimate Critique: Autobiographical Literary Criticism* and *Confessions of the Critics* are exemplary here in challenging the separation of the autobiographical and the theoretical, stretching and enlivening the boundaries of academic discourse by incorporating the autobiographical impulse and, in so doing, proving these categorical distinctions amorphous at best. It is here that Georges May's non-definition of autobiography is suggestive.[23] If autobiography is indeed 'a literary attitude, which we have come readily to recognize because we have all read so much autobiographical literature' (1978, 320), then one could also argue that with the amount of crossover in recent writing, it is also an easily recognizable academic attitude, the new meta-genre of 'personal criticism.'

One wonders, however, particularly in the backlash against political correctness, whether some forms of this autobiographical academic output attempt to be more equal than others. In order to weigh their respective equalities, the designation of autobiographical writing, as opposed to an amorphous non-definition of autobiography, can weigh in, not as a generic category as such but rather as a critical reading strategy. When we read texts with an eye towards considering them autobiographical writing, we are interrogating their depiction of relationships: with themselves, with important others, and with cultures at large. As I stated in the Introduction, we are reading empathetically in search of empathy. In other words, we are attempting to measure them by the critical yardstick of Walter Benjamin's rather enigmatic 'moral exhibitionism,' a quality that acts to counterbalance what Richard Wolin has considered 'perhaps the greatest deficiency of affirmative cultural criticism': 'its shameless fetishization of the concept of culture itself: its treatment of culture as something independent, divorced from the life-process of society. In truth, culture is valuable only when it remains true to its implicit critical capacities. Its independence from society allows it the breathing-space required to reflect on society with critical acumen, rather than to turn its back on the social world in the celebration of eternal verities' (1995, 41). Whereas Wolin's interest is the legacy of this century's European totalitarianism and philosophy and its lessons for the American (academic) mindset, my ears have been listening for the echoes of this legacy in the disturbingly unthinking exuberance in much of the recent autobiographical outpourings. 'I write this as part of a community of creative critics refusing to be co-opted by the usual critical conventions of impersonality coupled with one-upmanship and the linear "logic" that keeps the poetic and personal from the professional and theoretical,' declares Diane Freedman at the end of 'Border Crossing as Method and Motif in Contemporary American Writing, or, How Freud Helped Me Case the Joint' (21), the lead essay in *The Intimate Critique*. She continues: 'We must write out of that psychically unrestful juncture – a juncture dangerous for tenure, publication, and promotion – of the personal and the theoretical, in the realm where knowledge is not separated from poetry, where borders of self and other and one genre or language and another collide' (21). What kind of 'we' is Freedman referring to? To what extent is the danger she describes rhetorical and to what extent is it real? Does the collision of borders she describes elide or open up critical breathing space? Is this a case not of eternal verities being celebrated, but truths that, if successfully implemented, threaten to become as monolithic as the system they would replace?[24] In contrast to my reading of Moi's and Felman's work, I do not get the impression from Freedman's essay that a personal methodology has been cobbled together from thoughtful, individual study. Elisabeth Young-Bruehl also insists on this distinction: 'Identity is not insight. And autobiography that ends where it began, that defensively or offensively armours an identity rather than journeys in search of one, is simply a weapon, not an education' (1991, 17).

The direction indicated by our opening theoretical signpost, Hal Foster's 'anti-aesthetic,' is now discernible. In determining whether critique 'destructures the order of representations in order to reinscribe them' (1983, xv), the focus is thus directed at the manner in which the order of representations are reinscribed, if at all, and whether a critical threshold of independence has been attained, that critical threshold before which declarations of interdependence are dangerous and after which they are imperative.

The quantity and spectrum of recent autobiographical output on the part of academics is an extraordinary development, begging the question of why it should be that, as the technologically enhanced vice of cultural homogenization and commodification has tightened, it has been matched or perhaps even surpassed in fervent written declarations of identity.[25] It has not been my purpose in this study to analyse or account for this trend, and it would therefore be presumptuous at this point to pretend I have an answer. As impetus for further study, however, I offer a preliminary diagnosis: that postmodernity is suffering from an Alzheimer's disease of the soul characterized by the same progressive memory and identity loss as its physiological counterpart, and that it is in need of antibodies such as the autobiographical writings of the six subjects of this study. These women do not presume to tell their readers how to live, or how to write. They simply recount how they have lived and what they feel life has taught them, how they pulled themselves out of the various beds of quicksand life scattered across their paths, with the tacit assumption that this knowledge will somehow be of use. As Deidre Bair notes: 'If [Beauvoir's] answers and actions disappointed others, she had a simple yet abrasive answer for them: "Well, I just don't give a damn. It's my life and I lived it the way I wanted. I'm sorry to disappoint all the feminists, but you can say that it's too bad so many of them live only in theory instead of in real life. It's very messy in the real world, and maybe they should learn that"' (1990, 642–3, n14). When confronted with others and their less than godlike dimensions, one is faced with choices and with messiness, which some choose to acknowledge and others do not. As the textual representation of those choices is a paramount choice in and of itself, · readings of autobiographical texts that reconstruct them in terms of those choices will have gone a long way to counteract the perverse potential of both art and life to go beyond good to evil.

Notes

Introduction: Zarathustra's Sisters

1 '[E]ines Morgens stand [Zarathustra] mit der Morgenröthe auf, trat vor die Sonne hin und sprach zu ihr also: "Du grosses Gestirn! Was wäre dein Glück, wenn du nicht Die hättest, welchen du leuchtest! Zehn Jahre kamst du hier herauf zu meiner Höhle: du würdest deines Lichtes und dieses Weges satt geworden sein, ohne mich, meinen Adler und meine Schlange"' (Vorrede, 1, *Zarathustra*). All translations of Nietzsche are mine, based on both the Kaufmann and Hollingdale translations. When the name Zarathustra appears italicized, it should be taken as referring to this text, otherwise Nietzsche's prophet is meant.

2 'Gefährten sucht der Schaffende und nicht Leichname, und auch nicht Heerden und Gläubige. Die Mitschaffenden sucht der Schaffende, Die, welche neue Werthe auf neue Tafeln schreiben. Gefährten sucht der Schaffende, und Miterntenden: denn Alles steht bei ihm reif zur Ernte. Aber ihm fehlen die hundert Sicheln: so rauft er Ähren aus und ist ärgerlich. Gefährten sucht der Schaffende, und solche, die ihre Sicheln zu wetzen wissen. Vernichter wird man sie heissen und Verächter des Guten und Bösen. Aber die Erntenden sind es und die Feiernden' (Vorrede, 9, *Zarathustra*).

3 'Von sich *absehn* lernen ist nöthig, um *Viel* zu sehn: – diese Härte thut jedem Berge-Steigenden Noth' (Der Wanderer, *Zarathustra*; italics in original).

4 See, for example, Johnson's review, 'La Grande Sartreuse' (1981).

5 Works such as Schmidt Machey's 1956 *Lou Salomé, inspiratrice et interprète de Nietzsche, Rilke et Freud*, Angela Livingstone's 1984 biography *Lou Andreas-Salomé. Her Life (as Confidante of Freud, Nietzsche and Rilke) and Writings (on Psychoanalysis, Religion and Sex)* and Werner Ross's 1992 *Lou Andreas-Salomé:*

Weggefährtin von Nietzsche, Rilke, Freud indicate that this tendency is quite consistent across national boundaries.

6 I intend 'force field' as it has been developed in the work of Adorno and critical theorists, that is, referring to 'a relational interplay of attractions and aversions that constitute the dynamic, transmutational structure of a complex phenomenon' (Jay 1984, 14).

7 This is not to imply that the second half of the twentieth century has been any less tragic, nor to create the misleading impression that, with the exception of Lou Andreas-Salomé, these women no longer lived to see it. As it is primarily the turbulence up to and including the Second World War which set the course for their writing, however, it is that period I wish to draw attention to here.

8 While these educations may seem enviable from a late twentieth-century North American perspective, one should note that compared with those available to their male contemporaries, they are not particularly remarkable. Toril Moi's *Simone de Beauvoir: The Making of an Intellectual Woman* (1994) offers a thorough account of the educational opportunities available to Beauvoir and her contemporaries.

9 It is not my intention in this study to tackle the psychoanalytic implications of the particular familial constellations in question. Readers who find the biographies as they are presented here to be psychoanalytically suggestive are encouraged to consult Jessica Benjamin's *Like Subjects, Love Objects: Essays on Recognition and Sexual Difference*, particularly chapter 4, 'Father and Daughter, Identification with Difference: A Contribution to Gender Heterodoxy.' Benjamin turns the tables on interpretations of penis envy, which emphasize the girl's need to identify with the father as a *figure* of separation from the pre-oedipal mother and argues that it is the father, not the phallus, that matters in both boys' and girls' psychic development: 'The rapprochement girl's wish for a penis is not a self-evident response to anatomical difference. She desires it even as the boy cherishes it ... because she is struggling to individuate. Girls seek what toddler boys recognize in their fathers and wish, through identification, to affirm in themselves – recognition of their own desire. And their ambivalence around separation may be more intense than that of boys because of the bond of likeness between mother and daughter. All the more reason for them, too, to seek a different object in whom to recognize their independence. This other object is very often the father, whose otherness is guaranteed and symbolized by his other genital.' The process of identification can be successful only when it is reciprocal, however, that is, when the father identifies with his child and makes himself available as a mirror of desire. Problems often arise for girls,

according to Benjamin, when patriarchal fathers are less than forthcoming in this regard and refuse their daughters recognition. Benjamin's hypothesis that 'incorporation is a means of becoming the ideal object rather than an end in itself' and her question of whether 'a more positive father-daughter relationship [could] in fact allow a different integration of identification' receive striking confirmation in the cases of 'Zarathustra's sisters' (1995, 125, 129, 126).

10 A continuum marked by rupture and disjuncture is not paradoxical but modern.

11 I am alluding here to Smith and Watson's collection, *Getting a Life: Everyday Uses of Autobiography*. The exponential increase in both autobiographical writing and scholarship since the end of the Second World War is a noteworthy and suggestive trend, nicely captured in the entry on 'autobiography' in the 1991 edition of the *Penguin Dictionary of Literary Terms and Literary Theory*: 'Since the Second World War almost anyone who has achieved distinction in life – and many who have not – has written an account of his [*sic*] life; especially politicians, statesmen and high-ranking members of the services' (73). An indication of the growth in the scholarship on this topic is to be found in the MLA bibliography where the number of references for autobiography grew from 617 in 1963–80 to 5,549 in 1981–98. Similar growth is also to be found for memoirs (596 to 1,887) and for life-writing (18 to 143). These numbers take into consideration only work on autobiography, not the increasingly autobiographical nature of academic work in general.

12 I should add that postmodernity is understood here, as so masterfully spelled out in Inderpal Grewal and Caren Kaplan's *Scattered Hegemonies: Postmodernity and Transnational Feminist Practices*, as a historical situation 'characterized by the global reach of late commodity capitalism, the widespread bureaucratization of all aspects of corporate life, the shift to electronic communications networks that are altering notions of time and space, the condition of cultural asymmetries, and the interrogation of received concepts of a universal, rational, and autonomous humanist self' (cited in Smith and Watson 1996, 3).

13 Anaïs Nin is a particularly exemplary case in point.

14 I allude here, of course, to Jürgen Habermas's assault on Nietzsche as chief promulgator against the enlightenment project, its rationality, and progressive emancipation. Nietzsche has been heralded as a 'turning point' towards the postmodern, if not the postmodern herald incarnate. For a concise synopsis of the debate surrounding Nietzsche's role in Habermas's critique of the postmodern condition, see Nagl (1989).

15 To take but two examples: Axel Honneth distinguishes Nietzschean affirmation from Hegelian recognition in 'Pluralization and Recognition: On the Self-Misunderstanding of Postmodern Social Theories' in *The Fragmented World of the Social: Essays in Social and Political Philosophy*, while Gilles Deleuze, in *Nietzsche and Philosophy*, similarly emphasizes that 'The lesson of the eternal return is that there is no return of the negative. The eternal return means that being is selection. Only that which affirms or is affirmed returns' (1983, 189).

16 'Der aber hat sich selber entdeckt, welcher spricht: Das ist *mein* Gutes und Böses: damit hat er den Maulwurf und Zwerg stumm gemacht, welcher spricht: "Allen gut, Allen bös" ... "Das – ist nun *mein* Weg – wo ist der eure?" so antwortete ich Denen, welche mich "nach dem Wege" fragten. *Den* Weg nämlich – den giebt es nicht!' ('Vom Geist der Schwere,' 2, *Zarathustra*; italics in original).

17 In the concluding chapter of this study I will return to Georges May's assertion that '[a]utobiography is neither a genre, nor a form, nor a style, nor even a language, as has been argued – often with considerable skill – by one or the other of the chief contemporary theorists of this kind of literature. Rather it is something much vaguer and more general: a *literary* attitude, which we have come readily to recognize because we have all read so much autobiographical literature, but which simply does not lend itself to the would-be scientific approaches featured in most trends of contemporary literary theory' (1978, 320, italics added). What I question here is precisely this 'self-evident' understanding of the autobiographical as primarily literary, and I suggest, in the wake of Lejeune's autobiographical pact, which May also cites, that that understanding can also be ethical.

18 Marlene Kadar discusses this point in her introduction to the 1992 collection *Essays on Life Writing: From Genre to Critical Practice.*

19 I am indebted to Johanna Meehan for driving home the importance of this point to me in Prague.

20 This position has been notably staked out by Habermas.

21 For a good discussion of the debate between Gadamer and Derrida, see Michelfelder and Palmer (1989).

22 While it is true that these others have tended to be male, I am not arguing here for any kind of *écriture feminine autobiographique*, nor attributing the fact that these categories do not fit the subjects of this study solely to their gender. Obviously there are many women writers whose writings do mesh well with these categories.

23 Beauvoir saw herself as a socially committed writer. Lou Andreas-Salomé's interest was not in creating beautiful prose but in offering well-reasoned

critiques of, among others, Ibsen, Nietzsche, and, later, Freudian theory. Her fictional work was published reluctantly, and only from financial considerations. Neither Mandel'shtam nor Nijinsky considered themselves writers at all, while Lacis remained firmly rooted in the pedagogic potential of the theatre. The only one for whom the designation 'literary artist' could be considered is Maitreyi Devi. However, although she certainly paid great attention to the aesthetic element of her autobiographical text, the woman she creates is never considered to be an artist as such.

24 See Mozejko (1998) for a discussion of the tendencies of the different national scholarships. For concrete examples, see Nicholls (1995), Nouss (1995), and Zima (1997).

25 The set of Bill Clinton dolls, which appeared at the apex of the Lewinsky scandal, in which the smallest doll is not a miniature version of Clinton but a cigar, is an example of how both trendy and politically aware these dolls can be.

26 It is perhaps worth noting in passing that R.J. Hollingdale, one of the noted English translators of Nietzsche, would surely object to this usage on grounds of sloppiness. In 'The Hero as Outsider,' he makes much of the difference between legend and myth: 'Legend is fiction presented as truth. The word is often used as if it were synonymous with myth, but legends differ from myths in that, while myths, being fictions about gods, are necessarily set in what is imagined as the very remote past, legends, being fictions about heroes, can attach themselves to the people or events of any period, including the most recent' (1996, 72–3). My usage of this term in not in keeping with Hollingdale but follows from Barthes and semiotics.

27 The work of Mary Oppen, wife of American poet George Oppen, is the only other possible candidate for inclusion I found. This difficulty in finding additional subjects for the study is a result of the fact that 'partners,' particularly Americans, tend to resemble not the irrepressible Mrs Oppen but Elizabeth Bacon Custor, of whom Shirley Leckie writes: 'all the factors in Elizabeth's early life, including her family, her education, and the books she read reinforced her attachment to the prevailing middle-class ideology, based on nineteenth-century domestic ideals' (1993, xix).

28 Translation of the term *Übermensch* is hazardous at best. Given that the subjects of this study are female, 'superman' and 'over-man' are inappropriate. More gender-conscious solutions would include possibilities such as 'overperson' and 'over-human.' In lieu of an unprovocative translation, the term is rendered here in the original.

29 '*Der* nämlich bin ich von Grund und Anbeginn, ziehend, heranziehend, hinaufziehend, aufziehend, ein Zieher, Züchter und Zuchtmeister, der sich

nicht umsonst einstmals zusprach: "Werde, der du bist!"' (*Das Honig-Opfer*, *Zarathustra*; italics in original).

30 For a bibliography of work to 1994, in which the question of Nietzsche and women is addressed, see Burgard 1994. There is a section in Pauline Johnson's 'Nietzsche Reception Today' on 'Feminist Readings' (1996) and, for an eastern European perspective, see Tadeusz Slawek's 'The Eye and the Body: Some Remarks on the Philosophy of the *Baba*' (1997). On the question of Nietzsche, postmodernism and postfeminism, see Behler (1996), Buhr (1990), Call (1995), and Patton (1993).

31 Anna Alexander's 'The Eclipse of Gender: Simone de Beauvoir and the *Différence* of Translation' provides a concise overview of Beauvoir reception and how it has been affected by translation.

32 Nehamas prefers Kaufmann's translation. I have opted for *eternal return*, since I am not intending to invoke events or series, for which *recurrence* is admittedly better suited. While one could just as easily speak of having one's life recur as one assembles an autobiography, it is more common to speak of returning to the past, and I want to emphasize the more active connotations of returning, rather than the involuntary implications of recurring.

33 For a good discussion of the concept of 'persona' in autobiography, see Renza (1977).

34 Cf. Agnes Heller's *An Ethics of Personality*: 'Whether Nietzsche had syphilis or not, no one knows. But what one can know is that he manoeuvred himself into a philosophical situation (and philosophy was his entire life) where madness was the only escape left' (1996, 301, n50).

35 If I might be pardoned a rather pop analogy, in effect what Nietzsche is doing is likening the Christian tradition to HMS *Titanic* and warning people that when it sinks, as he is convinced it *must*, they had better be prepared to rescue themselves because that particular religious tradition, while it preaches equality and tolerance, when push comes to shove, will turn out to be a sham and seating will be reserved in the too few lifeboats, and those so privileged will simply sit there and let the underprivileged drown. As we know from our vantage point at the other end of an increasingly genocidal century, he was not far wrong.

36 When first introducing the *Übermensch*, in his speech to the folk gathered in the marketplace, Zarathustra also equates it with meaning: 'Behold, I teach you the *Übermensch*! The *Übermensch* is the meaning of the earth.'

37 Here is but one example of why it is wrong to read John Caputo's distinction in *Against Ethics* between heteromorphism (*heteros* in the sense of multiplicity, difference as discharge, as forces differentiating themselves à la

Deleuze and Nietzsche) and heteronomism (*hetero* as *alter*, as alterity to be respected, before which one is responsible à la Levinas) as fixed, as Eva Plonowska Ziarek does in 'Toward a Radical Female Imaginary: Temporality and Embodiment in Irigaray's *Ethics*.' One must not overlook the fact that Caputo's Dionysus is as rabbinical as his rabbi is Dionysian (see Caputo 1993, chapter 3).

38 Nor is it in either J. Hillis Miller's deconstructive or John Barbour's theocratic vein.

Prologue

1 'Seltsam ist's, Zarathustra kennt wenig die Weiber, und doch hat er über sie Recht! Geschieht diess desshalb, weil beim Weibe kein Ding unmöglich ist? Und nun nimm zum Danke eine kleine Wahrheit! Bin ich doch alt genug für sie! ... Du gehst zu Frauen? Vergiss die Peitsche nicht!' ('Von alten und jungen Weiblein,' *Zarathustra*).

2 By highlighting this one factor, I am not minimizing the importance of other factors, such as the question of Nietzsche's relationship with Wagner. However, consideration of the myriad ways all the various biographical factors have been received would be unwieldy, not to mention overkill.

3 Like Angela Livingstone in her biography of Lou Andreas-Salomé, I find myself faced with a dilemma in deciding how to refer to this first of my subjects. Livingstone's solution and her reasoning are as follows: 'On most occasions I am calling the subject of this book by her Christian name, firstly because she was herself particularly attached to it and used it prominently, secondly because, while not a feminist, she was a very independent woman whom it seems wrong to call by her father's or her husband's name, and thirdly because the other possible alternatives have distinct disadvantages: There are inappropriate connotations to "Salomé," Andreas-Salomé is long and awkward, and "Lou A.-S." sounds cold' (1984, 'Prefatory Notes'). While it is admittedly rather long, I will be referring to her by her full name, since it is the name under which she wrote her memoir, and I too find Pfeiffer's 'Lou A.-S.' cold. 'Lou Salomé' will be reserved for the young girl whose name it was when she first encountered Nietzsche.

4 Because of the liberties taken by the English translator of *Lebensrückblick* (hereafter cited LRB), the quotations here are my own translation followed by the pages numbers from both the original and the English translation.

5 Pfeiffer (1970); hereafter cited Dok.

6 For concise accounts see Montinair (1984–5) and Warner (1985).

7 For alternative perspectives on the matter of approach, see Kreide (1996),

Matarasso (1987), McCafferty (1995), Schultz (1994), and Welsch and Wiesner (1988).

8 By her part, I mean both the role she played in its inception and in its reception. Her 1894 *Friedrich Nietzsche in seinen Werken* was one of the first and the most influential early interpretations, providing a substantial alternative to Elisabeth Nietzsche's multi-volume ode to her brother, which begins with the 1895 *Das Leben Friedrich Nietzsches*. Ernst Behler's contribution to the 1996 *Cambridge Companion to Nietzsche*, 'Nietzsche in the Twentieth Century,' offers a succinct comparison and contextualization of these two interpretations.

1: Lou Andreas-Salomé

1 'Still ist der Grund meines Meeres: wer erriethe wohl, dass er scherzhafte Ungeheur birgt! Unerschütterlich ist meine Tiefe: aber sie glänzt von schwimmenden Räthseln und Gelächtern' ('Von den Erhabenen,' *Zarathustra*).

2 Koepcke identifies her study of Spinoza at this time as the foundational experience of her inner life (1986, 40–3).

3 The factor of poor health, of both Lou Andreas-Salomé and those around her, such as Nietzsche, should not be overlooked in understanding the dynamics of their relations. The aura of frailty and death can serve to accentuate a strong character and add romance to an otherwise staid atmosphere. Such a theme provides the cultural book-ends for the second half of the nineteenth century, from the 1848 *La Dame aux camélias* by Alexandre Dumas fils to the 1896 premiere of Puccini's *La Bohème*. It also forms the backbone of Lou Andreas-Salomé's own analysis of Nietzsche.

4 That Lou correctly understood Nietzsche's intentions in this regard can be seen by the following: '"I have the hope that she will become my pupil" wrote Nietzsche early in the summer to Malwida von Meysenbug, "and if my life should not go on forever, my spiritual heiress"' (cited in Andrews 1972, 55).

5 For a comprehensive account of Rilke's relationship with Russia, see Asidowski (1986).

6 It should perhaps be noted that in return he expected her to accept the illegitimate child he had with their housekeeper Marie, which she did.

7 L. Cavani's 1977 film, *Al di là del bene e del male*, G. Sinopoli's 1981 opera, *Lou Salomé*, R. Jaccard's 1982 novel, *Lou*, Lars Gustafsson's 1982 poem, 'Vor einem Porträt von Lou Andreas-Salomé,' Irvin Yalom's 1992 novel, *When Nietzsche Wept*, and Robert Langs's new play, *Freud's Bird of Prey*, are cases in point.

8 'Erlebnis' seems to have an almost magical quality for Lou Andreas-Salomé; the focus is the incommensurability and unrepeatability of each event, in contrast with 'Erfahrung,' where events pool into a pond of greater knowledge and even wisdom.

9 For example, in Flaubert, Laforgue, Mallarmé, and Wilde, who in turn served as inspiration for Richard Strauss.

10 Littau's 'Refractions of the Feminine: The Monstrous Transformation of Lulu' is a helpful overview of recent Lulu reception, but, typically, it does not mention the connection with Lou Andreas-Salomé.

11 I intend this term in the spirit of Ross's concluding chapter, 'Das Märchen von der schönen Lou' (The Fairytale of Lovely Lou).

12 Lou Andreas-Salomé was no stranger to such shenanigans, having been duly initiated by Nietzsche's sister: 'It is worth remembering that Lou, who kept well out of all controversy and never attempted to justify herself or to answer Elisabeth publicly, certainly knew that her character was torn to shreds in books that many people were reading ... Fifty years later (in May 1932) Freud wrote to Lou: "Often and often I have felt angry on finding your relationship to Nietzsche mentioned in a way that was obviously hostile to you and could not possibly be in accord with the truth. You have endured it all, you have been much too noble; won't you finally, in the most dignified manner, come to your own defence?"' (Livingstone 1984, 56).

13 Freud provides an instructive counter-example. As Martin reminds us, their friendship was Lou Andreas-Salomé's 'only pedagogical relation that displaced that hierarchical gender divide and inevitable appropriation characterizing other pedagogical exchanges, other all-too-conventional scenes of seduction and tragedy' (1991, 190).

14 Or not, as the case may be. Remember that Lou Andreas-Salomé did not allow herself to become a mother, choosing to initiate a miscarriage when she found herself carrying Pineles's child. Her oblique confession in her memoirs reads: 'There can be no doubt that the failure to experience motherhood bars a person from the most valuable part of being a woman. I remember how astonished someone once was when, in a long discussion of similar matters in my later years, I confessed, "Do you know I never dared to bring a child into the world?"' (LRB 35–6/18).

15 She again identifies herself as 'a stranger' when joining Freud's psychoanalytic circle: 'A stranger simply entered the room, was received without love or hate, was calmly introduced to the work at hand – and was exposed to something more overwhelming than anyone can imagine who had not experienced it firsthand. The years passed, age thinned the ranks of my contemporaries as the war had thinned the ranks of the young – and the stranger stayed' (LRB 183/115).

16 'Together with the title *Looking Back* is already indicated what these pages are not intended and shouldn't be: gossip' (Koepcke 1986, 382).

2: Simone de Beauvoir

1 '"Warum?" sagte Zarathustra. "Du fragst warum? Ich gehöre nicht zu Denen, welche man nach ihrem Warum fragen darf. Ist denn mein Erleben von Gestern? Das ist lange her, dass ich die Gründe meiner Meinungen erlebte. Müsste ich nicht ein Fass sein von Gedächtniss, wenn ich auch meine Gründe bei mir haben wollte? Schon zuviel ist mir's, meine Meinungen selber zu behalten; und mancher Vogel fliegt davon"' ('Von den Dichtern,' *Zarathustra*).

2 Previous efforts comparing these two women have tended to be on a much smaller scale; see the articles by Light (1995) and Moortgat (1977).

3 Lucie is her maternal grandmother, Ernest-Narcisse her paternal grandfather, and Marie the Virgin Mary; Simone was simply a popular name at that time.

4 *All Said and Done* (1974); hereafter cited ASD.

5 Sartre's other star student from that time, Lionel de Roulet, would later marry Simone's sister Hélène and their harmonious relationship would provide 'The Family' with some much-needed stability. Bost, who later married Olga, remained the most steadfast of Beauvoir's friends and lovers. In the 1980s, after Olga's and Sartre's deaths, he became Beauvoir's favorite drinking companion.

6 That this is an all-male list serves to highlight the exception that Beauvoir was.

7 Circumstance does make it appear that Beauvoir simply mimicked Sartre, as she did with partners in other relationships. Although her friendship with Sylvie le Bon began casually, they became closer in the fall of 1963 after the death of Beauvoir's mother, just as Sartre was growing closer to Arlette. However, she waited until after Sartre's death in 1980 to adopt Sylvie.

8 I mean her affair with the country as well as with Algren. Her 1948 travel diary, *L'Amérique au jour le jour*, makes clear her fondness for the country.

9 It went unclaimed for the eighth time since its inception in 1901, the other years being 1914, 1918, 1935, and 1940–3.

10 *The Prime of Life* (1962); hereafter cited PL.

11 It has been calculated that Beauvoir made 143 journeys between 1929 and 1962 (Vintges 1996, 190, n10).

12 This tendency, which Moi links to that of patriarchal ideology to denounce women as 'epistemological impostor(s)' and 'false intellectual(s)' (1994, 92),

is equally operative in the demonizing that dominated the early reception of Lou Andreas-Salomé. In fact, all of the ploys that Moi identifies in her chapter, 'Clichés and Commonplaces in the Reception of Simone de Beauvoir' are equally relevant to the reception of Lou Andreas-Salomé, as amply demonstrated by Biddy Martin (1991, 20–2).

13 I am referring here to academic readings that target her autobiographical texts (such as Baisnée and Hewitt), not to work that incorporates these texts into, for example, the larger interventions currently pushing to establish Beauvoir on the philosophical, not only literary and feminist, map (see Bergoffen 1997; Tidd 1999; and the special issue of *Hypatia* (Fall 1999) on Beauvoir).

14 The only later novel, *Les Belles Images*, was written in 1965 after a car accident and resulting hospitalization, and it is by far the shortest of all her novels. Neither does the only philosophical essay written subsequently, the admittedly not insubstantial 1970 *Old Age*, approach the tome-like dimensions of *The Second Sex*.

15 Baisnée's is perhaps the most thorough demonstration of how much of Beauvoir's autobiographical writing is prefigured in her fictional and philosophical work.

16 Vintges phrases it well: 'Various authors have remarked that, in her autobiography, Beauvoir is extremely economical with the truth' (1996, 89). Beauvoir herself admits in *Force of Circumstance* to touching her story 'up improvingly here and there in the telling' (1965, 363), an example of which is the following: 'Sarraute questioned SdB's reliability as "a historian of her time," saying, "Every time she mentioned me in her memoirs she made some comment about my 'blue' hat or dress or suit. She knew very well that I seldom if ever wore blue, always green." I questioned SdB about this, and she said unhesitatingly, "But I always *think* of her as blue"' (Bair 1990, 459; italics in original).

17 If one can judge from his withering responses, the fictional account of their time together seems, if anything, to have been closer, and more revealing, than its autobiographical counterpart (cf. Bair 1990, 500, 658, n10).

18 William Barrett wrote in 1958: 'French Existentialism, as a cult, is now as dead as last year's fad. Its leaders, to be sure, are still flourishing: Sartre and Simone de Beauvoir are still phenomenally productive, though in the case of Sartre we feel that he has already made at least his penultimate statement, so that now we have his message pretty completely' (8).

19 Kate and Edward Fullbrook have done much valuable work in this regard.

20 The somber, depressing tone of the tome as a whole, especially the famous, controversial closing, 'I was gypped,' are correspondingly downplayed.

21 *Memoirs of a Dutiful Daughter* (1959); hereafter cited MDD.

22 In their correspondence, he was the 'crocodile,' while she was his 'frog wife.'

23 This is the subject of the third part of Moi's study, which addresses the psychic costs for Beauvoir in becoming 'a woman admired by a whole world for her independence' (1994, 252).

3: Maitreyi Devi

1 'Sie sind lustig, begann er wieder, und wer weiss? vielleicht auf ihres Wirthes Unkosten; und lernten sie von mir lachen, so ist es doch nicht *mein* Lachen, das sie lernten. Aber was liegt daran! Es sind alte Leute: sie genesen auf ihre Art, sie lachen auf ihre Art; meine Ohren haben schon Schlimmeres erduldet und wurden nicht unwirsch. Dieser Tag ist ein Sieg: er weicht schon, er flieht, *der Geist der Schwere*, mein alter Erzfeind! Wie gut will dieser Tag enden, der so schlimm und schwer begann!' ('Die Erweckung,' 1, *Zarathustra*; italics in original).

2 A comparison suggests itself at this point with Nietzsche, who was appointed to the philology chair in Basel at age twenty-four on the recommendation of Friedrich Richl, with whom he had studied in Bonn and Leipzig.

3 *It Does Not Die* (1976), hereafter cited DND.

4 The purpose of Eliade's trip was to immerse himself in Indian philosophy and religion, and his main area of interest was yoga. His dissertation, which was later published in French as *Le Yoga: Immortalité et Liberté*, includes a section (vi), 'Yoga and Tantrism – Mystical Eroticism, Maithuna and the Conjunction of Opposites.' Maithuna is defined as the sexual rite by which the human couple become a divine couple (260). Like Eliade, Dasgupta dedicated his work on yoga, the 1924 *Yoga as Philosophy and Religion*, to the Maharaja.

5 *Maitreyi* enjoyed a renaissance in the late 1960s in Romania when it was removed from the list of banned books, and became 'a novel of the seventies, not unlike some Russian novels of the sixties (such as *The Master and Margarita*) which, although written in the twenties or the thirties, established themselves in Soviet literary consciousness only after the end of the Stalinist period' (Spariosu 1980, 350).

6 The title of Eliade's half of this autobiographical duo, *Bengal Nights*, as well as its publication credits betray a belief that the French translation was, in fact, the original. As translator Catherine Spencer, unlike Ricketts and Johnson, has provided neither a translator's preface nor notes of any kind, one is left to speculate on the translation's inception.

7 That the film *La Nuit Bengali* was made two years after Eliade's death is also suggestive that such legal provisions were taken.

8 In an interview, Eliade was to say of himself: 'I wasn't English, luckily, and I came from a country that had never had any colonies, from a country that had in fact been treated like a colony itself for centuries. So I had no reason to have an inferiority complex. But, simply as a European, I did feel shame' (1982, 53).

9 Eliade's penchant for legends, mystery and magic becomes, in its turn, an object of ridicule, in Devi's romance. When in the final episode Amrita enters Mircea Euclid's office at the University of Chicago, he is portrayed as unable to deal with this concrete manifestation of his dreams and descends into absurd angst:

> I entered the room. At once the old man made a sound, 'Ohh!', and sprang to his feet. Then he sat down and got up again and then turned his back towards me ...
> 'Mircea, why are you standing with your back towards me?'
> 'I am waiting for someone else.'
> 'Who are you waiting for, Mircea?'
> 'For an Income-Tax Officer.'
> 'Income-Tax Officer!'
> 'Yes, yes, yes.' (DND 251)

Two pages later, Mircea has still refused to look at her, and Amrita is becoming increasingly exasperated: "I don't want to listen to all this chatter. Turn around, Mircea, I want to see you." He is standing but unsteady – there is about three yards space between us – so I raise my voice. We are quite old, maybe our hearing is weak. He appears confused. "How can I see you? Did Dante ever think he would see his Beatrice with eyes of flesh?" I am trembling. I am angry at his confusion. This man really lives in an unreal world of fantasy. From where does he bring in Dante and Beatrice?' (253). Whether Amrita is right or not, whether she was 'a simple little girl who sometimes played the philosopher,' not an enigma, whether the mystery was all Mircea's creation or not, the point remains that she is unable to 'free him from his world of fantasy,' to awaken him, to make him see her in 'this real world' (255).

10 Her husband, like F.C. Andreas, came from a family in which men were not expected to be lords and masters: 'I was pleasantly surprised to know the men folk of my husband's family. They never lorded it over others, women were the real mistresses of their homes. I had noticed in many other families that all the best things were reserved for the master of the house. This

could never happen here: the men would take no advantage over the women. On the contrary, when the wife was cooking the husband tried to fan her in spite of her embarrassed protests! In fact I had never before seen so many good people in one family' (DND 168).

4: Asja Lacis

1 Gefährten suchte einst der Schaffende und Kinder seiner Hoffnung: und siehe, es fand sich, dass er sie nicht finden könne, es sei denn, er schaffe sie selber erst. Also bin ich mitten in meinem Werke, zu meinen Kindern gehend und von ihnen kehrend: um seiner Kinder willen muss Zarathustra sich selbst vollenden. Denn von Grund aus liebt man nur sein Kind und Werk; und wo grosse Liebe zu sich selber ist, da ist sie der Schwangerschaft Wahrzeichen: so fand ich's ('Von der Seligkeit wider Willen,' *Zarathustra*).

2 She was hospitalized for a neural disorder, not, as her German memoir would have it, because of a nervous breakdown. The immediacy of Lacis's impact on Benjamin can be felt in the dedication of *One-Way Street* to her, 'who as an engineer laid it through the author.'

3 This story was related to me in August 1998 in private conversation with one of her favorite actresses, Maria Kalnina, née Adamova.

4 Neither has yet been published in English. The page numbers given here are from the original texts.

5 *Krasnaia Gvozdika* (*The Red Carnation*) (1984); hereafter cited RC.

6 *Revolutionär im Beruf* (*A Revolutionary by Profession*) (1971); hereafter cited RP.

7 The appalling reception of Lacis in German scholarship is discussed in my article, 'The Writing of Asja Lacis,' forthcoming in *New German Critique*.

8 Just as Sartre headed to Berlin in 1933 to study phenomenology in German and Eliade headed to Calcutta in 1928 to study yoga in Sanskrit, Benjamin's flirtation with Marxism in part motivated his trip to Moscow in the winter of 1926–7. Benjamin's lack of commitment (to both Marxism and Lacis) is reflected linguistically in the fact that he never acquired as much as a reading knowledge of Russian. Sartre's stay in Berlin was also marked by a decided lack of commitment, both politically and romantically: 'a listless affair with the wife of a fellow student at the French Institute whom he and Beauvoir agreed to nickname "the Moon Woman" because of her round face and dreamy disposition' (Bair 1990, 189). Of the three, only Eliade would make the following type of claim about his stay abroad: 'I became politically aware in India. Because there I witnessed the repression' (1982, 53).

9 I will later question the extent to which Lacis's Russian editors exercised ideological vigilance. That vigilance does not detract, however, from the fact that the subject matter and direction taken in *The Red Carnation* are her own, not her editor's, as is the case in the German.

10 It would perhaps be more accurate to say that Lacis would be upset by communist criticism and proud of 'bourgeois, western' criticism; that serves only to support my contention, however, not to contradict it.

11 As I discuss in 'The Writing of Asja Lacis,' the Russian variant (RC) is more lively and the figure of Benjamin takes on a different, less klutzy and more sophisticated, form. In the German edition, the initial description reads: 'My first impression: eye-glasses which threw off beams like little head-lights, thick, dark hair, narrow nose, clumsy hands – he dropped the packages. In general – very much the intellectual, one of the well-off ones. He accompanied me home, took his leave and asked whether he could be permitted to pay me a visit' (RP 42).

12 Not unlike Beauvoir, who commented that her father 'had destined me to a life of study' (MDD 181); 'I loved my father and my father loved books: he had filled my mother with a religious respect for them' (ASD 7). Lou Andreas-Salomé's father, on the other hand, had a much more laissez-faire approach to his daughter's education: 'In her later school years, when Russian was the compulsory language of instruction and Lou, who spoke German and French at home, felt her Russian was not up to it, her father arranged for her to *hospitieren* (attend lessons without doing homework or exams), laughing and saying "*She* doesn't need the compulsion of school"' (Livingstone 1984, 22; italics in original).

13 In the German version the father comes off sounding more progressive; he 'was a resourceful worker. He found work in Riga in a carriage factory. He participated in the revolutionary struggles of the year 1905' (RP 13). In the Russian version, on the contrary, he can't even provide for his family: 'Father found a job in a factory, but he was often sick, and in order to earn enough for the family, Mama opened a little store' (RC 17).

14 The poetry of Sarojini Naidu (1879–1949) was highly acclaimed in England in the first half of the twentieth century. Many considered the poems in her collections, *The Golden Threshold*, *The Bird of Time*, and *The Broken Wing*, second only to those of Tagore.

15 See Hellbeck (1996, 27), for a discussion of the Nietzschean influence on the Soviet revolution.

16 Hellbeck's German translation, *Tagebuch aus Moskau, 1931–1939*, is of the entire diary. An English excerpt can be found in *Intimacy and Terror: Soviet Diaries of the 1930s* (1995, 291–331).

17 As we will see in the next chapter, Nadezhda Mandel'shtam was decidedly not of this profile, considering revolutionary change far from being either necessary or possible.

Part 3

1 Quotations from Nadezhda Mandel'shtam are taken from Max Hayward's translation of *Hope Abandoned* (1974), in consultation with *Vtoraia Kniga* (1987), hereafter cited HA; the first volume of her memoirs, *Hope against Hope: A Memoir* (1970); the 'Third Book,' *Kniga Tret'ia* (1987), hereafter cited KT.

5: Nadezhda Mandel'shtam

1 'Diese Vorsehung ist über meinem Schicksal, dass ich ohne Vorsicht sein muss. Und wer unter Menschen nicht verschmachten will, muss lernen, aus allen Gläsern zu trinken; und wer unter Menschen rein bleiben will, muss verstehn, sich auch mit schmutzigem Wasser zu waschen. Und also sprach ich oft mir zum Troste: "Wohlan! Wohlauf! Altes Herz! Ein Unglück missrieth dir: geniesse diess als dein – Glück!"' ('Von der Menschen-Klugheit,' *Zarathustra*).

2 In the introduction to her first volume of memoirs, Clarence Brown stresses the magnitude of this accomplishment: 'Had [she] not lived, or had she been less valorous, intelligent and loving than she is, Mandelstam would no doubt have died several years earlier, and his work, that great concealed body of poetry and prose that never emerged in public print, would almost certainly have perished' (HAH xiii).

3 Schultz (1993). See the articles by Brender and Mitscherlich-Nielson, respectively. In order to appreciate the type of cultural company the Mandel'shtams are now travelling in, let me enumerate these other pairs: Marilyn Monroe and Arthur Miller, Susette Gontard and Friedrich Hölderlin, Dorothea Veit and Friedrich Schlegel, Oscar Wilde and Lord Alfred Douglas, Stella Patrick Campbell and George Bernard Shaw, Bella Rosenfeld and Marc Chagall, Wallis Simpson and Edward VIII, Eleonara Duse and Gabriele D'Annunzio, Felice Bauer and Franz Kafka, Clara Wieck and Robert Schumann, Gertrude Stein and Alice B. Toklas, Eva König and Gotthold Ephraim Lessing, and Mary Wollstonecraft and William Godwin.

4 *Women's Works in Stalin's Times* (1993b) is more correctly only half a book, since Lidiia Chukovskaia's *Notes on Akhmatova* shares the stage with Mandel'shtam's memoirs.

5 Feminist historians, such as Beth Holmgren and Judith Robey, tend to downplay and re-evaluate this aspect of Mandel'shtam's writing.

6 Further examples include: 'As regards achieving the status of a classic, I have been taught by M. to scorn the very idea, but when it comes to money I have some sympathy for them' (HA 214); 'M. taught me to beware of any kind of authoritarianism, and I hate a metallic note of command in anybody's voice, much preferring reasoned argument, or even the passionate appeal of genuine conviction' (HA 227); 'M. had knocked out of me the idea that I had a right to be happy, but I cannot advise anybody to court suffering or to take pride in it' (HA 286); 'He taught me that even people who had written only two or three real poems (such as Mei) were part of Russian poetry' (HA 99).

7 Holmgren (1993a) discusses this point at length.

8 Others of the multitude of examples include: 'Since he was also not in the least prone to melancholia, Ivask and Lurye are wrong to derive M.'s black sun, which created such a stir in the years just before the Revolution, from Nerval' (132); 'There is as much truth in this as in her yarn about someone pointing M. out to her as he stood among other "modernists" in a Moscow salon frequented by the Symbolists – at the time in question he was still going to school in Petersburg, satchel in hand, and never went anywhere near Moscow' (141); 'As I never tire of pointing out, the order of the poems in *Tristia* is completely haphazard' (75); 'Now that a demand has grown up for it, apart from the balderdash published abroad we also have the native variety to contend with. One must distinguish between the various kinds of lying: the pernicious ... and the innocuous' (55).

9 Further examples include: 'M. was the only person I knew who was absolutely devoid of all pretensions or affectations, always remaining utterly true to his own natural self' (355); 'There was something about him that I have never seen in anybody else, and it is time to say that what distinguished him from all the people around us (the Fedins and Fadeyevs of this world) was not irresponsibility, but this infinite sense of joy ... Everybody else was always after something – but not he. He just lived his life and reveled in it' (291); 'I only know that M. had a hard core, a deep bedrock of principles, which set him apart from anyone of his own or later generations' (160).

10 The resonance of the expression 'we' in Soviet literature should be noted. Zamiatin's science fiction novel, *We*, is one of the most significant anti-utopian novels of this century. The prototype for George Orwell's 1948 *Nineteen Eighty-Four*, it was the first novel to be banned by the Soviet censorship board, Glavlit, which was established in 1922.

11 It is to be noted that the philosophers Mandel'shtam draws on include Sergei Bulgakov, Berdiayev, and Bergson, but that Bakhtin receives no mention, indicating that his work was not yet known in the Soviet Union. This emphasis correlates with Caryl Emerson's contention that the current recuperation of Bakhtin by Russian and Anglo-American scholars is proceeding along much different lines: 'The Bakhtin one increasingly sees in Russian contexts, then, is no apostle of carnival and certainly not of trend-setting literary theory. He is being read, rather, as an old-fashioned "philosopher of life" with roots in the pre-Romantics, a disputant with Kant and Henri Bergson rather than a Marxist or semiotician in a twentieth century sense of the word. To contemporary Russians, Bakhtin now seems to matter not as a revolutionary or radical destabilizer but as a bridge to their own deeply felt but long-suppressed religious humanism' (1993, 14–15).

6: Romola Nijinsky

1 'Ich würde nur an einen Gott glauben, der zu tanzen verstünde ... Ich habe gehen gelernt: seitdem lasse ich mich laufen. Ich habe fliegen gelernt: seitdem will ich nicht erst gestossen sein, um von der Stelle zu kommen. Jetzt bin ich leicht, jetzt fliege ich, jetzt sehe ich mich unter mir, jetzt tanzt ein Gott durch mich' ('Vom Lesen und Schreiben,' *Zarathustra*).

2 The extent of this attention, it should be noted, is limited to the sphere of her husband's profession. The only work, to my knowledge, that focuses on Romola as its primary subject is her daughter Tamara's biography, *Nijinsky and Romola*, hereafter cited as N&R.

3 Romola's mother recorded her given names as such in her prayer book (N&R 1).

4 *Nijinsky* (1933); hereafter cited as N.

5 The uncertainty surrounding Vaslav's exact date of birth, due to the probability of his mother's having changed it so that he might avoid military duty, is discussed in Ferguson (1983).

6 Like Gustav von Salomé, de Pulsky's ancestry can be traced back to the Huguenot expulsion. His family (at that point called de la Poule) did not flee via the Baltic to St Petersburg, however, but via Poland to Hungary, where both titles and landed estates were bestowed upon it by the Habsburgian empress, Maria Theresia.

7 There is some question as to the veracity of Romola's account of her interview with Bleuler. According to Ostwald's examination of Vaslav's medical records: 'Prof. Bleuler never made the statement that Waslaw was incurably insane' (N&R 204).

8 Zsenia Anastazia Marie de la Consolation Madeleine Nijinsky was born on 14 June 1920 and at her father's insistence called Tamara (N&R 208). The rumors that not Vaslav but rather the doctor who was attending him was in fact her father are convincingly dismissed by Acocella in her introduction to the English translation of the unexpurgated version of Vaslav's *Diary*.

9 Romola's petit aristocratic upbringing had aimed at marriageability, that is, it was precisely the 'career' trajectory from which Simone de Beauvoir had been spared by her family's fall on hard times. The extent to which Romola internalized this socialization is indicated in a letter to her daughter, Tamara: 'It is not right nor proper for a woman to wander through life without a supporter or protector' (N&R 337). In a letter to Tamara's daughter, Kinga, upon the latter's completion of high school in Pheonix, Arizona, in the 1960s, she reiterates this sentiment, but with a qualification: 'In my opinion, marriage is the best solution, if one finds a good partner. But even that is not easy' (N&R 460).

10 *The Last Years of Nijinsky* (1952); hereafter cited LYN.

11 This meeting occurred late in 1960, on the last day of Romola's stay in the country; it is reputed to having been followed by her airplane's being delayed at the airport, so that a full-length sable coat could be delivered to her, with Krushchev's compliments (N&R 419–22).

12 Tamara Nijinsky's biography of her parents ends with her account of the bureaucratic fight in which she was (and, one presumes, still is) embroiled in trying to get her parents into the same grave.

13 Buckle enumerates the other five as follows: Iliodor Lukiano, poisoned by his own hand at twenty-one; George Rosaai, dead of pneumonia at twenty-one, Grigori Babitch, killed by a jealous husband at twenty-three, Mikhail Feodorov, dead of tuberculosis at twenty-six; Nijinsky, insane at thirty-one (1971, 4).

14 This polarization is something she had in common with her mother: 'No one could remain impartial to Emilia Markus; people either went into raptures and worshipped her or ... despised her' (N&R 6).

15 How much Bronislava privately supported, or even got along with, Romola is to be viewed with some scepticism: 'Bronislava has confided ... that she had distrusted Romola on a number of issues and could never rid herself of the feeling that Romola had been partly to blame for Vaslav's insanity' (N&R 476). Public displays of family loyalty were a priority among the Nijinskys, however, and Bronislava's public criticism of her sister-in-law was muted, at worst.

16 For a detailed review of these productions, see my 'Nijinsky: From Modern Love to Postmodern Madness' (2000).

17 Kyril FitzLyon's English translation appeared in 1999 under the expert editorship of New York dance critic, Joan Acocella.

18 The episode has the following denouement: 'Next morning, Vaslav found me in the Prado and begged me to return, saying, "It shall be as you wish." From that day on, Kostrovsky and H. never entered our home any more' (N 301).

19 This is something they learned from their mother: 'Frugality, economy of means were unknown [to Emilia Markus] ... It was said that the Emperor Franz-Joseph often reached into his purse to help his favourite Hungarian actress' (N&R 36).

20 The fate of Guiseppi Garibaldi's godson, Count Karoly de Pulszky, is certainly unexpected given his promising start. Charlie, as he was commonly called, became the scapegoat in a political plot against his brother, Agost, then minister of justice. Unfairly convicted of improprieties in the purchase of an Italian painting by Piombo, Charlie spent a year and a half in a sanatorium and then, even though his wife refused to accompany him, pressure from the Pulszkys forced him to go into exile. He travelled alone, first to England and then to Australia, where, after the collapse of the insurance company he tried to start, he committed suicide in 1899 at age forty-six. He was posthumously exonerated by the Hungarian courts (see N&R, 14–28; Shapcott 1984).

21 Not only were both his parents Polish, his sister relates that his early education was also in that language: 'At the beginning of 1894, Stassik [their older brother, who was seven at the time] and Vatsa [who was almost five] began to learn to read and write, both in Polish and Russian' (1992, 19).

22 These priorities were to change in the face of the changing geopolitical realities. When she was thinking of sending Kyra to her grandparents in 1925, her written instructions to them were that 'for six to eight weeks, Kyra should learn English and French, nothing else' (N&R 226).

23 While it is far from my intention to offer any type of psychological or psychoanalytic commentary on any of the subjects of this study, it is difficult to refrain from at least drawing attention to the obvious nature of the repetition complex involved in Romola's struggles.

24 It might be argued that Diaghilev is also a somewhat less than pristine figure. While this is undoubtedly true, Romola does indicate that Diaghilev behaved admirably towards them both in America and in Spain and that the conflicts that ensued in both places were due to contractual disputes: 'We tried to forget the disagreeable fact that Diaghilev owed Vaslav half a million francs, for which we would be obliged to fight. Vaslav would have preferred to drop the matter altogether, but, thinking of his family, he felt

he could not do it, and left the whole case in my hands' (N 259, 302). There is a great deal of respect in her account of 'his amazing hypnotic power' (N 296), for which there are no equivalent descriptions of her mother.

25 According to Tamara Nijinsky, her grandmother was, not surprisingly, debilitated with shock upon reading Romola's account of their relations in the first biography (N&R 252).

26 Romola's younger sister, Tessa, did not fare any better. Her marriage to tenor Eric Schmedes collapsed, owing to the latter's alcoholism. She was as ill equipped as her sister to support herself and usually managed poorly, often by pawning items from Romola's shaky resources. The ensuing sibling acrimony played itself out brutally: 'Tessa suffered from arteriosclerosis and because of Romola's financial straits had to be placed in a psychiatric clinic in Gest' (N&R 405) where she died of pneumonia on 19 March 1963.

27 The United States was also to prove the final destination of both Romola's daughters: Kyra settled in San Francisco and Tamara in Phoenix. Vaslav's sister, Bronislava, who died of a heart attack in 1972 in Los Angeles, could also be mentioned in this regard, as could her daughter Irina, who is 'happily settled in Pacific Palisades, California and [has] two grown children' (N&R 487).

28 See also the newspaper articles by Howard and Gilbert. All clippings are available in the Romola de Pulszky Nijinska file at the New York Public Library for the Performing Arts.

29 But not by way of children. Like Lou Andreas-Salomé and Simone de Beauvoir, both Nadezhda and Romola felt procreation neither necessary nor desirable. Romola's poor relationships with her daughters stem from her decided lack of enthusiasm about motherhood and children in general. Upon finding herself pregnant shortly after their marriage, Romola admits a long, considered contemplation of abortion. Conception of her second daughter (who receives scant attention in either the biographies or in real life and makes much of this fact in her biography of her mother) was an attempt to cure her husband's illness. When her granddaughter miscarried her first child, Romola was quick to 'comfort' her in a letter: 'Believe me, in our century, in our times, it is almost criminal to create a child' (N&R 500).

30 Ostwald's documentation of Nijinsky's institutionalization offers a much different portrayal, with entries from the supervising physicians such as 'Often he is unclean, smearing urine all over the floor' (1991, 280). I am not implying that Nadezhda's characterization is equally misleading but simply offering a concrete example of the creative aspect of these portrayals.

31 Further examples include: 'As the spring began we prolonged our walks,

and through Vaslav I learned to love nature. Each flower, each tree, had a meaning for him; he could find an expression of beauty in them, which he made me understand' (N 229); 'Nijinsky would watch their [the animals'] movements for a long time, and made me notice everything lovely around us. It seemed to me that life began to have a new meaning. Suddenly I realized that so much beauty surrounds us which, before, I had failed to observe' (N 203).

32 Buckle further characterizes Romola as 'courageous,' 'dauntless,' and 'indomitable' (1971, 501, 507, 519). Romola has also received praise in Russian criticism: 'The eccentric and extravagant woman did herself perform miracles of patience, devotion and courage' (Krasovskaya 1979, 344).

Conclusion

1 'Verstandet ihr diess Wort, oh meine Brüder? Ihr seid erschreckt: wird euren Herzen schwindlig? Kläfft euch hier der Abgrund? Kläfft euch hier der Höllenhund? ... Habt ihr Muth, oh meine Brüder? Seid ihr herzhaft? Nicht Muth vor Zeugen, sondern Einsiedler- und Adler-Muth, dem auch kein Gott mehr zusieht? Kalte Seelen, Maulthiere, Blinde, Trunkene heissen mir nicht herzhaft. Herz hat, wer Furcht kennt, aber Furcht zwingt, wer den Abgrund sieht, aber mit Stolz. Wer den Abgrund sieht, aber mit Adlers-Augen, wer mit Adlers-Krallen den Abgrund fasst: Der hat Muth' ('Vom höheren Menschen,' 2/4, Zarathustra).

2 If Alice B. Toklas had written The Autobiography of Alice B. Toklas and thereby come into the same kind of cultural capital as the subjects of this study, that process would correspond to the mechanism I am trying to elucidate. Stein's having written it herself disqualifies the text because she was using her autobiography not as cultural collateral but rather as aestheticist, modernist self-expression.

3 As we have seen in each section, it is precisely this paradoxically committed lack of commitment that makes them such awkward, slippery subjects for feminist scholars.

4 'Wie geschieht diess doch! so fragte ich mich. Was überredet das Lebendige, dass es gehorcht und befiehlt und befehlend noch Gehorsam übt?' ('Von der Selbst-Überwindung,' Zarathustra).

5 Gregg Horowitz's reading of art in the aesthetic theories of Kant and Adorno is even more evocative of the parallel between art and women's lives: 'autonomous art criticizes society just by being there because the "there" where it is is no "proper" place' (1997, 264).

6 Both Ricoeur and Taylor highlight the dialogic, narrative, ethical nature of

identity in their works. Taylor states: 'We think of this fundamental moral orientation as essential to being a human interlocutor, capable of answering for oneself' (1989, 29), while for Ricoeur: 'The capacity of the moral subject to impute his own actions *to himself* is based on his capacity to assume *narratively* the story of his own life' (1995, 397; italics added). Thus for both Ricoeur and Taylor, as for Nietzsche, to engage in the autobiographical process of determining one's identity is to be faced with a narrative and ethical imperative; put differently, the duty to oneself for oneself to come to terms with who one thinks one is is what makes the autobiographical act, whether written or simply thought out, an ethical as well as aesthetic one.

7 As in the Prologue, I refer to Osip Mandel'shtam's essay 'On the Addressee.'

8 'Frei nennst du dich? Deinen herrschenden Gedanken will ich hören und nicht, dass du einem Joche entronnen bist' ('Vom Wege des Schaffenden,' *Zarathustra*).

9 That it need not be told from this perspective is evidenced by the following account: 'In the spring of 1899 Rilke set off for three months in Russia in her company and that of her official husband, Dr Friedrich Carl Andreas. *She had decided* that Rilke could earn his living as a translator from the Russian and *she obliged him* to learn the language. While in Moscow the three of them called on Tolstoi at tea, and in Saint Petersburg she introduced Rilke to her family and her friends. This was not all that *she accomplished*. *She* also implanted in his mind the suggestion that Russia was his true spiritual home, however slight his understanding of the Russian soul might be' (247–8; bold and italics added). In Wayne Andrews's *Siegfried's Curse: The German Journey From Nietzsche to Hesse* (1972), men are generally portrayed as victims of this fearsome specimen of womanhood, who sizes them up (or down, as the case may be) and disposes of them accordingly.

10 After the controversy surrounding her 1993 memoir, *French Lessons*, a chastised Alice Kaplan soberly notes in 'The Trouble with Memoir,' that 'breaking down the boundary between private and public life is essential to memoir, but keeping that boundary secure is essential for well-being in life' (1997, B5).

11 'Ich lehrte sie all mein Dichten und Trachten: in Eins zu dichten und zusammen zu tragen, was Bruchstück ist am Menschen und Räthsel und grauser Zufall, – als Dichter, Räthselrather und Erlöser des Zufalls lehrte ich sie an der Zukunft schaffen, und Alles, das *war* –, schaffend zu erlösen' ('Von alten und neuen Tafeln,' 3, *Zarathustra*; italics in original).

12 In likening such divergent approaches, I am not minimizing their substantial differences. It is precisely because of their differences, however, that this

point of commonality can be seen as evocative of the larger zeitgeist, or what Heidegger (and Richard Bernstein, among others, in his wake) would call a *Stimmung*, or mood.

13 Eakin's latest work, in which he recoups for both sexes the relationality that Mary Mason's ground-breaking 1980 essay, 'The Other Voice: Autobiographies of Women Writers,' claimed for women, is part of a larger wave of relational criticism. Although Nancy Chodorow's work is often cited in this context, Kenneth Gergen's work on the 'saturated self' has yet, to my knowledge, to receive any attention and might prove a fruitful area of investigation.

14 For a sense of this shattered non-identity, one could consult the films of Atom Egoyan, in which it is effectively presented and critiqued (I am grateful to Monique Tschofen for drawing my attention to this point).

15 Their doing so is in keeping with the way Nietzsche unites the personal and political: 'If we understand *Kultur* as the German equivalent to the Greek *paideia*, then [Henning] Ottman is right to say that "was Nietzsche suchte, war die Überwindung der Entfremdung, die Wiedergewinnung der allseitigen Persönlichkeit und der Dominanz der Kultur über Ökonomie und Politik"' (cited in Rosen 1995, 257, n43: what Nietzsche was looking for was to overcome alienation and regain a complete personality and the domination of culture over the economy and politics).

16 'Wachet und horcht, ihr Einsamen! Von der Zukunft her kommen Winde mit heimlichem Flügelschlagen; und an feine Ohren ergeht gute Botschaft' ('Von der schenkenden Tugend,' 2, *Zarathustra*).

17 The following citations are from Edmund Jephcott's English translation. The original can be found in the *Gesammelte Schriften*, vol. ii, 1, 295–310.

18 I intend these remarks in the spirit of Irving Wohlfarth's warning: 'To apply Benjaminian categories to the present without also trying to rethink them in the light of intervening history is ... not merely to remain trapped within the coordinates of his thought, but to arrest the recasting process that it sought to initiate' (cited in Wolin 1995, 56). In his letter of 9 December 1923 to Christian Rang, Benjamin describes criticism (where it is identical with interpretation and the opposite of all current methods of art appreciation) as 'the mortification of works of art' (1994, 224). Gregory Ulmer's essay, 'The Object of Post-Criticism,' is particularly illuminating in this context. Under the headings of Collage/Montage, Grammatology, Allegory, and Parasite/Saprophyte, he analyses 'the application of the devices of modernist art to critical representations' (1983, 83) to support Barthes's contention that when there are only writers, the categories of literature and criticism can no longer be kept apart. After first quoting Rosalin Krauss on

'paraliterature': 'If one of the tenets of modernist literature had been the creation of a work that would force reflection on the conditions of its own construction, that would insist on reading as a much more consciously *critical* act, then it is not surprising that the medium of a *post*modernist literature should be the critical text wrought into a paraliterary form' (from 'Poststructuralism and the "Paraliterary,"' *October* 13 (1980): 40; italics in Ulmer), he then concludes that 'The insight of paraliterature is that although by the 1960s the collage revolution seemed to have run its course, it was in fact being renewed in critical discourse, which was itself finally being affected by experiments with representation. Indeed, as Elizabeth Bruss proposes in *Beautiful Theories* (concerned with the criticism of Susan Sontag, William Gass, Harold Bloom and Roland Barthes), theory is not only the most interesting of contemporary literary forms, it is the mode best suited for moving out of the impasse reached by the modernist movements in the arts' (1983, 107–8, n10).

19 It is a lovely irony that Heidegger, with his penchant for the productive aspect of *Destruktion*, has led the pack in terms of scandal (cf. Wolin 1993). The trend towards discrediting academic work on an 'ad hominem' continues to gather momentum and is a deserving topic for in-depth study.

20 See Evans (1996, 9), for an example of 'discomfort' with such constructions of Beauvoir.

21 While Vintges takes passion as her overriding theme, she does not explore any of the implications of her subject's passion. Rather, at her book's end she leaves Beauvoir literally suspended and in process: 'Beauvoir thought it strange that people did not want to believe in "intellectual passions" (FoC 200). As Sartre once said, she was capable of shedding "metaphysical tears," and her passion was sometimes infectious: "I found myself alone with Sartre in the streets of Paris at dawn. I began to sob over the tragedy of the human condition; as we crossed the Seine, I leaned on the parapet of the bridge. 'I don't see why we don't throw ourselves into the river!' 'All right, then, let's throw ourselves in!' said Sartre, who was finding my tears contagious and had shed a few himself" (119). But they simply continued on their way over the Seine' (1996, 177). One possible line of enquiry would lie in recalling Lacan's final seminar in *The Ethics of Psychoanalysis*: 'I think that throughout this historical period the desire of man [*sic*], which has been felt, anaesthetized, put to sleep by moralists, domesticated by educators, betrayed by the academies, has quite simply taken refuge or been repressed in that most subtle and blindest of passions, as the story of Oedipus shows, the passion for knowledge. That's the passion that is currently going great guns and is far from having said its last word' (1992, 324).

22 Sidonie Smith and Julia Watson's *Women, Autobiography, Theory* is an extremely important resource in anthologizing and providing a bibliography of this work. That this trend has not been greeted by universal enthusiasm is evidenced by David Simpson's cynical comment: 'Literary critics are busier writing about themselves than they have ever been before, to the point that the award of tenure now seems to bring with it a contract for one's autobiography' (1995, 25).

23 I would not like to create the impression that his is the only such observation, but it is particularly felicitously worded for present purposes. Paul de Man's essay on autobiography begins in a similar vein: 'Empirically as well as theoretically, autobiography lends itself poorly to generic definition: each specific instance seems to be an exception to the norm; the works themselves seem to shade off into neighbouring or even incompatible genres and, perhaps, most revealing of all, generic discussions, which can have such powerful heuristic value in the case of tragedy or of the novel, remain distressingly sterile when autobiography is at stake' (1979, 919).

24 Richard Bernstein reminds us that 'it is Hegel who teaches us over and over again to be alert to the uncanny way in which radical gestures of opposition and negation are complicit with, and parasitic upon what they are presumably rejecting' (1992, 308).

25 Not only written. New types of radio and television programs, not to mention internet sites, whose sole raison d'être is self-expression, continue to mushroom.

Bibliography

Section I: The Women and Their Autobiographical Writing: Primary and
Secondary Sources

Lou Andreas-Salomé

Andreas-Salomé, Lou. 1951. *Lebensrückblick, Grundriß einiger Lebenserinnerung-
en*. Zürich: Insel; Frankfurt: Insel, 1968, 1979.

RELEVANT WORKS
Andreas–Salomé, Lou. 1983. *Fenitschka. Eine Ausschweifung: Zwei Erzählungen*.
Frankfurt: Ullstein (*Fenitschka and Deviations: Two Novellas*. Trans. Dorothee
Einstein Krahn. Lanham: University Press of America, 1990).

TRANSLATIONS (FROM UNESCO'S *INDEX TRANSLATORUM*)
Il mito di una donna. 1975. Trans. Uta Olivieri. Firenze, Rimini: Guaraldi.
Ma vie: esquisse de quelques souvenirs. 1977. Trans. Dominique Miermont and
Brigitte Vergne. Paris: Presses universitaires de France.
Mit liv. 1979. Trans. Luise Pihl. Copenhagen: Hernov.
Mirada restrospectiva.1980. Trans. Alejandro Venegas. Madrid: Alianza
Editorial.
Carnets intimes des dernières années. 1983. Trans. Jacques Le Rider. Paris:
Hachette (trans. of *Eintragungen, letzte Jahre*).
Looking Back: Memoirs. 1991. Ed. Ernst Pfeiffer. Trans. Breon Mitchell. New
York: Paragon House, 1991.

SECONDARY LITERATURE
Andrews, Wayne. 1972. *Siegfried's Curse: The German Journey From Nietzsche to
Hesse*. New York: Atheneum.

Asadowski, Konstantin, ed. 1986. *Rilke und Rußland: Briefe, Erinnerungen, Gedichte*. Trans. Ulrike Hirschberg. Frankfurt: Insel.

Binion, Rudolph. 1968. *Frau Lou: Nietzsche's Wayward Disciple*. Foreword by Walter Kaufmann. Princeton: Princeton University Press.

Brender, Irmela. 1993. '"Aus allem Schönen gehst Du mir entgegen": Lou Andreas-Salomé und Rainer Maria Rilke.' In *Liebespaare: Geschichte und Geschichten*. Ed. Hans Jürgen Schultz. Munich: Deutscher Taschenbuch Verlag.

Cavani, Liliana, dir. 1977. *Al di là del bene e del male (Beyond Good and Evil)*. Starring Dominque Sanda, Erland Josephson, and Robert Powell.

Etkind, Aleksandr. 1993. *Eros Nivozmozhnogo: Istoria psixoanaliza v Rossii (Eros of the Impossible: The History of Psychoanalysis in Russia)*. St Petersburg: Medyza.

Gane, Mike. 1993. 'In Transcendence: Friedrich Nietzsche and Lou Salomé.' In *Harmless Lovers? Gender, Theory and Personal Relationships*. London and New York: Routledge.

Gropp, Rose-Maria. 1988. *Lou Andreas-Salomé mit Sigmund Freud: Grenzgänge zwischen Literatur und Psychanalyse*. Weinheim and Basel: Beltz.

Gustafsson, Lars. 1982. 'Vor einem Porträt von Lou Andreas-Salomé.' *Die Stille der Welt vor Bach, Gedichte*. Munich (*The Stillness of the World before Bach: New Selected Poems*. Ed. Christophe Middleton. Trans. Robin Fulton et al. in collaboration with L. Gustafsson. New York: New Directions, 1988).

Hahn, Barbara, ed. 1994. *Frauen in den Kulturwissenschaften: Von Lou Andreas-Salomé bis Hannah Arendt*. Munich: Beck.

Haines, Brigid. 1995. 'Masochism and Femininity in Lou Andreas-Salomé's *Ausschweifung*.' *Women In German Yearbook* 10: 97–115.

– 1991. 'Lou Andreas-Salomé's *Fenitschka*: A Feminist Reading.' *German Life and Letters* 44.5 (Oct.): 416–25.

– 1993. '"Ja, so würde ich es auch heute noch sagen": Reading Lou Andreas-Salomé in the 1990s.' *Publications of the English Goethe Society* 62: 77–91.

Hillebrand, Bruno. 1987. 'Porträt von Lou Andreas-Salomé.' *Neue deutsche Hefte* 34: 114–31.

Jaccard, R. 1982. *Lou*. Paris: Grasset.

Koepcke, Cordula. 1986. *Lou Andreas-Salomé. Leben*Persönlichkeit*Werk. Eine Biographie*. Frankfurt: Insel.

Kreide, Caroline. 1996. *Lou Andreas-Salomé: Feministin oder Antifeministin? Eine Standortbestimmung zur whilhelminischen Frauenbewegung*. New York: Peter Lang.

Langs, Robert. 2000. *Freud's Bird of Prey: A Play in Two Acts*. New York: Zeig, Tucker & Theisen.

Light, John. 1995. 'Lou Andreas-Salomé and Simone de Beauvoir: The Mystic and the Intellectual.' *Simone de Beauvoir Studies* 112 (1995): 52–8.

Littau, Karin. 1995. 'Refractions of the Feminine: The Monstrous Transformation of Lulu.' *Modern Language Notes* 110. 4 (Sept.): 888–912.

Livingstone, Angela. 1984. *Lou Andreas-Salomé. Her Life (as Confidante of Freud, Nietzsche and Rilke) and Writings (on Psychoanalysis, Religion and Sex)*. London: Gordon Fraser Gallery.

Martin, Biddy. 1991. *Woman and Modernity: The (Life)styles of Lou Andreas-Salomé*. Ithaca, NY: Cornell University Press.

Matarasso, Michel. 1987. 'Anthropoanalysis and the Biographical Approach: Lou Andreas-Salomé.' Trans. Jeanne Ferguson. *Diogenes* 139 (Fall): 127–64.

McCafferty, Susan. 1995. 'Psychobiography of Lou Andreas-Salomé.' Dissertation 3454B, Massachusetts School of Professional Psychology.

Meltzer, Françoise. 1987. *Salome and the Dance of Writing: Portraits of Mimesis in Literature*. Chicago and London: University of Chicago Press.

Montinair, Mazzino. 1984–5. 'Zu Nietzsches Begegnung mit Lou Andreas-Salomé.' *Blätter der Rilke Gesellschaft* 11–12: 15–22.

Moortgat, P. 1977. 'Lou Andreas-Salomé et Simone de Beauvoir.' *Revue d'Allemagne* 5: 385–401.

Peters, H.F. 1962. *My Sister, My Spouse: A Biography of Lou Andreas-Salomé*. New York: Norton.

– 1977. *Zarathustra's Sister: The Case of Elisabeth and Friedrich Nietzsche*. New York: Crown Publishers.

Pfeiffer, Ernst, ed. 1970. *Friedrich Nietzsche, Paul Reé, Lou Andreas-Salomé: Die Dokumente ihrer Begegnung*. Frankfurt: Insel.

Ross, Werner. 1992. *Lou Andreas-Salomé: Weggefährtin von Nietzsche, Rilke, Freud*. Berlin: Siedler.

Schaffner. Roland. 1965. 'Die Salome-Dichtungen von Flaubert, Laforgue, Wilde und Mallarmé.' Dissertation, Würzburg.

Schmidt Machey, I. 1956. *Lou Salomé, inspiratrice et interprète de Nietzsche, Rilke et Freud*. Paris: Nizet, 1956.

Schultz, Karla. 1994. 'In Defense of Narcissus: Lou Andreas-Salomé and Julia Kristeva.' *German Quarterly* 67.2 (Spring): 185–94.

Sinopoli Staub, Giuseppe. 1981. *Lou Salomé, eine Oper: Programmheft der Bayerischen Staatsoper*. Zusammenstellung und Gestaltung Klaus Schultz. Munich.

Sorell, Walter. 1975. *Three Women: Lives of Sex and Genius*. Indianapolis/New York: Bobbs-Merill Company.

Wäcker, Erika. 1993. 'Die Darstellung der tanzenden Salomé in der bildenden Kunst zwischen 1870 und 1920.' Dissertation, Freie Universität Berlin.

Warner, William. 1985. '"Love in a Life": The Case of Nietzsche and Lou Salomé.' *Victorian Newsletter* 67 (Spring): 14–17.

Wedekind, Frank. 1994. *Werke: Kritische Studienausgabe*. Ed. Elke Austermühl, Rolf Kiesor, and Hartmut Vinçon. Darmstadt: J. Häuser.

Welsch, Ursula, and Michaela Wiesner. 1988. *Lou Andreas-Salomé. Vom 'Lebensurgrund' zur Psychoanalyse*. Munich and Vienna: Verlag Internationale Psychoanalyse.

Yalom, Irvin. 1992. *When Nietzsche Wept. A Novel of Obsession*. New York: Harper Collins.

Simone de Beauvoir

Beauvoir, Simone de. 1958. *Mémoires d'une jeune fille rangée*. Paris: Gallimard.
– *La force de l'âge*. 1960. Paris: Gallimard.
– *La force des choses*. 1963. Paris: Gallimard.
– *Une morte très douce*. 1964. Paris: Gallimard.
– *Tout compte fait*. 1972. Paris: Gallimard.
– *La cérémonie des adieux*. 1981. Paris: Gallimard.
– *Lettres à Sartre*. 1990. Paris: Gallimard.

RELEVANT WORKS
Beauvoir, Simone de. 1954. *Les Mandarins*. Paris: Gallimard (*The Mandarins: A Novel*. Trans. Leonard M. Friedman. Cleveland: World Publishing, 1956).

TRANSLATIONS
Memórias de uma moça bem comportada. 1959. Trans. Sergio Milliet. São Paulo: Difusão Euroopéia do Livro.
Memorias de una joven formal. 1959. Trans. Silvina Bullrich. Buenos Aires: Sudamericana.
Memoirs of a Dutiful Daughter. 1959. Trans. James Kirkup. Cleveland: World; London: André Deutsch and Weidenfeld & Nicolson.
Memoiren einer Tochter aus gutem Hause. 1960. Trans. Eva Rechel-Mertens. Reinbek bei Hamburg: Rowohlt.
Memorie d'una ragazza per bene. 1960. Trans. Bruno Fonzi. Torino: Einaudi.
Pamietnik stetecznej panienki. 1960. Trans. Hanna Szumanska-Grossowa. Warsaw: Panstv. Instytut Wydawn.
Egy Jóházból Való Urilány Emléki. 1961. Trans. Péter Nagy. Budapest: Magvetö.

Aru onna no kaiso. Musume jidai. 1961. Trans. Tomiko Asabuki. Tokyo: Kinokuniya shoten.

En Familjeflickas Memoarer. 1962. Trans. Eva Alexanderson. Stockholm: Bonnier.

Al-Umm. 1962. Trans. Muhammad Fat'hi. Al-Qahirah: Matba'at lajnat al-Ta'lif wal-Tarjamah.

Uspomene dobro odgojene djevojke. 1962. Trans. Agica Curcic. Zagreb: Mladost.

Amintirile Unei Fete Cuminti. 1965. Trans. Anda Boldur. Bucharest: Editura pentru literatura universala.

En Velopdragen ung piges Erindringer. 1966. Trans. Bibba Jørgen Jensen. Copenhagen: Vinten.

Memoires. Herinneringen van een welopgevoed meisje. 1967. Trans. Jan Hardenberg. Hilversum: De Boer.

Pameti Sporádané Divky. 1969. Trans. A.M. Liehm. Prague: Czech. spisovatel.

Cheonyeo sijeol. 1976. Trans. Jeon Seong Ja. Seoul: Munye Pub.

Bir genç kizin anilari. 1976. Trans. Seçkin Cilizoglu. Istanbul: Payel Yayinevi.

Memórias de uma menina bem comportada. 1976. Trans. Maria João Remy Friere. Amadore: Bertrand.

Bir genc kizin anilari. 1983. Trans. Seçkin Cilizoglu. Istanbul: Payel Yayinevi.

Een welopgevoed meisje. 1986. Trans. Jan Hardenberg. Houten: Agathon.

Memorias de uma moça bem comportada. 1987. Trans. Sergio Milliet. São Paulo: Circulo do Livro.

Perhetytön muistelmat. 1987. Trans. Annikki Suni. Helsinki: Kirjayhtymä.

Waga ane bobowaru. 1991. Trans. Hukui Mituko. Tokyo: Heibonsya.

Amintirile unei fete cuminti. 1991. Trans. Anca-Dominica Ilea. Timisoara: Editura de Vest.

Spomeni na edno porjadacno momice. 1992. Trans. Marija Koeva. Sofia: Fama.

Chayuroun yoja. 1993. Trans. Yi Yong-shin. Seoul: Sanho.

Uspomene lepo vaspitane devojke. 1994. Trans. Mirjana Vukmirovic. Belgrade: Prosveta.

La plenitud de la vida. 1961. Trans. Silvina Bullrich. Buenos Aires: Sudamericana.

La Fôrça da idade. 1961. Trans. Sergio Milliet. Rio de Janeiro: Nova Fronteira.

L'età forte. 1961. Trans. Bruno Fonzi. Torino: Einaudi.

The Prime of Life. The Second Volume of Her Autobiography. 1962. Trans. Peter Green. Cleveland; World; London: André Deutsch and Weidenfeld & Nicolson.

Onna zakari; aru onna no kaiso. 1962. Trans. Tomiko Asabuki & Husa Ninomiya. Tokyo: Kinokuniya shoten.

Zrelo doba. 1962. Trans. Stanko Lasic. Zagreb: Mladost.

W sile wieku. 1962. Trans. Hanna Szumanska-Grossawa. Warsaw: Panstw. Instytut Wydawn.

A kor hatalma. 1965. Trans. Pál Réz. Budapest: Magwetö kiadó.

Samvaer med Sartre. 1966. Trans. Jørgen Breitenstein. Copenhagen: Hasselbalch.

Na-Eui Gyeyag Gyeolhon. 1967. Trans. Hyeon-A Lee. Seoul: Jeongeunsa (*Gyeyag Gyeolhon*. Trans. Bongseon Lee. Seoul: Minyesa, 1978).

Memoires. De bloei van het leven. 1968. Trans. Jan Hardenberg. Hilversan: De Boer.

In den besten Jahren. 1969. Trans. Rolf Soellner. Reinbek bei Hamburg: Rowohlt.

Gyeyag gyeolhon. 1978. Trans. Bongseog Lee. Seoul: Minyesa.

De bästa åren. 1984. Trans. Anne-Marie Edéus. Stockholm: AWE/Geber.

De bloei van het leven. 1984. Trans. Jan Hardenberg. Weesp: Agathon.

Najlepsa leta. 1986. Trans. Marjeta Novak. Murska Sobota: Pomurska zalozba.

Voiman vuodet. 1986. Trans. Anna-Maija Viitanen. Helsinki: Kirjayhtymä.

Kyeyak kyolhon. 1995. Trans. Yi Sok-pong. Seoul: Hansong midio.

Najbolje godine. 1995. Trans. Mirjana Vukmirovic. Belgrade: Prosveta.

Force of Circumstance: The Third Volume of Her Autobiography. 1965. Trans. Richard Howard. New York: Putnam, London: André Deutsch and Weidenfeld & Nicolson.

Sob o signo da história. 1965. Trans. Sergio Milliet. São Paulo: Difusão Européia do Livro.

Aru sengo. 1965. Trans. Tomiko Asabuki and Fusa Ninomiya. Tokyo: Konokuniya shoten.

Der Lauf der Dinge. 1966. Trans. Paul Baudisch. Reinbek bei Hamburg: Rowohlt.

La fuerza de las cosas. 1966. Trans. Ezequiel de Olaso. Buenos Aires: Sudamericana.

A Körülmények Hatalma. 1966. Trans. Klára Szöllösy and Katalin Rayman. Budapest: Magvetö Kiadó.

La forza delle cose. 1966. Trans. Bianca Garufi. Torino: Einaudi.

Snaga Stuari. 1966. Trans. Stanko Lasic. Zagreb: Mladost.

Sila Rzeczy. 1967. Trans. Jerzy Panski. Warsaw: Panstw. Instytut Wydawn.

Memoires: De druk der omstandigheden. 1968. Trans. L. Witsenburg. Bussun: De Boer.

Kadinligimin hikâyesi. 1977. Trans. Erdogan Tokatli. Istanbul: Payel Yayinevi (trans. of *La force de l'âge* and *La force des choses*).

Världen öppnas. 1986. Trans. Kerstin Hallén. Stockholm: AWE/Geber.

De druk der omstandigheden. 1986. Trans. L. Witsenburg. Houton: Agathon.

Maailman meno. 1991. Trans. Anna-Maija Viitanen. Helsinki: Kirjayhtymä.

Ein sanfter Tod. 1965. Trans. Paul Mayer. Reinbek bei Hamburg: Rowohlt.

Odayakana shi. 1965. Trans. Toshio Sugi. Tokyo: Konokuniya shoten.

Een zachte Dood. 1965. Trans. Jan Hardenberg. Hilversum: De Boer.

Avled Stilla. 1965. Trans. Lily Vallquist. Stockholm: Bonnier.

Una muerta muy dulce. 1965. Trans. Maria Elena Santillán. Buenos Aires: Sudamericana.

Väga Kerge Surm. 1965. Trans. Hemno Rajandi. Tallin: Periodika.

A Very Easy Death. 1966. Trans. Patrick O'Brian. New York.

Lempeä Kuolema. 1966. Trans. Outi Kasurinen-Badji. Helsinki: Kirjayhtymä.

Una morte dolcissima. 1966. Trans. Clara Lusignoli. Torino: Einaudi.

Una mort molt dolça. 1966. Trans. Ramon Zuriguera. Barcelona: Proa.

Môt cái chēt rāt diu dàng. 1966. Trans. Vū-dình-luu. Saigon: Eds Van.

Velice Lehká Smrt. 1967. Trans. Eva Pilarová. Prague: Czech. spisovatel.

Uma morte serena. 1967. Trans. Luisa Dacosta. Lisbon: Estampa.

Ochen' legkaja smert.' 1968. Trans. N. Stoljarova. Moscow: Progress.

Lijepe Slike. Vrlo blaga smrt. 1969. Trans. Ivo Klaric and Smiljka Sucic. Zagreb: Naprijed.

Budeureoun jugeum. 1977. Trans. Gweon Yeong Ja. Seoul: Pyeongminsa.

Lempeä kuolema. 1979. Trans. Outi Kasurinen-Badji. Helsinki: Kirjayhtymä.

En lett og rolig død. 1982. Trans. Bente Christensen. Oslo i.e. Lysaker: Solum.

Mawet qal me'od. 1983. Trans. Micha Frankel. Jerusalem: Keter.

En skånsom død. 1984. Trans. Karen Mathiasen. Copenhagen: Vinten.

Uma morte muito suave. 1984. Trans. Alvaro Cabral. Rio de Janiero: Nova Fronteira.

Een zachte dood. 1986. Trans. Greetje van den Bergh. Houten: Agathon.

Arumdaun chukum. 1986. Trans. Kyon Yong-cha. Seoul: Haengrimchulpansa.

Yae pwet pamar. 1989. Trans. (from English) Mya Than Tint. Yangon, Myanmar: Sar Chit Ths Sarpay.

Kyol, kurigo ibyollui pyonjugok. 1990. Trans. Sok-pong Lee. Seoul: Minyesa.

Ocen' legkaja smert.' 1992. Trans. L. Zonina, et al. Moscow: Respublika.

Grazus paveiksle. 1994. Trans. Aldona Merkyte. Vilnius: Zaltvyksle.

A conti fatti. 1973. Trans. Bruno Fonzi. Torino: Einaudi.

All Said and Done. The Final Volume of Her Autobiography. 1974. Trans. Patrick O'Brian. Harmondsworth, U.K.: Penguin.

Alles wel beschouwd. 1977. Trans. Pieter Grashoff. Bussum: Agathon.

Alles in allem. 1980. Trans. Eva Rechel-Mertens. Reinbek bei Hamburg: Rowalt.

Balanço final. 1980. Trans. Bertha Mendes. Amadora: Bertrand.

Final de cuentas. 1984. Trans. Ida Vitale. Barcelona: Edhasa.

Saranggwaa yohaengui gin choldae. 1987. Trans. Chong Sosong. Seoul: Myongjisa.

Balanco final. 1990. Trans. Rita Braga. Rio de Janeiro: Nova Fronteira.

Alles welbeschouwd. 1992. Trans. Pieter Grashoff. Houton: Agathon.

A cerimonia do adeus & Entrevistas con Jean-Paul Sartre. 1982. Trans. Rita Braga. Rio de Janiero: Nova Frontiera, 1982.

I-byeol-eui yangsig. 1982. Trans. Sang Lu Lee. Seoul: Jung-ang-ilbosa.
La ceremonia del adiós. 1983. Trans. J. Sanjosé Carbajosa. Buenos Aires: Sud-
   americana.
*Het afscheid: een kroniek van Jean-Paul Sartre's laatste jaren & gesprekken over litera-
   tuur, filosofie, politiek, vriendschap, liefde.* 1983. Trans. Frans de Haan. Utrecht:
   Bijleveld.
Veda töreni. 1983. Trans. Nesrin Altinova. Istanbul: Varlik Yayinlari.
Die Zeremonie des Abschieds & Gespräche mit Jean-Paul Sartre. 1983. Trans. Uli
   Aumüller and Eva Moldenhauer. Kornwestheim: Bibliothek der Buchfreude.
Adieux: A Farewell to Sartre. 1984. Trans. Patrick O'Brian. New York: Pantheon
   Books.
Wakare no gishiki. 1984. Trans. Sankichi Asabuki. Kyoto: Jinbun shoin.
A cerimonia do adeus: conversas com Jean-Paul Sartre. 1986. Trans. Helena Leonor
   M. dos Santos. Lisbon: Bertrand.
Letters to Sartre. 1992. Trans. Quintin Hoare. New York: Arcade.

SECONDARY LITERATURE

Alexander, Anna. 1997. 'The Eclipse of Gender: Simone de Beauvoir and the
   Différence of Translation.' *Philosophy Today* (Spring): 112–22.
Bair, Deirdre. *Simone de Beauvoir: A Biography.* New York: Simon and Schuster.
Baisnée, Valérie. 1997. *Gendered Resistance: The Autobiographies of Simone de
   Beauvoir, Maya Angelou, Janet Frame and Marguerite Duras.* Amsterdam:
   Rodopi.
Barrett, William. 1958. *Irrational Man: A Study in Existential Philosophy.* New
   York: Anchor Books.
Bergoffen Debra B. 1997. *The Philosophy of Simone de Beauvoir: Gendered Pheno-
   menologies and Erotic Generosities.* New York: State University of New York
   Press.
Brosman, Catharine Savage. 1991. *Simone de Beauvoir Revisited.* Boston: Twayne.
Cohen-Solal, Annie. 1987. *Sartre: A Life.* Ed. Norman MacAfee. Trans. Anna
   Cancogni. New York: Pantheon Books (*Sartre.* Paris: Gallimard, 1985).
Evans, Mary. 1996. *Simone de Beauvoir.* London: Sage.
Fallaize, Elizabeth, ed. 1998. *Simone de Beauvoir: A Critical Reader.* New York
   and London: Routledge.
Francis, Claude, and Fernande Gontier. 1987. *Simone de Beauvoir: A Life ... A
   Love Story.* Trans. Lisa Nesselson. New York: St Martin's Press (*Simone de
   Beauvoir.* Paris: Perrin, 1985).
Fullbrook, Kate and Edward Fullbrook. 1993. *Simone de Beauvoir and Jean-Paul
   Sartre: The Remaking of a Twentieth-Century Legend.* New York: Harvester
   Wheatsheaf.

– 1998. *Simone de Beauvoir: A Critical Introduction*. Cambridge: Polity Press.

Hewitt, Leah D. 1990. *Autobiographical Tightropes: Simone de Beauvoir, Nathalie Sarraute, Marguerite Duras, Monique Wittig and Maryse Condé*. Lincoln and London: University of Nebraska Press.

Johnson, Douglas. 1981. 'La Grande Sartreuse.' *London Review of Books*. 15 Oct. – 4 Nov. 20–1.

Lamblin, Bianca. 1996. *A Disgraceful Affair: Simone de Beauvoir, Jean-Paul Sartre, & Bianca Lambin*. Trans. Julie Plovnick. Boston: Northeastern University Press. (*Mémoires d'une jeune fille derangée*. Paris: Gallimard, 1993).

Mitscherlich-Nielsen, Margarete. 1993. '"Ein einziger Vorsatz belebte uns: Alles erfassen, von allem Zeugnis ablegen": Simone de Beauvoir und Jean Paul Sartre.' In *Liebespaare: Geschichte und Geschichten*. Ed. Hans Jürgen Schultz. Munich: Deutscher Taschenbuch Verlag.

Moi, Toril. 1994. *Simone de Beauvoir: The Making of an Intellectual Woman*. Oxford, U.K., Cambridge, Mass.: Blackwell.

Sartre, Jean-Paul. 1946. *The Flies*. Trans. Stuart Gilbert. London: H. Hamilton (*Les mouches*. Paris: Gallimard, 1943).

– 1949. *Nausea*. Trans. Lloyd Alexander. Norfolk, Conn.: New Directions (*La nausée*. Paris: Gallimard, 1938).

– 1963. *Saint Genet: Actor and Martyr*. Trans. Bernard Frechtman. New York: G. Braziller (*Saint Genet: comédien et martyr*. Paris: Gallimard, 1952).

– 1964. *The Words* Trans. Bernard Frechtman. New York: G. Braziller (*Les mots*. Paris: Gallimard 1964).

– 1966. *Being and Nothingness: A Phenomenological Essay on Ontology.* Trans. Hazel E. Barnes. New York: Washingon Square Press (*L'être et le néant, essai d'ontologie phenomenologique*. Paris: Gallimard, 1943).

– 1976. *Critique of Dialectical Reason*. Trans. Alan Sheridan-Smith. London: NLB (*Critique de la raison dialectique: précédé de 'Question de méthode.'* Paris: Gallimard, 1960).

– 1977. *Life/Situations, Essays Written and Spoken*. Trans. Paul Auster and Lydia Davis. New York: Pantheon Books (*Situations X*. Paris: Gallimard, 1975).

– 1981. *The Family Idiot: Gustave Flaubert, 1821–1857*. Trans. Carol Cosman. Chicago: University of Chicago Press (*L'idiot de la famille: Gustave Flaubert de 1821–1857*. Paris: Gallimard, 1971).

– 1988. *Mallarmé, or The Poet of Nothingness*. Trans. Ernest Sturm. University Park: Pennsylvania University Press (*Mallarmé: la lucidé et sa face d'ombre*. Paris: Gallimard, 1986).

– 1992. *Notebooks for an Ethics*. Trans. David Pellauer. Chicago and London: University of Chicago Press (*Cahiers pour une morale*. Ed. Arlette Elkaïm-Sartre. Paris: Gallimard, 1983).

– 1992, 1993. *Witness to My Life: The Letters of Jean-Paul Sartre to Simone de Beau-
voir, 1926–1939.* Trans. Lee Fahnestock and Norman MacAfee. New York:
Scribner's; *Quiet Moments in a War: The Letters of Jean-Paul Sartre to Simone de
Beauvoir, 1940–1963.* Trans. Lee Fahnestock and Norman MacAfee. New
York: Scribner's (*Lettres au Castor, et a quelques autres.* Ed. Simone de Beau-
voir. Paris: Gallimard, 1983).
Tidd, Ursula. 1999. *Simone de Beauvoir, Gender and Testimony.* Cambridge, U.K.
and New York: Cambridge University Press.
Vintges, Karen. 1996. *Philosophy as Passion: The Thinking of Simone de Beauvoir.*
Trans. Anne Lavelle. Bloomington and Indianapolis: Indiana University
Press (*Filosofie als passie. Het denken van Simone de Beauvoir.* Amsterdam:
Prometheus, 1992).

Maitreyi Devi

Devi, Maitreyi. 1976. *It Does Not Die: A Romance.* Calcutta: P. Lal; Chicago and
London: University of Chicago Press, 1994 (*Na Hanyate.* Calcutta: Manisha
Granthalaya, 1974).

TRANSLATIONS
Dragostes nu moare. 1992. Trans. Stefan Dimitru and Theodor Handoca.
Bucharest: Românul.
Mircea. 1993. Trans. Elzbieta Walterowa. Warsaw: Panstwowy Instytut
Wydawniczy.

SECONDARY LITERATURE
Dasgupta, Surendranath. 1921–55. *A History of Indian Philosophy in Five Volumes.* Cambridge: Cambridge University Press.
– 1970. *Yoga as Philosophy and Religion.* Port Washington, NY: Kennikat Press.
Eliade, Mircea. 1958. *Yoga: Immortality and Freedom.* Trans. Willard R. Trask.
New York: Bollington (*Le Yoga. Immortalité et Liberté.* Paris: Librarie Payot,
1954).
– 1977. *No Souvenirs. Journal, 1957–1969.* Trans. Fred H. Johnson, Jr. New York:
Harper & Row (*Fragments d'un journal.* Paris: Gallimard, 1973: 229–571).
– 1981. *Autobiography.* Vol. I: *1907–1937, Journey East, Journey West.* Trans. (from
the Romanian) Mac Linscott Ricketts. San Francisco: Harper & Row.
– 1982. *Ordeal by Labyrinth: Conversations with Claude-Henri Rocquet.* Trans.
Derek Coltman. Chicago and London: University of Chicago Press
(*L'Épreuve du Labyrinthe: Entretiens avec Claude-Henri Rocquet.* Paris: Pierre
Belfond, 1978).

– 1988. *Autobiography.* Vol. II: *1937–1960, Exile's Odyssey.* Trans. (from the Romanian) Mac Linscott Ricketts. Chicago and London: University of Chicago Press, 1988.

– 1994. *Bengal Nights.* Trans. Catherine Spencer. Chicago: University of Chicago Press (*La nuit bengali.* Paris: Éditions Gallimard, 1950. *Maitreyi.* Bucharest, 1933).

Mukherjee, Meenakshi. 1995. 'Mircea Eliade and India: A Reading of *Maitreyi.'* In *Framing Literature: Festschrift for Professor M. Sivaramakrishna.* Ed. Rama Nair, B. Gopal Rao, and D. Venkateswarta. New Delhi: Sterling Publishers.

Naidu, Sarojini. 1930. *Select Poems.* Chosen and edited by H.G. Dalway Turnbull. Bombay: Oxford University Press.

La Nuit Bengali. 1988. Dir. Nicolas Klotz. Starring Hugh Grant, John Hurt, and Supriya Pathak.

Spariosu, Mihai. 1980. 'Orientalist Fictions in Eliade's *Maitreyi.'* In *Fiction and Drama in Eastern and Southeastern Europe: Proceedings of the 1978 UCLA Conference.* Ed. Henrik Birnbaum and Thomas Eekman. Columbus, Ohio: Slavica.

Asja Lacis

Lacis, Asja. 1967. 'Brief an Hildegard Brenner.' *Alternative* 56–57 (Oct.–Dec.): 211–14.

– 1968. 'Das "Programm eines proletarischen Kindertheaters": Erinnerungen beim Wiederlesen.' *Alternative* 59–60 (Apr.–June): 64–7.

– 1969. 'Städte und Menschen: Erinnerungen.' *Sinn und Form* 21: 1326–57.

– 1971. *Revolutionär im Beruf: Berichte über proletarisches Theater, über Meyerhold, Brecht, Benjamin und Piscator.* Ed. Hildegard Brenner. Munich: Rogner & Bernhard (1976).

– 1984. *Krasnaia Gvozdika, Vospominaniia (The Red Carnation: A Memoir).* Riga: Liecma.

– 1989. *Profession: Révolutionnaire. Sur le théâtre prolétarien: Meyerhold, Brecht, Benjamin, Piscator.* Trans. and intro. Philippe Ivernel. Afterword by Hildegard Brenner. Grenoble: Presses Universitaires de Grenoble.

Lacis, Asja, and Walter Benjamin. 1973. 'Building a Children's Theater. 2 Documents.' Trans. Jack Zipes and Susan Buck-Morss. *Performance* 1: 22–32.

SECONDARY LITERATURE

Benjamin, Walter. 1979. *One Way Street and Other Writings.* London: New Left Books (*Einbahnstrasse.* Berlin: Ernst Rowohlt Verlag, 1928; Frankfurt: Suhrkamp, 1955).

– 1986. *Moscow Diary.* Ed. Gary Smith. Trans. Richard Sieburth. Cambridge,

Mass. and London: Harvard University Press (*Moskauer Tagebuch.* Frankfurt: Suhrkamp, 1980).

Garros, Véronique, Natalia Korenevskaya, and thomas Lahusen, eds. 1995. *Intimacy and Terror: Soviet Diaries of the 1930s.* New York: New Press.

Hellbeck, Jochen. 1996. 'Introduction.' In Podlubnyi (1996).

Kimele, Dagmara, and Gunta Strautmane. 1996. *Asja: Rezisores Annas Laces dekaina dzive.* Riga: Liktenstasti.

Mierau, Fritz, ed. 1991. *Russen in Berlin: Literatur, Malerei, Theater, Film, 1918– 1933.* Leipzig: Reclam.

Podlubnyi, Stepan. 1996. *Tagebuch aus Moskau, 1931–1939.* Trans. and ed. Jochen Hellbeck. Munich: Deutscher Taschenbuch Verlag.

Nadezhda Mandel'shtam

Mandel'shtam, Nadezhda. 1970. *Vospominania (Memoir).* Paris: YMCA Press.

– 1987. *Kniga Tret'ia (Third Book).* Paris: YMCA Press.

– 1990. *Vtoraia Kniga (Second Book).* Paris: YMCA Press; Moscow: Moskovskii robochii.

TRANSLATIONS

Hope against Hope: A Memoir. 1970. Trans. Max Hayward, with an Introduction by Clarence Brown. New York: Atheneum.

Stalins Mirakel: En bok om Osip Mandelsjtam. 1970. Trans. Hans Björkegren. Stockholm: Wahlström & Widstrand.

Das Jahrhundert der Wölfe: eine Autobiographie. 1971. Trans. Elisabeth Mahler. Frankfurt: S. Fischer; Vienna: Salzer.

L'epoca e i lupi: Memorie. 1971. Trans. Giorgio Kraiski. Milan: Mondadori.

La mie memorie (Osip M.). Poesie e altri scrittie. 1972. Trans. Serena Vitale. Milan: Garzanti.

Contre tout espoir. 1972. Trans. Maya Minoustchine. Paris: Gallimard.

Ihmisen Toivo. 1972. Trans. Esa Adrian Anisimoff. Helsinki: Otava.

Memoires. 1972. Trans. Kees Verheul. Amsterdam: Van Oorschot.

Memoires (2). 1973. Trans. Kees Verheul. Amsterdam: Van Oorschot.

Hope Abandoned. 1974. Trans. Max Hayward. New York: Atheneum.

Contre tout espoir (2). 1974. Trans. Maya Minoustchine. Paris: Gallimard.

Generation ohne Tränen: Erinnerungen. 1975. Trans. Godehard Schramm. Frankfurt: S. Fischer.

Erindringer. 1975. Trans. Peter Ulf Møller and Lene Tybaerg Schacke. Copenhagen: Arkiv for Ny Litteratur/Arena.

Nadzieja w beznadziejnosci. 1976. No trans. given. London: Polonia Book Fund.

Tiqwat ha-shir. 1977. Trans. I.M. Heshwan. Tel Aviv: Am Oved.
Ryûkei no shijin Mandel'shtam. 1980. Trans. Hiroshi Kimura and Takashi Kwasaki. Tokyo: Shinchosha.
Spomini. 1980. Trans. Aleksandar Skaza. Ljublijana: Cankarjeva zalozba.
Contra toda esperanza: memorias. 1984. Trans. Lydia K. de Velasco. Madrid: Alianza Editorial.
Emlekeim. 1990. Trans. Judit Pór. Budapest: Magvet.

SECONDARY LITERATURE
Althaus-Schönbucher, Silvia. 1981. 'Nadezhda Mandel'shtam: *Vospominanija* und *Vtoraja kniga.* Memoiren als Ergänzung der Literaturforschung.' In *Colloquium Slavicum Basiliense: Gedenkschrift für Hildegard Schroeder.* Ed. Heinrich Riggenbach and Felix Keller. Bern: Peter Lang.
Brodsky, Joseph. 1986. *Less Than One: Selected Essays.* New York: Farrar, Straus & Giroux.
Emerson, Caryl. 1993. 'Bakhtin and Women: A Nontopic with Immense Implications.' In Goscilo (1993).
Freidin, Gregory. 1987. *A Coat of Many Colors: Osip Mandelstam and His Mythologies of Self-Presentation.* Berkeley: University of California Press.
Goscilo, Helena, ed. 1993. *Fruits of Her Plume: Essays on Contemporary Russian Women's Culture.* Armonk and London: M.E. Sharpe.
Griffiths, Frederick T., and Stanley J. Rabinowitz. 1994. 'Stalin and the Death of Epic: Mikhail Bakhtin, Nadezhda Mandelstam, Boris Pasternak.' In *Epic and Epoch: Essays on the Interpretation and History of a Genre.* Ed. Steven M. Oberhelman, Van Kelly, and Richard J. Golsam. Lubbock: Texas Tech University Press.
Harris, Jane Gary. 1990. 'Autobiography and History: Osip Mandelstam's "Noise of Time."' In Harris, ed. (1990).
– ed. 1990. *Autobiographical Statements in Twentieth-Century Russian Literature.* Princeton, N.J.: Princeton University Press.
Heldt, Barbara. 1987. *Terrible Perfection: Women and Russian Literature.* Bloomington: Indiana University Press.
Holmgren, Beth. 1993a. 'The Creation of Nadezhda Iakovlevna Mandel'shtam.' In Goscilo (1993).
– 1993b. *Women's Works in Stalin's Time: On Lidiia Chukovskaia and Nadezhda Mandelstam.* Bloomington and Indianapolis: Indiana University Press.
Isenberg, Charles. 1990. 'The Rhetoric of Nadezhda Mandelstam's "Hope Against Hope."' In Harris, ed. (1990). (Also in *New Studies of Russian Language and Literature.* Ed. Anna Lisa Crone and Catherine V. Chvany. Columbus, Ohio: Slavica.)

– *Substantial Proofs of Being: Osip Mandelstam's Literary Prose*. Columbus, Ohio: Slavica.

Mandel'shtam, Osip. 1965. *The Noise of Time and Other Prose Pieces*. Collected, translated from the Russian and with introductions by Clarence Brown. London and New York: Quartet Encounters.

– 1997. 'On the Addressee.' In O. Mandel'shtam, *The Complete Critical Prose*. Trans. Jane Gary Harris and Constance Link. Ann Arbor, Mich.: Ardis.

– 1980. *Poems*. Chosen and translated by James Greene, with forewords by Nadezhda Mandelstam and Donald Davie. London: Granta.

Margolina, Sofia. 1993. '"Ich, die niemals richtig weinen konnte, ich weine, ich weine": Nadeshda Jakowlewna Chasina und Osip Mandelstam.' In Schultz (1993).

Pratt, Sarah. 1996. 'Angels in the Stalinist House: Nadezhda Mandelstam, Lidiia Chukovskaia, Lidiia Ginzburg and Russian Women's Autobiography.' *Engendering Slavic Literatures*. Ed. Pamela Chester and Sibelan Forrester. Bloomington and Indianapolis: Indiana University Press. (Also in *a/b: Auto-Biography-Studies* 11, 2 (Fall, 1996): 68–87.)

Proffer, Carl R. 1987. *The Widows of Russia and Other Writings*. Ann Arbor, Mich.: Ardis.

Rifkind, Donna. 1990. 'Literary Widows.' *American Scholar* 59: 531–46.

Robey, Judith. 1998. 'Gender and the Autobiographical Project in Nadezhda Mandelstam's *Hope Against Hope* and *Hope Abandoned*.' *Slavic and East European Journal* 42.2: 231–53.

Schultz, Hans Jürgen, ed. 1993. *Liebespaare: Geschichte und Geschichten*. Munich: Deutscher Taschenbuch Verlag.

Shtempel',' N.E. 1987. 'Mandel'shtam v Voronezhe.' *Novyi mir* 10: 207–34.

Zamiatin, Evgenii. 1970. *We*. Trans. Bernard Guilbert Guerney. London: Jonathan Cape.

Romola Nijinsky

Nijinsky, Romola. 1933. *Nijinsky*. London: Victor Gollancz.

– 1952. *The Last Years of Nijinsky*. London: Victor Gollancz.

– 1956. 'Commentary.' In *Diaghilev-Nijinsky and Other Vignettes*. By Maurice Sandoz. Prefatory note by Walter Terry. New York: Kamin.

– ed. 1937. *The Diary of Vaslav Nijinsky*. By Vaslav Nijinsky. Berkeley and Los Angeles: University of California Press, 1936, London: Victor Gollancz.

TRANSLATIONS

Nijinsky. 1951. Trans. (from the Hungarian) Gastão Cruls. Brazil: n.p.

Nizinski o theos tou khorou. 1951. Trans. E. Bakalopoulos and M. Stauros. Athens: Ikaros.

Journal. 1953. (V.N.). Trans. G. Solpray. Paris: Gallimard.

Vida de Nijinsky. 1953. Trans. (from the Hungarian) F. Oliver Brachfeld and Rafael Vázquez Zamora. Barcelona: Destino.

Der Clown Gottes (Tagebuch d. Waslaw Nijinskij). 1957. Trans. Leonore Schlaich. Stuttgart: Klett.

Nizinski. 1961. Trans. (from the Hungarian) Y. Winizqi. Tel Aviv: Ziw (1963).

Nijinsky no shuki. 1971. Trans. Ichikawa Miyabi. Tokyo: Gendai shichosha.

Dagboek. 1972. (V.N.). Trans. A.M.H. Brinkhuysen. Amsterdam: Bezige Bij.

Nijinsky: der Gott des Tanzes, Biographie. 1974. Trans. Hans Bütow. Frankfurt: Insel.

Godoghan yeonghoneui gil. 1975. (V.N.). Trans. Lee Deog-Heui. Seoul: Munye chulpansa.

Sonogo no Nijinsky. 1977. Trans. Ichikawa Miyabi. Tokyo: Gendai shichosha (LYN).

Journal. 1980. (V.N., Nouv. éd.). Trans. Georges S. Solpray. Paris: Gallimard.

Nizinski sekä Nizinskin viimeiset vuodet. 1984. Trans. Irma Vienola-Liindfors. Helsinki: Otava.

Der Clown Gottes: ein Tagebuch. 1985. Trans. Leonore Schlaich. Munich: Schirmer-Mosel.

Dnevnik Vatslava Nizhinskogo: Vospominania o Nizhinskom. 1995. Trans. (from the French) M. Viv'en and S. Orlova. Introduction and commentary by V. Gaevskogo. Moscow: Artist. Rezhisser. Teatr.

Nijinski: Cahiers Le Sentiment – version non-expurgée. 1995. Trans. (from the Russian) Christian Dumais-Lvowski and Galina Pogojeva. Arles: Actes Sud.

The Diary of Vaslav Nijinsky. 1999. Unexpurgated edition, edited with an introduction by Joan Acocella. Trans. Kyril FitzLyon. New York: Farrar, Straus & Giroux.

SECONDARY LITERATURE

Bourman, Anatole (with D. Lyman). 1937. *The Tragedy of Nijinsky.* London: Robert Hale.

Buckle, Richard. 1971. *Nijinsky.* London: Weidenfeld & Nicolson.

Fergeson, Ian. 1983. 'Nijinsky's Birthday?' *The Dancing Times* (Aug.): 862–4.

Ingram, Susan. 2000. 'Nijinsky: From Modern Love to Postmodern Madness.' *Slovo: An Interdisciplinary Journal of Russian, Eurasian and East European Affairs* 12: 104–16.

Kirstein, Lincoln. 1975. *Nijinsky Dancing.* New York: Farrar, Straus & Giroux.

– 1991. *By With To & From: A Lincoln Kirstein Reader.* Ed. Nicholas Jenkins. New York: Farrar, Straus & Giroux.

Krasovskaya, Vera. 1979. *Nijinsky.* Trans. John E. Bowlt. New York: Schirmer Books.

Lifar, Sergei. 1994. *Diaghilev i c Diaghilevem.* Moscow: Izdatelstva 'Art.'

Nijinska, Bronislava. 1981. *Early Memoirs.* Trans. and ed. Irina Nijinska and Jean Rawlinson. Introduction by and in consultation with Anna Kisselgoff. Durham and London: Duke University Press, 1992 (*Mémoires: 1891–1914.* Trans. Gérard Mannoni. Paris: Ramsey, 1983).

Nijinsky, Tamara. 1991. *Nijinsky and Romola: Biography.* London: Bachman and Turner.

Ostwald, Peter. 1991. *Vaslav Nijinsky: A Leap into Madness.* New York: Lyle Stuart.

Reiss, Françoise. 1960. *Nijinsky: A Biography.* Trans. Helen and Stephen Haskell. London: Adam & Charles Black (*Nijinsky ou la Grace, Tome 1: La Vie de Nijinsky.* Paris: Éditions d'histoire et d'art, 1957).

Sert, Misia. 1953. *Misia and the Muses.* New York: J. Day.

Shapcott, Thomas. 1984. *White Stag of Exile.* London: Allen Lane.

Stevenson, Florence. 1965. 'Romola in Russia.' New York Ballet Program (Jan.): 10, 22.

Ware, Walter. 1938. 'Vaslav Nijinsky: Fact or Fiction?' *American Dancer* (March): 12, 39.

SECTION II: Autobiography, Modernity, Nietzsche

Angelou, Maya. 1969. *I Know Why the Caged Bird Sings.* New York: Random House.

Ansell-Pearson, Keith. 1992. 'Who is the *Übermensch*? Time, Truth, and Woman in Nietzsche.' *Journal of the History of Ideas* 53: 309–31.

Barbour, John D. 1992. *The Conscience of the Autobiographer: Ethical and Religious Dimensions of Autobiography.* London: Macmillan.

Barthes, Roland. 1972. *Mythologies.* Selected and trans. Annette Lavers. New York: Hill & Wang (*Mythologies.* Paris: Éditions du Seuil, 1957).

– 1977. *Roland Barthes.* Trans. Richard Howard. London: Macmillan (*Roland Barthes par Roland Barthes.* Paris: Seuil, 1975).

Behler, Diana. 1993. 'Nietzsche and Postfeminism.' *Nietzsche Studien* 22: 355–70.

Behler, Ernst. 1996. 'Nietzsche in the Twentieth Century.' In *The Cambridge Companion to Nietzsche.* Ed. Bernd Magnus and Kathleen M. Higgins. Cambridge: Cambridge University Press.

Benhabib, Seyla. 1992. *Situating the Self: Gender, Community and Postmodernism in Contemporary Ethics*. London and New York: Routledge.

– 1996. *The Reluctant Modernism of Hannah Arendt*. London: Sage.

Benjamin, Andrew, ed. 1989. *The Problems of Modernity: Adorno and Benjamin*. London and New York: Routledge.

Benjamin, Jessica. 1995. *Like Subjects, Love Objects: Essays on Recognition and Sexual Difference*. New Haven, Conn., and London: Yale University Press.

Benjamin, Walter. 1978. 'Surrealism: The Last Snapshot of the European Intelligentsia.' In *Reflections: Essays, Aphorisms, Autobiographical Writings*. Ed. with an introduction by Peter Demetz. Trans. Edmund Jephcott. New York: Schocken Books.

– 1994. *The Correspondence of Walter Benjamin, 1910–1940*. Ed. Gershom Scholem and Theodor W. Adorno. Trans. Manfred R. Jacobson and Evelyn M. Jacobson. Chicago and London: University of Chicago Press. (*Gesammelte Briefe*. Ed. Christoph Godde and Henri Lonitz. Frankfurt: Suhrkamp, 1995).

Bernstein, Jay. 1989. 'Art Against Enlightenment: Adorno's Critique of Habermas.' In Benjamin (1989).

– 1997. 'Fragment, Fascination, Damaged Life: "The Truth about Hedda Gabler."' *The Actuality of Adorno: Critical Essays on Adorno and the Postmodern*. Ed. Max Pensky. Albany: State University of New York Press.

Bernstein, Richard J. 1992. *The New Constellation: The Ethical-Political Horizons of Modernity/Postmodernity*. Cambridge, Mass.: MIT Press.

Buhr, Manfred, ed. 1990. *Moderne – Nietzsche – Postmoderne*. Berlin: Akademie Verlag.

Burgard, Peter J., ed. 1994. *Nietzsche and the Feminine*. Charlottesville and London: University Press of Virginia.

Bürger, Peter. 1994. *Theory of the Avant-Garde*. Trans. Michael Shaw. Minneapolis: University of Minnesota Press (*Theorie der Avantgarde*. Frankfurt: Suhrkamp, 1974).

Call, Lewis. 1995. 'Woman as Will and Representation: Nietzsche's Contribution to Postmodern Feminism.' *Women in German Yearbook* 11: 113–30.

Caputo, John D. 1993. *Against Ethics: Contributions to a Poetics of Obligation with Constant Reference to Deconstruction*. Bloomington and Indianapolis: Indiana University Press.

Cavell, Stanley. 1976. *Must We Mean What We Say?* Cambridge: Cambridge University Press.

Deleuze, Gilles. 1983. *Nietzsche and Philosophy*. Trans. Hugh Tomlinson. New York: Columbia University Press (1962).

de Man, Paul. 1979. 'Autobiography as De-Facement.' *Modern Language Notes* 94.5: 919–30.

Dews, Peter. 1989. 'Adorno, Poststructuralism and the Critique of Identity.' In Benjamin (1989).

D'haen, Theo. 1996. 'Dis/Coursing Post/Modernism: Science, Magic, (Post)-Modernity.' *Canadian Review of Comparative Literature / Revue Canadienne de Littérature Comparée* 23.1: 189–97.

Eakin, Paul John. 1999. *How Our Lives Become Stories: Making Selves*. Ithaca, NY, and London: Cornell University Press.

Elliot, Bridget Jane, and JoAnn Wallace. 1994. *Women Artists and Writers: Modernist (Im)positionings*. London and New York: Routledge.

Felman, Shoshana. 1993. *What Does a Woman Want? Reading and Sexual Difference*. Baltimore and London: Johns Hopkins University Press.

Foster, Hal, ed. 1983. *The Anti-Aesthetic: Essays on Postmodern Culture*. Seattle, Wash.: Bay Press.

Freedman, Diane P. 1993. 'Border Crossing as Method and Motif in Contemporary American Writing, or, How Freud Helped Me Case the Joint.' In Freedman, Frey, and Murphy (1993).

Freedman, Diane P., Olivia Frey, and Frances Murphy Zauhar, eds. 1993. *The Intimate Critique: Autobiographical Literary Criticism*. Durham, S.C., and London: Duke University Press.

Gasparov, Boris. 1992. 'The "Golden Age" and Its Role in the Cultural Mythology of Russian Modernism.' In *Cultural Mythologies of Russian Modernism: From the Golden Age to the Silver Age*. Ed. B. Gasparov, Robert P. Hughes, and Irina Paperno. Berkeley: University of California Press.

Gergen, Kenneth J. 1994. *Realities and Relationships: Soundings in Social Construction*. Cambridge, Mass., and London: Harvard University Press.

– 1996. 'Technology and the Self: From the Essential to the Sublime.' In *Constructing the Self in a Mediated World*. Ed. Debra Grodin and Thomas R. Lindlof. London: Sage.

Goethe, Johann von Wolfgang. 1949. [1811–12] *Dichtung und Wahrheit aus meinem Leben*. Munich: Carl Hanser.

Grewal, Inderpal, and Caren Kaplan, eds. 1994. *Scattered Hegemonies: Postmodernity and Transnational Feminist Practices*. Minneapolis: University of Minnesota Press.

Habermas, Jürgen. 1983. 'Modernity: An Incomplete Project.' Trans. Seyla Ben-Habib. In Foster (1983).

– 1987. *The Philosophical Discourse of Modernity*. Trans. Frederick Lawrence Cambridge, Mass.: MIT Press (*Der philosophische Diskurs der Moderne. Zwölf Vorlesungen*. Frankfurt: Suhrkamp, 1985).

Heller, Agnes. 1988. *General Ethics*. Oxford and Cambridge, Mass.: Blackwell.

– 1990. *A Philosophy of Morals*. Oxford and Cambridge, Mass.: Blackwell.

– 1996. *An Ethics of Personality.* Oxford and Cambridge, Mass.: Blackwell.

Hobsbawm, Eric, and Terence Ranger, eds. 1983. *The Invention of Tradition.* Cambridge: Cambridge University Press.

Hodge, Joanna. 1989. 'Feminism and Postmodernism: Misleading Divisions Imposed by the Opposition Between Modernism and Postmodernism.' In Benjamin (1989).

Hollingdale, R.J. 1965. *Nietzsche: The Man and His Philosophy.* London: Routledge & Kegan Paul.

– 1996. 'The Hero As Outsider.' In *The Cambridge Companion to Nietzsche.* Ed. Bernd Magnus and Kathleen M. Higgins. Cambridge: Cambridge University Press.

Honneth, Axel. 1995. *The Fragmented World of the Social: Essays in Social and Political Philosophy.* Ed. Charles W. Wright. Albany: State University of New York Press.

Horowitz, Gregg M. 1997. 'Art History and Autonomy.' In *The Semblance of Subjectivity: Essays in Adorno's Aesthetic Theory.* Ed. Tom Huhn and Lambert Zuidervaat. Cambridge, Mass. and London: MIT Press.

Irigaray, Luce. 1991. *Marine Lover of Friedrich Nietzsche.* Trans. Gillian C. Gill. New York: Columbia University Press (*Amante marine.* Paris: Les Éditions de Minuit, 1980).

Jay, Martin. 1984. *Adorno.* Cambridge, Mass.: Harvard University Press.

Johnson, Pauline. 1996. 'Nietzsche Reception Today.' *Radical Philosophy* 80 (Nov–Dec.): 24–33.

Kadar, Marlene, ed. 1992. *Essays on Life Writing: From Genre to Critical Practice.* Toronto: University of Toronto Press.

Kaplan, Alice. 1993. *French Lessons: A Memoir.* Chicago and London: University of Chicago Press.

– 1997. 'The Trouble with Memoir.' *Chronicle of Higher Education* 5 Dec.: B4–5.

Kaufmann, Walter. 1968. *Nietzsche: Philosopher, Psychologist, Antichrist.* 3rd ed. Princeton, N.J.: Princeton University Press.

Kingston, Maxine Hong. 1976. *The Woman Warrier: Memoirs of a Girlhood Among Ghosts.* New York: Knopf.

Lacan, Jacques. 1992. *The Seminar of Jacques Lacan. Book VII: The Ethics of Psychoanalysis 1959–1960.* Ed. Jacques-Alain Miller. Trans. Dennis Porter. New York and London: W.W. Norton.

Leckie, Shirley A. 1993. *Elizabeth Bacon Custer and the Making of a Myth.* Norman and London: University of Oklahoma Press.

Leiris, Michel. 1992. *Manhood: A Journey from Childhood into the Fierce Order of Virility.* Trans. Richard Howard, with a foreword by Susan Sontag. Chicago: University of Chicago Press (*L'âge d'homme.* Paris: Gallimard, 1939).

Lejeune, Philippe. 1989. *On Autobiography.* Trans. Katherine Leary. Minneapolis: University of Minnesota Press (*La pacte autobiographique.* Paris: Gallimard, 1975).

Marcus, Laura. 1994. *Auto/biographical Discourses: Theory, Criticism, Practice.* Manchester, U.K., and New York: Manchester University Press.

Mason, Mary. 1980. 'The Other Voice: Autobiographies of Women Writers.' In *Autobiography: Essays Theoretical and Critical.* Ed. James Olney. Princeton, N.J.: Princeton University Press.

May, Georges. 1978. 'Autobiography and the Eighteenth Century.' In *The Author in His Work: Essays on a Problem in Criticism.* Ed. Louis L. Martz and Aubrey Williams, with an introduction by Patricia Meyer Spacks. New Haven, Conn., and London: Yale University Press.

McCarthy, Mary. 1951. *The Groves of Academe.* New York: Harcourt, Brace & World.

Michelfelder, D., and R.E. Palmer. 1989. *Dialogue and Deconstruction: The Gadamer-Derrida Debate.* Albany: State University of New York Press.

Miller, J. Hillis. 1987. *The Ethics of Reading.* New York: Columbia University Press.

Miller, Nancy K. 1991. *Getting Personal: Feminist Occasions and Other Autobiographical Acts.* New York and London: Routledge.

– 1994. 'Representing Others: Gender and the Subjects of Autobiography.' *Differences: A Journal of Feminist Cultural Studies* 6.1: 1–27.

Modleski, Tania. 1998. *Old Wives' Tales and Other Women's Stories.* New York and London: New York University Press.

Mozejko, Edward. 1998. 'Literary Modernism: Ambiguity of the Term and Dichotomy of the Movement.' *Canadian Review of Comparative Literature / Revue Canadienne de Littérature Comparée* 25.1.2: 123–43.

Nagl, Ludwig. 1989. 'The Enlightenment – a Stranded Project? Habermas on Nietzsche as a "Turning Point" to Postmodernism.' *History of European Ideas* 11: 743–50.

Nehamas, Alexander. 1985. *Nietzsche: Life as Literature.* Cambridge, Mass., and London: Harvard University Press.

nichol, bp. 1988. *Selected Organs: Parts of an Autobiography.* Windsor, Ont.: Black Moss Press.

Nicholls, Peter. 1995. *Modernisms: A Literary Guide.* Berkeley and Los Angeles: University of California Press.

Nietzsche, Friedrich. 1961. *Thus Spoke Zarathustra.* Trans. with an introduction by R.J. Hollingdale. London: Penguin. (Also in *The Portable Nietzsche.* Selected and translated with an introduction, prefaces and notes by Walter Kaufmann. New York: Viking Press, 1954.)

– 1988. 'Ecce Homo.' In *Sämtliche Werke, kritische Studienausgabe*, vol. 6. Berlin and New York: Walter de Gruyter.

– 1994. *Also sprach Zarathustra. Ein Buch für Alle und Keinen*. Stuttgart: Reclam.

Nouss, Alexis. 1995. *La modernité*. Paris: Presses Universitaires de France.

Nussbaum, Martha C. 1990. *Love's Knowledge: Essays on Philosophy and Literature*. New York and Oxford: Oxford University Press.

Olshen, Barry N. 1995. 'Subject, Persona, and Self in the Theory of Autobiography.' *a/b: Auto/Biography Studies* 10.1: 5–16.

Oppen, Mary. 1978. *Meaning A Life: An Autobiography*. Santa Barbara, Calif.: Black Sparrow Press.

Osborne, Peter. 1989. 'Adorno and the Metaphysics of Modernism: The Problem of a "Postmodern" Art.' In Benjamin (1989).

Overall, Christine. 1998. *A Feminist I: Reflections from Academia*. Peterborough: Broadview Press.

Pascal, Roy. 1960. *Design and Truth in Autobiography*. Cambridge, Mass.: Harvard University Press.

Patton, Paul, ed. 1993. *Nietzsche, Feminism and Political Theory*. New York and London: Routledge.

Paz, Octavio. 1991. *Children of the Mire: Modern Poetry from Romanticism to the Avant Garde*. Cambridge, Mass., and London: Harvard University Press.

Renza, Louis A. 1977. 'The Veto of the Imagination: A Theory of Autobiography.' *New Literary History* 9.1: 2–26.

Ricoeur, Paul. 1992. *Oneself as Another*. Trans. Kathleen Blamey. University of Chicago Press (1990).

– 1995. *The Philosophy of Paul Ricoeur*. Ed. Lewis Edwin Hahn. Chicago and La Salle, Ill.: Open Court.

Rosen, Stanley. 1995. *The Mask of Enlightenment: Nietzsche's Zarathustra*. Cambridge: Cambridge University Press.

Rousseau, Jean-Jacques. [1800] 1938. *Confessions*. Paris: Librarie Larousse.

Simpson, David. 1995. *The Academic Postmodern and the Rule of Literature: A Report on Half-Knowledge*. Chicago and London: University of Chicago Press.

Slawek, Tadeusz. 1997. 'The Eye and the Body. Some Remarks on the Philosophy of the Baba.' In *Studia slavistica et humanistica in honorem Nullo Minissj*. Ed. Ireneusz Opacki, Aleksandr Wilkoni, and Jolanta Zurawska. Katowice: Wydawnictwo Uniwersytetu Slaskiego.

Smith, Sidonie, and Julia Watson, eds. 1996. *Getting a Life: Everyday Uses of Autobiography*. Minneapolis: University of Minnesota Press.

Smith, Sidonie, and Julia Watson, eds. 1998. *Women, Autobiography, Theory: A Reader*. Madison, Wis.: University of Wisconsin Press.

Stein, Gertrude. 1933. *The Autobiography of Alice B. Toklas*. New York: Literary Guild.

Taylor, Charles. 1989. *Sources of the Self: The Making of the Modern Identity*. Cambridge, Mass.: Harvard University Press.

Tirrell, Lynne. 1994. 'Sexual Dualism and Women's Self-Creation: On the Advantages and Disadvantages of Reading Nietzsche for Feminists.' In Burgard (1994).

Ulmer, Gregory L. 1983. 'The Object of Post-Criticism.' In Foster (1983).

Veeser, H. Aram, ed. 1996. *Confessions of the Critics*. London and New York: Routledge.

Wolin, Richard, ed. 1993. *The Heidegger Controversy: A Critical Reader*. Cambridge, Mass.: MIT Press.

– 1995. 'Kulchur Wars: The Modernism/Postmodernism Controversy Revisited.' In *Labyrinths: Explorations in the Critical History of Ideas*. Amherst: University of Massachusetts Press.

Young-Bruehl, Elisabeth. 1991. 'Pride and Prejudice: Feminist Scholars Reclaim the First Person.' *Linga Franca* 1.3: 15–19, 33.

Ziarek, Ewa Plonowska. 1998. 'Toward a Radical Female Imaginary: Temporality and Embodiment in Irigaray's Ethics.' *diacritics* 28.1: 60–75.

Zima, Peter V. 1997. *Moderne/Postmoderne: Gesellschaft, Philosophie, Literatur*. Tübingen and Basel: A. Francke Verlag.

Index